CW01096245

Haynes

Restoration Manual

Jaguar XJ6 Series 1, 2 and 3

Dave Pollard

Other Haynes Publishing titles of interest:

Jaguar XJ6, XJ & Sovereign; Daimler Sovereign
(Saloon & Coupé, Series 1, 2 & 3) (0242)

Jaguar XJ6 & Sovereign
(3.2, 3.6 & 4.0 Saloon automatic) (3261)

First published by G. T. Foulis & Co as Jaguar XJ6 Purchase and Restoration Guide in 1997
Reprinted by Haynes Publishing with new cover and minor amendments as Jaguar XJ6 Restoration Manual in 2003
Reprinted 2009, 2011 (twice) and 2012

A catalogue record for this book is available from the British Library

ISBN 978 1 84425 020 2

Library of Congress catalog card number 97-72305

Haynes Publishing, Sparkford, Yeovil, Somerset BA22 7JJ, UK

Tel: 01963 442030
Fax: 01963 440001
Int. tel: +44 1963 442030
Int. fax: +44 1963 440001

E-mail: sales@haynes.co.uk
Website: www.haynes.co.uk

Haynes Publications Inc.
861 Lawrence Drive, Newbury Park,
California 91320, USA

Printed in the USA by Odcombe Press LP,
1299 Bridgestone Parkway, La Vergne, TN 37086

Jurisdictions which have strict emission control laws may consider any modification to a vehicle to be an infringement of those laws. You are advised to check with the appropriate body or authority whether your proposed modification complies fully with the law. the publishers can accept no liability in this regard.

While every effort is taken to ensure the accuracy of the information given in this book, no liability can be accepted by the author or publishers for any loss, damage or injury caused by errors in, or omissions from, the information given.

Contents

Acknowledgements

This book would not have been possible without the co-operation of many companies and individuals. These (and others too many to mention here, but included in the text of the book) have not only provided technical information and photographs, but also the intangible benefits of many years of Jaguar experience. My thanks to them all.

Phil Blundell of *PB Restorations* did most of the hard work for the non-specialised sections of this book. A true Jaguar enthusiast, he worked for more hours than there are in a day to bring the project to its highly successful conclusion despite constant 'must do it now' journalistic deadlines. Most of the spares Phil fitted were supplied by Jaguar Specialists, *SNG Barratt* – thanks to Richard Darcy for getting the right parts to the right location at the right time. Their stock of components, from nuts and bolts to complete body panel sections for all Jaguars is incredible, and their mail order service is ideal for the home restorer.

Tyres are of vital importance on a powerful heavy car like the XJ6. Trina Brindley, Katy Leese and Paul Bould of *Goodyear Great Britain* were extremely helpful in providing information and photographs relating to what tyres are suitable for which vehicles. *Pristine* at Woburn Sands turned water to wine by transforming our ratty old alloy wheels into 'pristine' wheels suitable for those tyres.

Clarke International is world-renowned for its huge range of power tools, notably welding and pneumatic products. Thanks to Ross Bernard for the supply of products, photos and information for the relevant sections. Hand tools from *Sykes-Pickavant* were used for many of the sections – my thanks to Christine Whitworth for technical help and photos.

The engine work was carried out by Tim Camp's highly skilled team at *VSE Engineering* in the heart of rural Wales. In three days they turned an oily, dirty and very tired 4.2 XK engine into a gleaming, purring pussycat, offering many technical asides and gems of information to aid the DIY engine-builder. The engine now drives through a comprehensively rebuilt automatic gearbox produced by Graham Whitehouse of *G. Whitehouse Autos Ltd* – moreover, it was thoroughly tested on their special rig before it was fitted to our car.

Spraying body panels is a black art, but its mastery was shown by father-and-son team, Nigel and Jeff Worker, at *Bedford Auto Panels*. Our XJ6 project car is now resplendent in British Racing Green.

Last, but definitely not least, my wife Ann has been instrumental in piecing everything together, checking and proofing, and generally putting up with endless discussions revolving around the Jaguar – how it works, when it changed and how it fits together.

Introduction

Currently often overshadowed by its Mark 2 predecessor, the XJ6 was the culmination of many years of effort by Jaguar to produce the ultimate luxury saloon car. Taking technical innovations from previous and (then) current models, together with the latest technology, they succeeded, and how – any car that can be said to be better than a Rolls-Royce can't be all bad! Moreover, Jaguar managed to achieve its usual party trick of providing unbelievable value for money, especially when compared with its European rivals. In an age when many mundane cars are referred to as classics simply because they are over 10 years old, the XJ6 can truly lay claim to that title.

This book covers the 'Series' XJ6 cars, dealing with the three models which appeared from the time of the car's introduction in 1968 to 1987. The change from first to last was very much a metamorphosis, a gradual honing of the shape and components, rather than sudden changes. Much of the space is given over to the 4.2 litre cars of various Series, largely because they were by far the most popular – outselling the smaller-engined versions by a ratio of almost eight to one.

Most enthusiasts of the XJ6 will be of a practical nature and prepared for the work that lays ahead of them. However, few of those owners will tackle a full restoration at one go; most being more likely to opt for a 'rolling restoration', whereby the various restoration tasks are tackled piecemeal. As such, owners are still able to gain pleasure from driving their pride and joy on a regular basis whilst replacing and/or uprating as required. To this end, most of the jobs shown within have been broken down into 'easy to swallow' sections, meaning that, if required, certain aspects can be repaired/restored whilst keeping the car on the road.

Obviously, there are certain things that have to be replaced together; dampers/springs should be replaced at least as a matched axle set and ideally as two matched axle sets. Similarly, it would be extremely dangerous to put a new disc and pads on one side but not on the other.

PLANNING

Mice and men may have little control over their destinies, but to enter into open-ended restoration is asking for trouble. If you're having your engine rebuilt professionally by a company such as VSE (see Chapter 6) then you need to plan ahead. Check with the company when they want the engine – i.e. when it will best suit their schedule – and when they expect to finish it. Clearly, with the engine out, the car won't go far, and so it's the time to consider bigger bodywork and other mechanical jobs. An engine bay-clean would probably be first on the agenda! Moreover, having taken out the engine and gearbox (they come out as a single unit), it might be an idea to ponder on the state of the latter. Whilst your bank balance may be wilting under the strain, it does make sense to effect any repair/replacement work while it is out, rather than putting the whole assembly back and then having to remove it again at a later date.

Chapter 1
Heritage

THE 'XK' SALOONS

The Jaguar name first appeared on a car in 1935, when the SS Jaguar 2½ litre saloon/drophead coupé was introduced. After the war the SS nomenclature had obvious and unpleasant connotations, and so 1945 saw the introduction of the first car to bear only the Jaguar name – the 1½ litre.

From 1951 (the Mk VII) until 1985, all Jaguar saloons were powered by a derivation of the incredible double-overhead-cam XK engine. Some may argue that this shows a stick-in-the-mud attitude, but the flip side of the coin reveals differently – the engine was much ahead of its time when it was introduced, and through a constant development programme, its performance, even in the last of the XJ6 saloons, was more than equal to that of the opposition.

▲ H1. This is a 3½ drophead, one of just 498 made between 1946-1949. Essentially this is a development of a pre-war design, but showing all the Jaguar hallmarks of luxury, performance and value for money. Rakish bonnet line with huge Lucas headlamps. The twin SU carburettors bolted directly on to the head – no manifold. There was also a 2½ litre version of this car which looked very similar.

The engine was first seen in 3.4 litre guise in the XK120 sports car which took the world by storm at the Earls Court Motor Show in 1948. The first saloon to receive the XK unit was the Mk VII (and its derivative, the Mk VIIM) produced from 1951-1957. This model followed on directly from the Mk V, there being no Mk VI because the name was already in use by Bentley. Incredible as it might seem, the only Jaguar ever to win the Monte Carlo Rally was not a fearsome E-type or ground–breaking XK120, but a Mk VII!

◀ H2. The Mk VII was the first saloon to receive a 3.4 litre version of the award-winning XK engine, that first saw service in this innovative XK120. (Ironically, the

XK was originally designed during the war for the Mk VII.) The Mk VII and the Mk VIIM were produced from 1951-57. Note the split windscreen. It's almost unbelievable that this was the only Jaguar ever to win the Monte Carlo Rally – in 1956! The Mk VIII version appeared in that year and was basically the same car but more luxurious and with more power (210 bhp) from the engine. Two years later saw the arrival of the Mk IX which was the first luxury car in the world to feature disc brakes all-round and the first Jaguar to feature standard power steering. The capacity of the XK engine was increased, for the first time, to 3.8 litres. With 220 bhp, the top speed was 114 mph.

▲ H3. 1956 was a busy year for Jaguar, for it was the time of the Mk 1 Jaguar compact saloon. There were two XK engine variants – a 122 bhp 2.4 litre and a 210 bhp 3.4 litre (the latter enabled the car to be the first Jaguar saloon to top 120 mph). In 1959 the Mk 2 arrived – this is a 1960 model. Note the four front lamps – something of a Jaguar trademark long before the XJ6 – and the wire wheels, still very much de rigueur.

The Mk VIII appeared in 1956 and was in production for three years. It utilised the Mk VII shell but added much more luxury to the basic Jaguar recipe. The engine, though still at 3.4 litres, had its power increased to 210 bhp.

Also in 1956 there appeared the first of Jaguar's compact saloons – the Mk 1. The original car featured a 122 bhp 2.4 litre version of the XK engine, with the 3.4 litre 210 bhp version available a year later. The latter became the first Jaguar saloon to top 120 mph.

In 1958, the Mk VIII became the Mk IX, having the distinction of being the first luxury car in the world to feature

disc brakes all-round and the first Jaguar to feature standard power steering. The capacity of the XK engine was increased for the first time to 3.8 litres, giving 220 bhp which, with 240 lb/ft of torque on tap, was enough to give the large car a top speed of 114 mph and a 0-60 mph time of just 11.3 seconds.

In 1959 the second Jaguar compact

saloon appeared, the Mk 2. Undeniably one of the most stylish Jaguars ever, it combined luxury and flowing lines with serious performance – the 3.8 litre version, with its 220 bhp, pushed the Mk 2 on to 126 mph. The 2.4 and 3.4 litre engines were also fitted, giving a wider choice of models.

◀ H4. The Mk 2 could hit 126 mph with a 220 bhp 3.8 litre engine up front. Not obvious in a black and white photo is the blue cylinder head. From the days of the XK120, Jaguar had taken to painting the heads with different colours (or deliberately not painting it but leaving it in a polished aluminium finish). The S-type, the Mk IX and the XK150 3.8 litre cars also had blue heads.

ALMOST THERE

With the arrival of the Mk 2, Jaguar was getting ever nearer its goal of producing the ultimate luxury car, one which combined grace, space and pace. There were just two more models to go before the work of decades culminated in the XJ6 – the Mk X and the S-type.

▶ H5. Having taken over Daimler, Jaguar soon realised that the company's compact V8 engine was just the right size to slot under the bonnet of the Mk 2– this is a 1960 car. Other than the source of motive power, the changes to the car were minimal, most in details such as the radiator grille and badging. The eight-pot power plant was short-lived, Jaguar preferring to rely on the already-legendary XK six-cylinder unit.

▼ H6. This is one of the last Mk 2 cars, produced in 1963, prior to the introduction of the S-type. Try as you might, it's hard to look at its stunning lines and not think of Inspector Morse!

▼ H8. Still lots of the chrome at the rear of the car, but check out those tail lamps – small by today's standards, but compare them with the Mk VII of only a few years earlier – and then with …

▲ H7. The leaping cat mascot, soon to be a victim of increasingly stringent American safety regulations and never seen (officially) on the XJ6, sits above a mass of chrome and the badge which declares this model to be powered by a 2.4 litre engine.

▲ H9. ... the Mk 2's successor, the S-type. This is a 1968, 3.4 litre car. You can clearly see the family resemblance here, though the S-type rear had been redesigned to take the independent rear suspension (first seen on the E-type) and to increase the boot space by 50 per cent, despite the installation of twin fuel tanks.

MARK X

British car-making is inextricably linked with American motoring; in more recent years it has been the impact of safety and emissions legislation, but more often it has been simply the search for USA sales. Launched in 1962, the Mk X was a car designed with America very much in mind as can be seen from its enormous dimensions; it was 16 ft 10 in long and a staggering 6 ft 4 in wide, a fact that made it the widest production car in the UK (a record it held until the launch of, ironically, another Jaguar, the stunning XJ220). Whilst such figures seem incredible to European eyes, it was just about right for the USA. In terms of styling, it was far from svelte and even further from being economical to run. However, in common with so many Jaguars over the years, it was very well priced and with an all-up sale ticket of just £2,500, it was up to 50 per cent cheaper than some of its immediate rivals.

Technically, there was plenty to commend the Mk X, not least that it used the independent rear suspension system which first saw service in the E-type sports car. Though this seemed to be over-engineered for a six-cylinder engine, Jaguar was pondering the possibilities of using a V8 or even a V12 engine in order to compete with the large-capacity V8 engines used by their American competitors. Certainly, there was no shortage of room under the vast bonnet. Despite that, it was introduced using the 3.8 litre XK engine fitted with three SU carburettors. Slotting it into the huge engine bay was easy, unlike the Mark 2 cars (where part of the offside inner wing had to be cut away to make room for the carburettors).

Inside, it was a mixture of typical Jaguar features (plenty of wood and leather) together with American-influenced items such as the single bench front seat, which offered precious little passenger support during 'press on' motoring.

In 1964, the Mk X received a 4.2 litre engine, with the bore size increased to 92.07mm. Though no power increase was claimed (it remained at 265 bhp at 3,000 rpm), the torque went up to 283 lb/ft at 4,000 rpm. Even though it had to lug all that bulk around, the automatic (curiously a better performer than the manual) could still top 60 mph in around 10 seconds and go on to 120 mph. Despite this, its sales were pretty poor; in America, it looked uncannily similar to the Hudson Hornet of 1948 and was plagued by a series of early reliability problems. In the UK, with its narrow roads, its sheer bulk put off many would-be buyers.

▼ H10. Also in production at the same time as the Mk 2 and the S-type was the non-too-slender Mk X (and later 420G). A leviathan of a car, it held the somewhat dubious record of being the widest UK production car until the introduction of another Jaguar – the XJ220!

In 1966 Jaguar attempted (and to some extent succeeded) in giving the Mk X a sales boost by transforming it into the 420G. Debates as to what the 'G' meant continue to this day. There was no official word, though the general consensus was that it stood for Grand. The 420G was essentially unchanged from the Mk X, but cosmetics included a different radiator grille (with a large vertical central strip), a chrome line along its flanks to help break up the bulky look, and new wheel trims. Inside the car, luxury is not a big enough word to describe it, with acres of wood veneer and just about every gadget available, including electric windows and a separate heating system for the rear seat passengers.

As a complete car, the Mk X/420G had many shortcomings but, taking it piecemeal, it is easy to see where much of the inspiration for the XJ6 came from. The interior gives one a definite sense of *déjà vu* and, squinting hard at the bloated bodywork, it's not hard to see shades of the XJ; look at the deep side sills, the twin headlamps alongside the chrome grille, the low, chrome front bumper, etc. All these show that Jaguar was getting very close to the ideal design for the luxury car.

S-TYPE

The other saloon around in the '60s at the time of the XJ6's gestation was the S-type, which hit the roads in October 1963 and, though clearly based on the much-loved Mk 2, the rear of the car had been subtly altered. This was largely to enable it to accommodate the independent rear suspension already used on the Mk X and E-type in place of the Mk 2's beam axle. In addition, the boot space was increased by a hefty 50 per cent, despite the fitting of twin fuel tanks. These alterations led to an increase in weight of around 330 lb (approx 150kg) and the decision not to offer an underpowered 2.4 litre version was certainly a wise one. The front was also visually different and the roofline changed in profile from that of the Mk 2.

▲ H11. *This front view shows how the S-type derived much of its styling from its Mk 2 predecessor. Like Mercedes and BMW, Jaguar have been adept at maintaining a corporate 'look' to successive models which has resulted in a continual supply of new buyers whilst retaining the existing owners. A neat trick if you can pull it off! The many detail changes included: indicators moved to an around-the-wing position, no top-mounted repeater lamps and different bumper and grille. Wire wheels were still en vogue,* even as the XJ6 was making its début.

The car was available with either 3.4 or 3.8 XK six-cylinder engine (of course!) which produced 210 bhp at 5,500 rpm or 220 bhp at 5,500 rpm respectively. As ever, most S-types were fitted with automatic transmissions, though manual box was available with power assistance and overdrive as options. These were unchanged from their spell in the Mk 2 although the S-type did gain new power steering.

In 1966 the 420 was introduced. This was confusing because, though this was based on the S-type (the production of which continued to run alongside it), the 420G was based on the Mk X! Visually, the 420 was an amalgam of styles, having an obvious kinship with the S-type, but with a front-end and grille owing more than a little to the Mk X. Production of both the S-type and 420 ceased in 1968, with the Daimler versions continuing for around another year, both dates coinciding with their XJ6 replacements.

JAGUAR XJ6 HISTORY

THE SERIES 1 (September 1968–July 1973)

The XJ6 glided seamlessly into UK motoring life at the British Motor Show in 1968, to become by far the most successful saloon model Jaguar ever made. In an industry where first impressions count, the XJ6 started with a full score sheet with styling straightaway so right. In fact, scrupulous attention had been given to all aspects of its design, from cylinder head cooling to its specially-designed tyres. Considerations had, of course, been given to American safety and emissions regulations, the need to compete head-on with competitors such as Mercedes and BMW, and the need to entice new Jaguar customers without alienating long-time Jaguar-istes.

▲ H12. The Press and public raved about it, and in the decade that was 'backing Britain' it seemed most appropriate that Jaguar should unveil its finest offering. A glance back at the Mk X shows many similarities – four headlamps in line, large central rectangular grille, low chrome bumper and lower wing mounted combined side/indicator lamp clusters. However, the proportions of the new car were far more pleasing and realistic. A slight reduction in the number of curves also gave the XJ6 a more modern appearance, an important factor in 1968. Note the lack of standard-fit door or wing mirrors and the LHD wiper pattern, which left an awkward unwiped area at the top right of the screen. This remained a feature until the Series 3 cars in 1979.

▲ H14. The leaping cat mascot may have gone, but it was there in spirit and on badges on the rear sections of the front wings. You can't keep a good cat down!

▲ H13. The 'squared-off' look was more apparent at the rear of the car. The first production cars were equipped with straight twin rear exhaust pipes, but problems with fumes entering the cabin led to a quick rethink, and a pair of more curvaceous pipes were fitted. Four silencers were fitted in order to keep the noise down. This is a late-model car which had larger reversing lamps with red reflectors fitted beneath the lamp clusters (earlier cars had smaller reversing lamps with the reflectors sitting alongside them). The number plate lights were set into the centre of the bumper and had a propensity for rot and water-related electrical problems as water dripped off the boot lid on to them. For the Series 2 and 3 models, the number plate lamp assembly was incorporated into the boot lock. Nowhere on the car was the word 'Jaguar', only a badge denoting its engine capacity. A 2.8 litre version was produced in order to undercut European tax legislation, but they were very much unloved and sold poorly compared to the 4.2 litre models.

The motoring public loved it, literally queuing up to buy it; the case of 20 Swiss business executives holding a noisy demonstration outside the London HQ of BLMC was extreme, but typical of the feelings of many who had been slow off the mark in getting down to their nearest Jaguar showroom. Without doubt, a huge part of its appeal was the price – at just under £2,500 it was serious value, and compared, say, to the contemporary Mercedes 220, it was bright sunshine on a dull day.

More important, perhaps, the motoring press – never easy to please – loved it just as much as the car-buying man-in-the-street. CAR magazine made it their 'Car of the Year' and Autocar reported that 'if Jaguar were to double the price of the XJ6 and bill it as the best car in the world, we would be right there behind them.' Overseas, the praise was no less forthcoming; in America, Road Test magazine said 'The Jaguar XJ sedan ushers in a new era in motoring excellence that will stand as the yardstick for the next decade', and down under in Australia, Wheels magazine came to the conclusion that the XJ6 was '… the best riding car we've ever driven.' The XJ6 was 'priced to sell' right from the start, continuing Jaguar's tradition of offering serious value-for-money packages.

Prices at launch were as follows:

2.8 litre de luxe	Manual	£1897
	Auto	£1999
4.2 litre de luxe	Manual	£2254
	Auto	£2398

By the time of the introduction of the Series 2, the prices had increased across the board by almost 50 per cent – a sign of the times!

DEVELOPMENT

Right from the start, great things were planned for the Mk X/420G replacement, to the extent that over £6m was invested in its development. For four years, Jaguar designers, engineers and stylists worked to produce a car that kept the good points of previous saloons and sports cars but also addressed their weaknesses. The 420G, for example, was often criticised for being overweight, over long and generally just being too much of everything – though the basic general styling was popular. The XJ6, therefore, was to go on a diet, the car eventually being some 380kg lighter than its predecessor.

In order to give a light, airy feel to the cabin, a large glass area was required and, to this end, very thin roof pillars were used. In theory, this should cause a real problem because most cars gain much of their structural strength from these pillars. However, the XJ6 had already gained masses of this from the fact that the rest of the shell was so rigid; the heavily ribbed floor pan was bounded by two large sills which, together with the transmission tunnel, provided the longitudinal strength required. This was then further enhanced by a front and rear box-section crossmember. The roof design, however, meant that a factory-fitted sunroof could not be offered until the Series 3 was introduced in 1979.

STYLE AND LUXURY – BODYWORK

The styling was, understandably, an instant success and the effect on public and press alike can easily be likened to that of the E-type Jaguar at the

beginning of the decade. Even 30 years later, the Series 1 cars stand up well as stylish, luxury cars, so just imagine the effect of such a machine in the late 60s!

Though clearly taking some styling cues from the 420G, the Series 1 XJ6 was considerably more pleasing to the eye, being more in proportion all round. And despite looking fresh and new, it also managed to evoke memories of Jaguars past – a neat trick if you can pull it off! The 420G ancestry was perhaps most noticeable at the front of the car, where the four-headlamp treatment was almost identical, with a similar large radiator grille, indicator lenses and narrow section chrome bumper.

The bonnet line was deliberately low to allow for the long-awaited and much-vaunted 12-cylinder engine. However, in order that the taller, six-cylinder XK motor would fit comfortably, a bulge from front to rear of the bonnet was required.

It's no use having a beautiful luxury car if it rattles like a can of marbles! Few know this better than Jaguar, and so great attention was paid to cutting down the noise for the cosseted occupants. Sound-deadening material was applied to the floors, box sections and doors, and it worked admirably, although as the cars got older, it had the unfortunate side-effect of holding moisture directly on to the steel pressings with the inevitable result – rust. This was particularly true on the floor panels.

Towards the end of its production run, a stretched version of the Series 1 was introduced to give the somewhat cramped rear seat passengers another 4 in of leg room. The cars, which ran alongside the existing short wheel base cars, were listed at XJ6L (and were also available in Daimler form). The extra length was put into the wheelbase at the back of the car, necessitating a longer rear door. The modifications resulted in a substantial weight gain of around 170 lb. This car effectively became the basis for most of the Series 2 range.

For some reason, presumably to favour export sales, the wiper pattern was wrong for RHD cars and, once the screen was dirty, visibility through the unswept

area at the top right of the screen was awkward and sometimes dangerous. Many foreign cars were imported into the UK with this problem, but it was most odd for Jaguar to follow suit. Despite much feedback about the subject, they stayed that way until the Series 3.

▲ H15. Twin fuel tanks (each of 11.5 gallons capacity) were fitted to all models. Burst-proof chrome filler caps were fitted, largely because of the influence of American legislation which concerned itself with the possibility of a fire in the event of a rear-end collision.

▲ H16. The Series 1 door handle was a typical chrome item with a separate lock which stayed through the Series 2 models but …

▲ H17. ... the Series 3 had to have flush-fitted door handles for safety. The simple lock remained, though, and it is still one of the key areas of insecurity. Note standard and heavily chromed door mirror.

SAFETY

Safety (a key consideration in the American markets, as we shall see) greatly affected many aspects of the XJ6 design and was the main reason for the deletion of the legendary 'leaping cat' mascot on the bonnet. However, despite this the name Jaguar did not appear anywhere on the car – just a chrome badge on the boot lid to indicate the engine size.

INTERIOR

Inside, the car was unmistakably Jaguar, with the designers picking and choosing the best aspects from previous models. The large speedometer and rev counter had chrome rings and were set into a wooden fascia. They were flanked by more modern warning lights, and the traditional Jaguar starter button had been ditched, starting now being literally on the key. There was a row of four auxiliary gauges, but they were not ideally placed for easy checking, being placed in the centre of the car, above the centre console. The steering column was collapsible and the wheel was reach-adjustable.

American safety regulations affected the design in the same way that the USA emission regulations affected the engine. For example, the 'trademark' row of toggle switches seen in earlier Jaguar models, was replaced by plastic rocker switches. Though they looked good,

especially to gadget-minded '60s drivers, there's no doubt that they could be confusing in use.

The designers were aware that comfort was one of Jaguar's key selling points; and on the grounds that the most comfortable place for most people is in bed, they brought in bed-manufacturers Slumberland to assist in the seat design! Early in its production life, the backs of the front seats were padded to prevent accident injury to rear seat passengers, and side-impact bars were built into the doors (except for the 2.8 litre models which were Europe-only vehicles). A long-time Jaguar fitment, rear passenger/front seat fold-down picnic tables were not fitted, again for crash safety reasons.

To counter criticisms of the heating on earlier saloons, the XJ6 utilised a proven Smiths system which 'breathed in' outside air via a chrome grille in front of the windscreen and heated it as required, passing it through a complex system of valves and flaps through the car. Overall, it was a great improvement, but many contemporary cars had better heating and ventilation. Anyone with £252 to spare could order the optional Delaney-Gallay air-conditioning system, one of the chief plus-points being that it had been designed to complement the car's own heating system and so not take up any valuable space. However, this was largely seen as an expensive frippery by '60s UK buyers, and in the USA, where air-con was seen more as a necessity, it was up against more efficient systems fitted to its main rivals.

When launched, static seat belts were standard at the front only, and the mountings were uprated shortly into the production run. Other interior safety items included a snap-off rear-view mirror, a quarterlight which opened with a plastic wheel (rather than a metal catch) and an energy absorbing surround for the instrument panel. In keeping with its role as budget model, and in an effort to make headway in the fleet sales market, the 2.8 litre cars had basic interiors; leather was not used, instead the door trim panels (no pockets for this car) and seats were finished in Ambla.

SUSPENSION

Many of the XJ6's underpinnings had already been used in previous models. For example, the 4.2 litre engine and the independent rear suspension (IRS) were to be found on the Mk X/420G. It was the modifications and the overall package that made the new Jaguar such an attractive package. The front suspension, for example, though based on that of the Mk X, utilised a much better anti-dive geometry set-up which allowed softer spring rates to be employed. As such, both the handling and the ride were improved. Also aiding the ride were shock absorbers mounted outside the coil springs (the dampers utilised greater displacement and thus offered better damping).

BRAKING

Stopping the car was down to a set of Girling brakes, a disc at each corner aided by a Type 100 vacuum servo unit. This included the master cylinder which featured two pistons in tandem, each with its own inlet and outlet ports, operating the front and rear discs respectively. If there were a failure of one set (if, say, a brake line fractured) the driver would still be left with some braking effect, albeit diminished. The front brakes were fairly conventional, but the rears, because of the use of the IRS suspension, were inboard and included a separate handbrake assembly on each rear disc with its own callipers and pads. The brake pads were Ferodo 2430, except for the M34 Mintex pads used on the handbrake. The discs were 11.18 in and 10.395 in diameter at the front and rear respectively.

STEERING

First used on the E-type, the Adwest rack and pinion steering was adapted for use on the XJ6, a first for a Jaguar saloon. Many criticised the steering for being too light and lacking in feel; though, as ever, Jaguar were aiming very much at the American market, where light steering is generally preferred. In line with (then) current safety thinking, universal joints were used in the system and the steering column was collapsible.

WHEELS AND TYRES

Yet another first for the XJ6 was the use of 6 in wide steel wheels – the widest to date on a Jaguar saloon. They were shod with Dunlop SP Sport E70VR radial tyres, which had been developed by the company specifically for Jaguar's new flagship. They had the twin benefits of offering incredible road-holding and, most important, an extremely quiet ride (even though there was more noise than a cross-ply tyre). This was largely because of the irregular tread pattern which broke down standard resonance patterns. It was a source of some delight to Jaguar (and Jaguar owners) that the XJ6 featured radial-ply tyres as standard some four years before Rolls Royce! No alloy wheel options were listed.

ENGINES

Several engines were mooted for the new car. A V8 was tried, not least because of the Daimler connection, but rejected because it was thought to be simply not smooth enough for a Jaguar. There was also a 3 litre, six-cylinder engine on the stocks but, although it produced plenty of power (almost as much as the 4.2 litre engine), it lacked any real torque and, once again, this was thought to be a key ingredient in any Jaguar. There was, of course, the possibility that the long-time-in-development V12 would go under the bonnet, but that was a long way off at that time.

As it transpired, the first XJ6 models were available with a choice of two engines, both, of course, XK six-cylinder variants. In common with other British vehicles, a viscous fan (with 12 blades) was fitted whereby at low speeds (up to around 2,500 rpm) it engaged and provided extra cooling. Above that engine speed, it 'freewheeled' as the air passing through the radiator would provide sufficient cooling. In fact, Jaguar had applied lots of thought to the cooling system in general, in order to avoid similar overheating problems to those experienced by some models of the Mk X and 420/G. The large crossflow radiator utilised a separate header tank so that the bonnet line could be kept low, though a

slight 'bulge' was necessary to cope with the extra height of the 4.2 litre engine (all bonnets, including the 2.8 litre versions, featured this).

The water pump was fitted with a larger impeller – to shift more water – and a smaller pulley, so that the impeller turned more quickly. In addition, the cylinder head porting was uprated in an effort to create a more even temperature around the inlet and exhaust valves. A bypass pipe led from the head to the radiator and helped keep the head cooler still.

Though the burble of a lightly-silenced six-cylinder Jaguar engine is music to the ears of the true enthusiast, for an up-market luxury carriage like the XJ6, silence is golden. To achieve this no fewer than four silencers were fitted, two in each of the two systems which ran down ether side of the car from the Siamesed manifold down-pipes. The result, as you might imagine, was a whisper quiet, silky smooth engine that required a glance at the tachometer to confirm that it was running. It is no coincidence that so many road-testers likened the XJ6 to the Rolls Royce!

The engine (whichever) was mounted on a subframe which took around 80 per cent of the weight of the unit. This effectively 'soaked up' vibration and road noise and was a major factor in obtaining the low level of interior noise.

SPECIFICATIONS – 4.2 litre (4325 cc, bore x stroke – 92.07 mm x 106 mm)

CR	Power	Torque
7:1	225 bhp at 5500 rpm	263 lb/ft at 5500 rpm
8:1	235 bhp at 5500 rpm	273 lb/ft at 3750 rpm
9:1	245 bhp at 5500 rpm (standard)	283 lb/ft at 3750 rpm

The 4.2 litre XJ6 produced an impressive set of statistics, cracking the 0-60 mph time in 9.7 seconds and hitting 100 mph in 26.4 seconds. With a little effort, it was possible to get close to 20 mpg, but driven in the way most drivers did, 15-16 mpg was a more realistic average.

SPECIFICATIONS – 2.8 litre (2,791 cc, bore x stroke – 83 mm x 86 mm)

Based around the old 2.4 litre motor, the smaller-engined XJ6 was never particularly popular in the UK. It was introduced primarily to pick up sales in Europe where its smaller capacity got it under a tax break. It was available in a choice of three compression ratios, namely:

CR	Power	Torque
7:1	160 bhp at 6,000 rpm	162 lb/ft at 3,750 rpm
8:1	170 bhp at 6,000 rpm (standard)	172 lb/ft at 3,750 rpm
9:1	180 bhp at 6,000 rpm	182 lb/ft at 3,750 rpm

Though these figures were reasonable, the car's overall lack of lugging power could be attributed to a deficit of around 100 lb/ft of torque compared to the 4.2 litre cars.

Before long, the 2.8 litre engines developed a reputation for holing pistons, and to combat this, new heavier pistons were fitted in 1970 (from engine number 7G.8849). This solved the original problem but created another – it made the smaller-engined Jaguar even slower, which led to them becoming even less popular than they were already. It was discovered that the problem only occurred on those cars which were treated 'kindly' and were pottered around town instead of being driven with some vigour, as the Jaguar test team had done. Carbon deposits built up on the tops of the pistons and, after a while, these deposits would start to detonate and ultimately burn holes through the tops of the pistons. By 1972, the 2.8 litre model had been deleted from the UK range, although it was available in Europe until the introduction of the Series 2.

TRANSMISSION

As on most luxury cars, the XJ6 and automatic transmission were synonymous. A 4-speed manual gearbox (as used in previous saloons, but modified to be quieter in operation) was advertised as being available on both cars, though this was largely a marketing ploy so that a lower basic price could be advertised ('… available from just …'). Of those who did order their XJ6 with a stir-it-yourself gearbox, almost all selected the Laycock overdrive option, which was only effective on top gear and activated by a switch in the top of the gear knob. Even worse for those in this select bunch – they had to wait for several months while the initial flurry of orders – almost all for automatic cars – was fulfilled.

Most 4.2 litre models were ordered with the three-speed Borg Warner Model 8 automatic gearbox; hardly a new and innovative unit, but there was nothing else available at the time to cope with the torque of the bigger engine. The 2.8 litre cars received the Model 35 box from the same company with, for the first time on any Jaguar, two drive positions – 1 and 2.

In 1969, European models were fitted with a revised rear axle ratio (3.31:1 for the 4.2 litre and 4.09:1 for the 2.8 litre) to suit the Borg Warner Model 12 automatic box. The improvements were many, including better acceleration (almost as good as a manual gearbox), the ability to select the lower two gears manually and a vacuum servo to replace the previous mechanical linkage. American cars were 2 years behind Europe in receiving the new gearbox.

AMERICA
Though much of the XJ6's design and build was in direct response to American legislation, it wasn't until the end of 1970 that export began, as the cars had to pass complex and stringent tests. American cars were fitted with two 175CD Stromberg carburettors, whereas European models had twin SU carbs. This was so that the cars would pass the already stringent emission regulations. However, in making the cars run leaner (one of the main elements in reducing exhaust emissions) it did tend to make the cars run hotter than normal. In addition, power output was down – Jaguar's figure was 246 bhp at 5,500 rpm for cars fitted with either SUs or Strombergs, but it is generally thought

that the American cars produced nearer 170 bhp (only 4.2 litre cars were exported to America).

DAIMLER
Because of staggeringly high demand for the Jaguar models, it was August 1969 before the first Daimler-badged car left the factory. In effect, the Daimler was a fully loaded XJ6, taking most of the options, apart from air-conditioning, as standard. From the outside, there were a few clues; a revised fluted front grille with a similar treatment for the boot lid plinth, Daimler badging carried through to the chrome hub caps and a central chrome strip on the bonnet. There was no doubt that the seemingly insignificant change of front grille was an extremely important sales tool, with buyers reckoning that it was far more becoming than the 'plain Jane' Jaguar versions. The Sovereign won the Motor Show Gold Medal for Bodywork in 1969 and 1970.

THE SERIES 2
(SWB: September 1973-November 1974/LWB: September 1973-February 1979/3.4 litre: April 1975-February 1979)
The Series 2 car was first shown at the Frankfurt Motor Show at the end of 1973. Early in its life, the car was made with the same wheelbase as the original Series 1, but production halted in

November 1974, after some 12,000 had been turned out. The Series 2 XJ6L, based on the same wheelbase as the LWB Series 1 car, became the 'standard' XJ6 and the cars were then badged as XJ 4.2.

From the front, a slightly different face was presented to the world, not withstanding the fact that it was still clearly an XJ6. The front bumper was raised from 12 in to 16 in, in order to meet new safety standards for pedestrians, the upshot of which was that the radiator grille became shallower

▼ H18. As much as anything, the strict American safety regulations dictated the new look to the front of the Series 2 models. At 12 in off the ground, the bumper of the Series 1 cars was deemed to be dangerous to pedestrians in the event of an accident and so it had to be raised to 16 in. This meant that (failing a 4 in hike in bonnet height!) the radiator grille had to become shallower and the grille beneath the bumper taller. In addition, the two 'air intakes', a key feature of the first model had to go. Note also that the large chrome bumpers were not pedestrian-friendly and were replaced by small rubber overriders. The new all-plastic indicator/sidelight assemblies remained in the wings, albeit moved down slightly to be below the bumper. Note the new style steel wheel with chrome centre cap.

and the lower grille became taller. The two intake grilles disappeared, the indicator/sidelight assemblies moved down the wing a little and the bumpers lost their chrome overriders to be replaced by small rubber appendages. A new design of steel wheel with chrome centre cap was fitted – chrome-plated wheels were an extra-cost option. The front window quarterlights were still fitted but, like those at the rear, were fixed rather than opening (as on the Series 1) in order cut down interior wind noise.

▲ H21. The chrome plinth which housed the bootlid lock became more chunky, not least because it now played host to the number plate lamps. These were moved from their original position in the bumper because of rust and water problems.

▲ H19. The difference between the Series 1 (at left) and Series 2 in this photo of the two together. The car to the right is actually a Daimler Vanden Plas version, denoted by the slightly larger grille, standard fog lamps in the lower grille and chrome central bonnet strip running from the grille toward the windscreen.

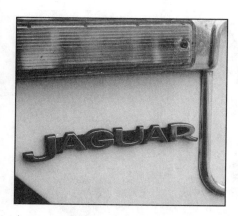

▲ H20. At the rear of the car, the bootlid gained the 'Jaguar' nomenclature for the first time, with the model and engine size (XJ6, 4.2) in the mirror image position on the other side of the bootlid.

At the rear there was little change – the number plate light migrated northwards to live in the revised chrome surround around the boot lid lock (as previously, this was fluted on Daimler versions). The prices at the 1973 launch were as follows, with the LWB versions being shown in brackets:

4.2 litre (saloon)	Manual + O/D	£3674 (£4124)
4.2 litre (saloon)	Auto	£3704 (£4154)
4.2 litre (coupé)	Manual + O/D	£4260
4.2 litre (coupé)	Auto	£4290

The most obvious difference when sitting in a Series 2 is that the Jaguar 'trademark' bank of rocker switches has disappeared from the centre of the dashboard. To many, these were (and still are) part of the Jaguar legend and their passing was regretted. However, by following the lead set by other manufacturers, putting many functions (including the floor-mounted dipswitch) on the steering column stalks did make life much easier and less confusing for the driver. The dials all moved to the console in front of the steering wheel where the driver could see them easily, but the bright plastic surrounds were distinctly down-market and out of place in an XJ6 – '70s or not! In the same vein, the exterior light control looked like an escapee from a rally spares accessory shop, looking very much like an afterthought and fitted under the dash to the left of the steering wheel.

Luxury was still a byword within the car, with lots of 'toys' available, including electric windows, inertia-reel seat belts standard across the range and fibre-optic lighting of various switches – a first for a British car. Initially, the central locking didn't include the boot.

Great attention was paid to the heating and ventilation system, something that came in for no small amount of criticism on the Series 1 cars. A very complex air-blending set-up utilising twin fans and servo motors was fitted, the amendments being so extensive that bodywork modifications were required. It also meant that the bulkhead was only single-skinned and plenty of sound-absorbing material (asbestos in the engine bay and bitumen/foam inside) had to be fitted to make sure that noise and resonance levels did not increase. The optional ventilated discs fitted to some Series 1 cars became standard fitting on the Series 2.

The 4.2 litre engines were being affected by American emission regulations and had to be fitted with a different air-cleaner and an air-intake system which used exhaust heat to reduce pollution.

The Borg-Warner Type 65 gearbox was a massive improvement on the Type 12 and was fitted to 4.2 litre models from the end of 1973. On the LWB cars the engine gave 170 bhp at 4,500 rpm and 231 lb/ft of torque at 3,500 rpm (the power output figures at this time changed to DIN readings, hence the apparent 'loss' of power compared with the earlier models).

In 1978 American cars were fitted with Lucas-Bosch D-Jetronic fuel injection (already tried on the V12 engine) and three-way catalyst exhaust systems in order to pass the ever more stringent emissions regulations. The more efficient system enabled the designers to increase the compression ratio to 8:1 (it had been reduced to 7.4:1 during previous attempts to cut down the emissions) and thus improve the performance and power output from 161 bhp to 176 bhp. By the end of 1978, some European 4.2 litre cars were being fitted with the same system, albeit without the catalytic exhaust.

3.4 LITRE

The 2.8 litre engine had already been dropped and, although it was still listed for a while, for two years, the choice was no choice at all – you had a 4.2 litre or nothing! However, in May 1975 the 3.4 litre model was introduced, Jaguar looking for sales in the lucrative executive fleet market, where a smaller-engined car would, theoretically at least, be more attractive.

The engine was essentially that used in Jaguars of yore, with the same bore and stroke but with better cooling, better internal oil flow and a totally new block – essential, as Jaguar had ditched the tooling for the original 3.4 litre unit.

Two SU HS8 carburettors were linked to an automatic choke and utilised the straight port head from the 4.2 litre model. With a bore x stroke the same as the 2.8 litre cars (83mm x 106mm), the actual capacity of the new engine was 3,442 cc, and with a compression ratio of 8:1 it produced 161 bhp at 5,000 rpm and 189 lb/ft of torque at 3,500 rpm. Like the 4.2 litre cars, a Type 65 Borg-Warner automatic transmission was used. With any luxury car, image is all-important and so it was vital that the car was not seen as a poor man's XJ6 – rather a *different* XJ6. The exterior give-aways are few – a boot badge 'XJ 3.4', the lack of a front-to-rear coachline and plain no-chrome steel wheels.

With the object of creating extra sales, it was important to reduce the base price. The simplest way to do this is to reduce the level of standard equipment, making much more extra-cost options. These included leather trim, front seat head rests and electric windows. Ultimately, it hit the streets costing some £400 less than the equivalent 4.2 litre model.

Fuel injection was fitted to US-spec cars from May 1978 – (though UK owners had to wait another three years for this).

TRANSMISSION

Manual cars were fitted with the five-speed gearbox taken from the contemporary Rover SD1 from October 1978 – one of dozens of examples of British Leyland utilising parts through different marques within the group. In theory, a good cost-saving idea, but not always viable in practice and the 'box did little to improve the performance, driveability or indeed, mpg of the XJ6.

THE DARK YEARS

It is perhaps fitting that the 'decade that taste forgot' should be the decade when Jaguar's quality control all but disappeared. The Series 2 is known as the most problematic Jaguar of them all. The confusion that reigned following the amalgamation of Jaguar into the melange that called itself British Leyland didn't help, and with management and

union problems throughout the '70s, it's a wonder that any XJ6s made it off the production line at all.

An example of the lack of quality control was the problem of water leakage, which affected most models. Rainwater seemed to be able to get in at a number of points simply because of inadequate sealing on the production line. Not unnaturally, owners were not best pleased when their carpets started to rot and the damp interior climate encouraged mould to form on the fittings.

Problems with the elderly paint plant in 1978 meant that late model Series 2 cars were available in any colour you liked – as long as you liked white, red or yellow!

That said, some cars *were* made to a reasonable standard, and many around today have had their bugbears sorted by either first owners (under warranty) and/or subsequent owners by regular applications of TLC. As such, the Series 2 cars don't always represent such a bad buy as you might imagine.

THE SERIES 3
(March 1979–April 1987)

Having invested almost £16m in new paint spraying facilities, BL was in no position to commission a 'new' XJ6, and so the Series 3 was very much based on the previous model; it utilised the floorpan (now overweight), the boot and the bonnet, though enough detail changes were made to make it distinctive. Italian stylists at the Pininfarina concern were employed to 'square-off' the car somewhat, and to this end the roofline was raised by around 3 in at the rear of the car (giving more rear passenger headroom), the quarterlights deleted and the front and rear screens were bonded into place in an effort to keep rainwater on the outside! The extra glass area gave a much more 'airy' feel for occupants, and the taller roof allowed the company to offer a sunroof as an option for the first time in an XJ6. All 4.2 litre cars were fitted with tinted glass as standard, it being an optional extra on the 3.4 litre models.

▲ H22. The difference between the Series 2 and 3 is less marked but still much at the behest of America, with rubber bumper inserts. The indicators have migrated to the bumpers themselves. This car has optional headlamp washers. Side repeater lamps on the front wings were standard throughout the range. New stainless wheel trims covered the entire wheel.

▲ H23. At the rear of the car there was a much more geometric look, as the angular boot lid was formed to bridge the two equally angular lamp clusters. Being a Daimler version, the boot lid lock/handle assembly is much more elaborate than on the 'mere' Jaguar versions. Note twin rear fog lamps built into either end of the bumper. The aerial had moved from the offside front wing (RHD) to the offside rear wing.

▶ H24. The 1982 40-hole alloys quickly became known as 'pepperpots' – for obvious reasons!

The new plant facilitated much more attention to be paid to rust-proofing, with bodyshells being sprayed with an anti-corrosion primer and wax injected into box sections. However, it took quite a while for the company to get to grips with the new equipment, and for two years the paint/primer/underseal finish varied wildly. It was 1982 (and into the Sir John Egan era) before quality paint finishes became the norm.

On the outside, the most obvious difference was the fitting of large, chrome-topped 'rubber' bumpers, once more required by USA crash regulations. Though clearly not as elegant and traditional as previous Jaguars, they were much more tastefully designed than on many models of the time. The indicators were fitted into the front bumper and the foglamps in the rear bumper, and the front wings each gained an indicator side-repeater lamp. The side lights were fitted into the outer headlamp housing.

The four-headlamp set-up remained; though, at last, they were quartz-halogen on all models except the 3.4. If the optional headlamp wipers were fitted, so was a larger (12.5 pint) washer bottle. Happily, a proper RHD wiper pattern was introduced, along with wash wipe as standard and the Econocruise cruise-control system as an optional extra.

The rear badging changed subtly – to the left of the number plate was the XJ6 derivation (Jaguar or Daimler) and to its right was the XJ6 legend together with the engine size – on Daimler models 'XJ6' was replaced by the 'Sovereign'.

Inside, there were plusher carpets, more comfortable front seats (with electric adjustment as an option), a clearer dash design and the option of cruise-control and electric door mirrors.

Inertia-reel seat belts were standard at the front but, curiously, rear belts were optional except on cars exported to America, Canada and France. Rationalisation of the car came together in many ways, as shown by the simple act of labelling the various switches with symbols – hence there was no need to swap and change on cars meant for foreign markets.

▲ H25. The Series 3 had a dashboard layout that was more tasteful than that of its predecessor, which seemed a bit tacky with a rather plasticky look to the dash and instrumentation. However, it's generally agreed that neither model can compete with the Series 1 for pure style.

All 4.2 litre cars were fitted with, Lucas-Bosch L-Jetronic fuel injection, but the 3.4 litre engines always used twin SU carbs. The compression ratio increased to 8.7:1 (from the previous 7.8:1, and achieved by use of 9:1 pistons as fitted in the E-type) which combined with earlier opening and larger inlet valves (1.875 in), Lucas-Bosch fuel injection and OPUS electronic ignition to produce a power output of 205 bhp at 5,000 rpm. Torque was 236 lb/ft at 3,750 rpm, but the most important aspect here was that almost all of that (231 lb/ft) was available as low as 1,500 rpm – only just over idling speed!

The Borg-Warner Type 65 gearbox was modified and became the Type 66 and, according to many experts, the best ever fitted to an XJ6.

The prices at launch were increased (naturally) and the most frequently quoted prices were base, not including many of the extras that no self-respecting Jaguar owner would want to be without.

3.4 litre	Manual + O/D	£11,189
4.2 litre	Manual + O/D	£12,326

At the top of the six-cylinder tree was the 4.2 litre Daimler Vanden Plas, which took a healthy chunk out of any bank balance at a steady £17,208.

GETTING IT RIGHT

The quality control bugbears continued into the early years of the Series 3, and it wasn't until Sir John Egan took the reins and started to make his presence felt in the early '80s that things began to turn around. Customer complaints were, in general, for niggling, small items that should either have been ironed out during production or, in many cases, weeded out during trials. Once more, the lack of cash from BL and the worker/management situation combined to make the worst of all worlds. However, the Egan Empire changed everything and, in fact, it was the Series 3 that effectively brought Jaguar back from the brink of extinction and provided the sound financial base for the development of new models so desperately required.

A CLASSIC COUPE

Taking a four-door saloon, especially one so aesthetically right, and making it into an equally stylish two-door coupé is no mean feat. Certainly, many manufacturers have tried and failed, but at the 1973 Frankfurt Motor Show Jaguar showed their beautiful, pillarless two-door coupé – technically the XJC. However, despite initial enthusiasm, its launch was delayed until 1975 because of problems getting the door windows to seal, by which time the model designation had changed to XJ4.2C (except for the V12-engined cars, of course!).

It was based on the original SWB Series produced in Series 2 guise. Of course, the two doors had to be much bigger than the original front doors of the four-door car and their extra weight (each door weighed around 200 lb!) meant that the door pillars and hinges had to be beefed-up to cope. At the show, the manual/overdrive model was listed at £4260 with the auto version costing £30 more – all XJ6Cs were fitted with 4.2 litre engines.

▲ H26. To some eyes (present company included) the XJ6 coupé (the XJ 4.2C) was the best-looking of all the models. It was available with 4.2 litre six-cylinder or 5.3 litre 12-cylinder engines; what a choice! The leaping cat mascot on this car is non-standard. The coupé was only ever available in Series 2 form.

▶ H27. 'Look Ma, no B-pillar!'. It was sealing problems with these pillar-less windows that caused the two-year delay from its début at the Frankfurt motor show in 1973 to its introduction in April 1975. Note that both front and rear windows have disappeared altogether – the rears not only go down, but also forward via a complex mechanism in order to clear the wheel arch. The dash, instrumentation and interior was much as for any other Series 2 car. The coupé remained in production for just two years by which time around 6,500 had been sold.

▲ H28. At one time, any Jaguar with a body kit would have been unthinkable. But thanks to the efforts of several major tuners, notably TWR, they have gained a new respectability. This car has been lowered and has had a bumper/sill/wheel-arch kit fitted, the colour-coding adding even more to the 'menacing' appearance the owner was doubtless seeking to achieve.

The lack of a 'B' pillar meant that much attention had to be paid to retaining the structural rigidity inherent in the original XJ6. Various areas were strengthened, including the roof at the 'C' pillar, and all production coupés featured that most '70s feature – the black vinyl roof.

Despite these attempts to replace the inherent strength of the XJ6 to the coupé, the car did not pass the USA crash tests – a big problem, as Jaguar had seen the North American market as an area ripe for sales. Because of the huge financial problems facing British Leyland at the time, no cash could be made available for what was seen as a 'plaything', and the limited market place was one of the major factors leading to its short life; production stopped in November 1977, with a tally of 6487 made.

▼ H29. Jaguar continued modifying and uprating the XK engine throughout the life of the XJ6. This is a concours example of a Series 3 4.2 litre unit. Right from the start there was plenty of extra room in the engine bay, as it was envisaged from the design stage that it would have to take the V12 engine. Note the heavily matt-black painted exhaust manifolds, more usually coloured rust brown!

▶ *H30. This is a 1983 Series 3 4.2 litre engine, by this time with a redesigned cylinder block (1979) and equipped with Lucas-Bosch L-Jetronic fuel injection (1981) to produce more power, better economy and lower emissions (North American cars had been fuel-injected since 1978).*

▶ *H31. Though inherently more complex than carburation, the fuel injection system remained 'on song' for longer and was considerably more efficient. Many owners feared troubles in the 'black box' – the ECU (electronic control unit) that deciphered the information received from sensors around the engine and gave instructions as to how much fuel to allow through the injectors. In truth, most fuel injection problems relate to sensor failure than to the ECU itself.*

JAGUAR XK SALOON PRODUCTION DETAILS

Model	Number	Produced from	Model	Number	Produced from
Mark VII	20,937	1951-57	420	10,236	1966-68
Mark VIIM	10,060	1951-57	240	4,430	1967-69
2.4 litre Mark 1	19,705	1956-59	340	2,804	
3.4 litre Mark 1	17,280	1956-59	**XJ6 Series 1**		1968-73
Mark IX	10,002	1958-61	2.8 litre	19,322	
2.4 litre Mark 2	26,322	1959-67	4.2 litre	59,951	
3.4 litre Mark 2	29,531	1959-67	**XJ6 Series 2**		1973-79
3.8 litre Mark 2	27,848	1959-67	3.4 litre	6,880	
Mark X 3.8 litre	12,961	1962-70	4.2 litre	69,951	
Mark X 4.2 litre	5,642	1964-70	**XJ Coupé (4.2 litre)**	6,487	1975-77
420G	5,542	1967-70	**XJ6 Series 3**		1979-87
S Type 3.4 litre	9,928	1964-68	3.4 litre	5,799	
S Type 3.8 litre	15,065	1964-68	4.2 litre	117,897	

XJ6 TECHNICAL SPECIFICATIONS

BASIC CONSTRUCTION

The XJ6 was introduced in 1968 and was initially available with the 2.8 litre or 4.2 litre XK, DOHC engine. The standard transmission was a four-speed manual gearbox with optional overdrive or a three-speed automatic gearbox being available as options.

SERIES 1
ENGINE

Six-cylinder in-line 'XK' engine, twin overhead cam engine with cast-iron block and aluminium cylinder head. Firing order 1, 5, 3, 6, 2, 4 – No. 1 cylinder is at the rear of the engine. Series 1 cars were available with 2.8 litre and 4.2 litre capacities, with details as follows:

2.8 litre

Capacity	2791cc
Bore x stroke	83mm x 86mm

4.2 litre

Capacity	4235cc
Bore x stroke	92.07mm x 106mm

The quoted power and torque figures were dependent on the compression ratios of the particular unit.

Comp ratio	Power	Torque
	Bhp at rpm	lb/ft at rpm
7:1	160/6000	162/3750
8:1 (standard)	170/6000	172/3750
9:1	180/6000	182/3750
4.2 litre		
7:1	225/5500	263/5500
8:1	235/5500	273/3750
9:1 (standard)	245/5500	283/3750

Dimensions	in	mm
Overall length	189.50	4812
Overall width	69.37	1762
Overall height	56.70	1440
Wheelbase	108.86	2765
Front track	58	1473
Rear track	58.9	1496
Turning circle	36 ft 0 in	11.0m

Overall weight	lb	kg
XJ6 2.8 litre	3668	1663
XJ6 4.2 litre	3696	1676

FRONT SUSPENSION

Independent wishbones with coil springs and anti-roll bar.

REAR SUSPENSION

Independent wishbones with coil springs and radius arms.

BRAKES

Servo-assisted Girling disc brakes all around.

STEERING

Power-assisted rack and pinion on all models.

TRANSMISSION

Rear wheel drive, with a choice of four-speed manual, four-speed manual with overdrive or automatic transmission.

GEARBOX RATIOS

See Chapter 7.

SERIES 2
ENGINE

Six-cylinder in-line 'XK' engine, twin overhead cam of 3.4 litre and 4.2 litre capacities.

4.2 litre

Details same as for Series 1 cars except for the following: Jaguar XJ6L (designated XJ 4.2 with effect from May 1975)

Power	Torque
Bhp at rpm	lb/ft at rpm
170/4500	231/3500

3.4 litre

Capacity	3442cc
Bore x stroke	83mm x 106mm

Comp ratio	Power	Torque
	Bhp at rpm	lb/ft at rpm
8.8:1	161/5000	189/3500

Dimensions	in	mm
Overall length XJ6 and XJ 4.2C	190.75	4844
Overall length XJ6L	194.68	4945
Overall width	69.3	1760
Overall height	54.10	1374
Wheelbase XJ6 and XJ 4.2C	109.10	2771
Wheelbase XJ6L	113.11	2873
Front track	58	1473
Rear track	58.9	1496
Turning circle	38 ft 0 in	11.6m

Overall weight	lb	kg
XJ6 3.4 litre	3717	1686
XJ6 4.2 litre SWB	3696	1676
XJ6 4.2 litre LWB	3808	1727
XJ 4.2C	3724	1689

GEARBOX RATIOS

See Chapter 7. Towards the end of the Series 2 production the Rover SD1 five-speed gearbox was introduced to replace the previous four-speed/overdrive 'box.

SERIES 3
The Series 3 models spanned March 1979-April 1987.

4.2 litre
Details same as for Series 2 XJ 4.2 except for the following:

Comp ratio	Power	Torque
	Bhp at rpm	lb/ft at rpm
8.7:1	200/5000	236/2750

3.4 litre
The engine remained the same specification as the Series 2 cars.

NOTE THAT Lucas-Bosch L-Jetronic fuel-injection was fitted to North American cars from 1978 and to UK cars from March 1979.

Dimensions	in	mm
Overall length	194.75	4947
Overall width	69.3	1760
Overall height	54.10	1374
Wheelbase	113.11	2873
Front track	58	1473
Rear track	58.9	1496
Turning circle	38 ft 0 in	11.6m

Overall weight	lb	kg
XJ6 3.4 litre	3892	1765
XJ6 4.2 litre	3965	1798

GEARBOX RATIOS
See Chapter 7.

LUBRICATION – ALL MODELS
ENGINE
Multigrade engine oil either SAE 10W/40 or 20W/50 or synthetic (see text).

TRANSMISSION
MANUAL GEARBOX
Four-speed
Hypoid gear oil to SAE 90EP.
Five-speed
Hypoid gear oil to SAE 75.
Hypoid gear oil to SAE 80EP (top-up only).*

*Where some baulking of gears is experienced with the five-speed gearboxes, it is permissible to drain and refill using Dexron II type ATF fluid.

AUTOMATIC GEARBOX
ATF (automatic transmission fluid) to M2C 33G.

FINAL DRIVE
Standard
Hypoid gear oil to SAE 90EP
Limited-slip differential
Powr-Lok approved gear oil to SAE 90.
Hypoid gear oil to SAE 90EP (top-up only).*

POWER STEERING
ATF fluid to M2C 33G.

BRAKE FLUID
Hydraulic fluid to SAE J1703D.

CLUTCH FLUID
Hydraulic fluid to SAE J1703D.

COOLING SYSTEM
Antifreeze all year round to BS 3150, BS 3152 or BS 6850. A mix of between 33-50% should be used.

IDENTIFY YOUR XJ6
The following table shows the starting chassis numbers for the various models.

Model	RHD	LHD
Series 1		
Jaguar 2.8 litre	IG1001	IG50001
Daimler 2.8 litre	IT1001	N/A
Jaguar 4.2 litre	IL1001	IL50001
Daimler 4.2 litre	IU1001	N/A
XJ6L	2E1001	2E50001
Daimler Sovereign	2D1001	N/A
Series 2		
Jaguar 4.2 litre (SWB)	2N1001	2N 50001
Daimler 4.2 litre (SWB)	2M1001	
Jaguar 4.2 litre	2T1001	2T50001
XJ 4.2C	2J1001	2J50001
Daimler Sovereign Coupé	2H1001	N/A
Jaguar 3.4 litre	3A1001	3A50001
Daimler 3.4 litre	3B1001	
Series 3		
Jaguar 3.4 litre	JAAL A 3CC	*
Jaguar 4.2 litre incl. Daimler, Sovereign and Jaguar Sovereign	JAAL P 7CC	*

*With the advent of the Euro VIN plate system, there was no distinction between models or RHD/LHD.

Chapter 2

Preparation

DISMANTLING – AND SPACE

Whether you're doing a complete restoration or, for example, tackling trim troubles, you'll soon find out that an enormous amount of space is required. If possible, allocate a section of your garage purely for storage of parts that have been removed and will either (a) be replaced as is or (b) cleaned/repaired, etc., before being replaced. In an ideal world it's good to have a separate place altogether for these parts, as this will stop them getting covered in swarf, dust and paint, as you work on the car. Some owners invest in a small (or not so small) shed just for this purpose. These are available second-hand quite cheaply and, of course, when the job is finished, it can be sold again – probably to another restorer!

HOME FROM HOME

A problem not often considered – until it's too late – is that of animals and birds making new homes in your dismantled Jaguar. Particularly in the winter, mice and even rats look for warmer climes, and that nicely padded rear seat in your garden shed will seem very tempting. The birds that don't fly down to Rio for the winter are also partial to bits of Jag. So it pays to seal your shed/workshop as much as possible (not forgetting the eaves) and make regular checks on your storage area to ensure you're not housing a few free-loading house guests!

▲ PR1. It's important to be methodical as you remove parts. At the time of dismantling it may be perfectly obvious which parts go where and in which order, but in three months' time, having dismantled hundreds of other components, it may not be quite so easy. Using old bits of wood, we cobbled together a simple but effective rack/storage system. It's advisable to mark all cardboard boxes with a thick marker pen to save rummaging through trying to find the part you require.

▶ PR2. Damp is always likely to be a problem in the UK, even in the summer as hot days create humidity, especially when combined with cool nights. Obviously, this moisture will rot perfectly good (if dirty) carpets and create even more rust that you originally had, so a dehumidifier is a good investment. This literally sucks in the air from the shed/garage, filters the water into an internal container and pushes the air back out again – usually around 2 degrees warmer. This is the Air Quality Products Super-Dri model. Check carefully when you buy that it is suitable for the space you have to deal with.

▲ PR3. Remember that damp starts at the bottom and works its way up, so anything placed directly on the floor will get damp. As you can see here, the leather seats have been placed on an old half pallet to stop them being damaged. The box on the right is for parts beyond further help, and the bumper is awaiting the step ladder to be hung on the rafter. Using 'natural' hanging rails, such as roof supports, is a good idea and good for storing pieces of carpet, sound deadening and awkward items such as bumpers.

▶ PR4. If not actually being restored, many XJ6s are used as weekend and/or fine-weather cars, meaning that the battery gets little or no use. Apart from the fact that a flat battery won't turn the engine, a battery that is allowed to fully discharge on a regular basis is going to wear out much more quickly than it should. Moreover, batteries left uncharged during the winter months can freeze and crack their casings. Worse still, a battery allowed to reach a condition of deep discharge may never accept its full charge again. Remembering to go out and start the car on a regular basis will help the battery, but running the engine at idle, on the choke will do the engine a power of no good. Enter the AG Products Battery Sava, a simple, effective and well-priced product aimed at saving your battery whilst the car is not being used. Looking like a calculator transformer, it clips on to the battery terminals (with the car's leads still in place) and then plugs into the mains. According to the makers, it costs a mere 4p per week in electricity. There are two versions – above and below 45AH batteries, to cater for the car and motorcycle markets respectively.

TIPS
– Try to store pieces of carpet and similar trim separately to allow them to dry out (if already damp) and to stay dry.
– Even if carpet pieces are damaged or dirtied beyond redemption, hang on to them; sometimes it is possible to have a local trim shop make up copies for you.
– The same principle applies to areas of sound deadening, where originals can also be used as templates.

– Once you've removed sub-assemblies which will have to be dismantled further at a later date (for example, the bumper), give it a good spray with Plus Gas or similar so that when you come to remove the nuts and bolts, they are more likely to be free.

WORKSHOP PROCEDURES AND SAFETY FIRST

Working on your Jaguar, whether it's simple maintenance and repair or a complete restoration, will give you immense satisfaction. However, it's important to take a leaf or two from the professional mechanic's book of safety. A logical approach to DIY motoring is essential as are the correct procedures and the use of the right tools for the right job.

PREPARATIONS

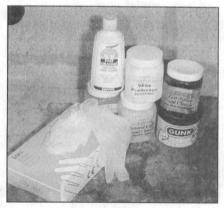

▲ SAF1. First things first – it's always wise to protect your hands, not least from the unpleasant effects of oil and grease, which are now known to be carcinogenic. Use a quality barrier cream before you dirty your hands so that any dirt on there will simply wash off. Better still, wear vinyl or latex gloves to keep dirt and oil off your skin altogether. When you wash your hands, use a purpose-made cleaner which will pull off the dirt without removing the skin's natural oils. When you're working on your car, always make sure that someone knows where you are, and ask them to check up on you on a regular basis – it could be your life-saver.

- Wear overalls, not least because there are less likely to be loose items of clothing to get caught in moving parts.
- Impose a NO SMOKING rule in your workshop at all times.
- Remove watches and jewellery where possible.
- Use barrier cream on your hands and arms before starting work on your car. Long-term contact with engine oil can be a health hazard.
- Keep things tidy – a workshop with cables and pipes running all over the floor is a recipe for disaster.
- Read the instructions! It's best to do this in the warmth of your living room, as you'll be more likely to skip bits out in a cold workshop.
- When cleaning components DON'T use petrol (gasoline). Use white (mineral) spirit, paraffin (kerosene) or purpose-made industrial cleaners.
- When using any power tools, or even hand tools where there is the danger of flying detritus (chiselling a seized nut, for example), wear goggles to protect your eyes, especially when using grinders, etc.

THE CAMERA NEVER LIES

If you're working on particularly complex items, make notes and diagrams as to where the various component parts should go. Alternatively, use a camera or even a video camera to show a dismantling procedure and replacement order. Using the latter also offers the opportunity to give a 'commentary' as well. Don't believe you'll remember everything – it's amazing how much the memory fades, even after just a week, and many restoration jobs will take months or even years.

UNDER THE CAR

You simply cannot be too careful when working under your car – 20 people die every year as a result of a car falling on them!

- Never work under your Jaguar when it is supported only by a jack. Use additional support from securely placed axle stands.
- Protect your eyes and hands using goggles/gloves.

- Don't attempt to loosen high-torque nuts or bolts while the car is off the ground. Torque them up when the vehicle is back on the floor.
- Never touch any part of the exhaust, manifolds or catalytic converter before ascertaining whether or not they are hot.
- Catalytic converters get extremely hot – don't park over dry grass, oily rags or any other material which may catch fire from the heat. Never run a catalyst-equipped engine without the heat shield in place.
- Although engine and transmission fluids should be warm in order to drain them properly, ensure that they are not hot enough to scald.

UNDER THE BONNET

- Make sure that the gearbox is in neutral, or 'Park' in automatic 'boxes, before starting the engine.
- Don't leave the key in the ignition while you're working on the car.
- Always remove the coolant filler cap with a cold engine. If you have to do it when the engine is warm, do it slowly, with a cloth for protection. Undo slightly and let the cap settle at the first indentation. This will release the pressure and steam – but remember that the steam will be even hotter than the escaping coolant.
- Keep brake fluid and anti-freeze off your paintwork. Wipe up spillages straight away.
- Never siphon fluids, such as anti-freeze or petrol (gasoline) by mouth – contact with skin as well as inhalation can damage your health. Use a suitable hand pump and wear gloves.

GENERAL SAFETY NOTES

- Take care not to inhale any dust, especially brake dust, which may contain asbestos.
- Wipe up oil or grease spillages straightaway. Use oil granules (cat litter will do the same job!) to soak up major spills.
- Use quality tools – an ill-fitting spanner could cause damage to the component, your car and, of course, to yourself!

- When lifting heavy items, remember the rule; bend your legs and keep your back straight. Know your limitations – if something is too heavy, call in a helper.
- Time is a vital element in any workshop. Make sure you've got enough to finish a job; rushed work is rarely done right.
- Children are naturally inquisitive but don't allow them to wander unsupervised round or in your car, especially if it is jacked up.

FINISHING

When you've finished, clean up the workshop and clean and replace all your tools. You'll reap the rewards in time saved next time out and in tools that last much longer and work much better.

FIRE

Always carry a fire extinguisher in the car and have another one available for use in your workshop. Choose a carbon dioxide type or, better still, dry powder, but never a water-type extinguisher for workshop use. Water conducts electricity and, in some circumstances, could actually make an oil- or petrol-based fire worse. Check the instructions for use before you need to use it and always direct the jet at the base of the flames.

Naked flames (when using gas welding equipment, for example) are an obvious threat, but petrol and its vapour can be ignited even by a spark. This could be caused by something as simple as a short circuit. This is why you should always disconnect the battery earth terminal before starting work. Other problem areas include sparks from a grinder or the striking of two metal surfaces against each other, the bulb in an inspection lamp or even a central heating boiler starting up.

MAINS ELECTRICITY

Mains power tools should be used with care outdoors. Use the correct type of plug with correct and tightly-made connections. Where applicable, make sure that they are earthed (grounded). Use an RCD – a residual circuit breaker –

which, in the event of a short circuit, cuts the power immediately to reduce the risk of electrocution. RCDs can be purchased from most DIY stores quite cheaply. Take special care when working in damp conditions, especially if you are using a mains extension lead. Wherever possible, work indoors and/or use battery powered tools.

FUMES
Never run your Jaguar in an enclosed space – the exhaust fumes contain deadly carbon monoxide and can kill within minutes. Treat all chemicals with great care, not least of which, petrol. Many cleaning agents and solvents contain highly toxic chemicals and should not be used in confined spaces or used for long periods without a break. Wear gloves when working with chemicals and if any is spilled on your skin, rinse off with water immediately.

HIGH TENSION IGNITION
Touching parts of the ignition system with the engine running (or being turned over), notably the HT leads themselves, can lead to severe electric shock, especially if the vehicle is fitted with electronic ignition. Voltages produced by electronic ignition systems are much higher than normal and could prove fatal, especially to those with cardiac pacemakers.

The likelihood of an electric shock is more pronounced in wet or damp conditions, when a spark can 'jump' to an earthing point – you! Take great care when performing a task which requires the engine to be running (setting the timing, for example) not to touch any ignition components.

PLASTIC MATERIALS
Working with fibreglass and other similar 'plastic' materials is opening up a whole new area of safety awareness. It is vital that the instructions for use be followed to the letter in order to avoid a dangerous situation developing. Substances such as polymers, resins and adhesives produce dangerous fumes (both poisonous and flammable) and skin irritants. In particular, do not allow

resin or two-pack hardener to come into contact with the skin. Make sure such materials are clearly labelled and stored safely away from the reach of children and/or under lock and key.

THE BATTERY
Most batteries give off a small amount of highly explosive hydrogen gas, so you should never allow a naked flame or a spark near your battery. Always disconnect the battery earth terminal whenever you are working on your car to remove the possibility of an accidental electrical short circuit. When charging the battery, remove both negative and positive leads. Unless otherwise advised, loosen the filler caps to allow excess gasses to escape.

The battery electrolyte level should be kept topped up (using only distilled water) to the point specified on the side of the battery. If any electrolyte is spilled, wipe it up immediately and wash off skin where applicable – it is highly corrosive. If you need to remove your battery, wear rubber gloves and goggles, always keeping it upright.

PETROL SAFETY
Petrol is a highly flammable, volatile liquid and should be treated with great respect. Even its vapour will ignite at the slightest provocation. When not actually in your fuel tank, it should be kept in metal cans (or approved 'plastic' cans) and stored where there is no danger of naked flames or sparks. Cans should have a ventilation hole to prevent the build-up of vapour. If you work in a pit, extra care is required, as petrol vapour is heavier than air and will tend to build-up in the bottom of the pit.

ENGINE OILS
There is some danger from contaminates that are contained in all used oil and, according to some experts, prolonged skin exposure can lead to serious skin disorders. You can offset this by always using barrier cream on your hands and wearing plastic or rubber gloves when draining the oil from your engine or transmission.

OIL DISPOSAL

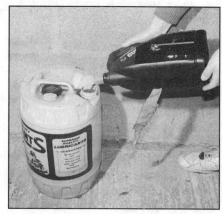

▲ SAF2. Never pour your used oil down a drain or on to the ground. Environmentally, it is very unfriendly and will render you liable to action from your local council. In most EC countries, including the UK, local authorities must provide free 'Oil Banks' as a safe means of oil disposal. If you're unsure where to take your used oil, contact your local Environmental Health Department for advice or ring the Oil Bank Line on freephone 0800 663366 for details of your nearest bank. To save transporting old oil five litres at a time, use a large drum (say 25 gals) as interim storage. When it is full, take it for safe disposal.

FLUOROELASTOMERS
Many items found on modern cars (e.g. oil seals, gaskets, diaphragms, and O-rings) appear to be rubber, but in fact they are made from a synthetic substitute which contains fluorine. The materials are called fluoroelastomers, and if heated to more than 315°C (599°F), they can decompose in a dangerous manner. Indeed, some decomposition can occur at temperatures of around 200°C (392°F). These temperatures would normally only be found on a car if it were to be set alight or if it were 'broken' by a vehicle dismantler using a cutting torch.

Where there is any water present, including atmospheric moisture, the heated fluoroelastomers produce extremely dangerous by-products.

The Health and Safety Executive says: 'Skin contact with this liquid or decomposition residues can cause painful and penetrating burns. Permanent irreversible skin and tissue damage can occur.'

Clearly, this is important to note if your car has caught fire, even if only partially, or if it has been stolen and 'fired' by the thieves. Even more caution is required if you are searching for used parts in a vehicle dismantlers.

Observe the following safety procedures:

1. Never touch blackened or charred pieces of rubber or anything that looks like it.
2. Allow all burnt or decomposed fluoroelastomer materials to cool down before inspection, investigations, tear-down or removal.
3. Ideally, don't handle parts containing decomposed fluoroelastomers. If you have to, be sure to wear goggles and PVC protective gloves. Never handle them unless they are completely cool.
4. Contaminated parts, residues, materials and clothing, including protective clothing and gloves, should be disposed of by an approved contractor to landfill or by incineration according to national or local regulations. Oil seals, gaskets and O-rings, along with contaminated material, must not be burned locally.

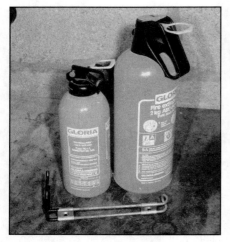

▲ SAF3. Always have a fire extinguisher to hand and know how to use it. There are so many things in your workshop and on your Jaguar that are flammable, you can't afford to be without one. Ideally, buy a smaller extinguisher to carry inside your vehicle and a larger model for workshop use.

RAISING YOUR JAGUAR SAFELY

▲ RAI1. A trolley jack, axle stands and ramps should be seen as essential Jaguar restoration and maintenance tools. Don't skimp on quality when you're buying, or on the safety aspects when you're using. According to latest statistics, 20 people die every year from being crushed under cars inadequately jacked up – don't get your name on that grim list.

▲ RAI2. Rolling about under your car on a cold concrete floor covered in dirt and oil isn't exactly appealing. A car 'creeper' not only keeps you off the floor but its castors make moving around much easier. (Courtesy Clarke International Limited)

RAMPS

▲ RAI3. When working underneath your Jaguar, the safest way to raise it is to use ramps. Always enlist the aid of a helper to ensure that you drive up the ramps squarely and with a wheel in the centre of each ramp. Drive up to the end stops on the ramps, but not beyond. Chock the wheels remaining on the ground. If the job entails using a jack, follow the procedure outlined in the previous paragraph. Note the strips of carpet wound round the end of the ramps which help the wheels get a purchase on the rungs and help prevent the ramps skidding.

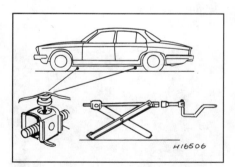

▲ RAI4. The original scissor jack supplied with the car should only be used for emergency wheel changing, or raising the car prior to supporting the car on axle stands. There are four jacking points beneath the body side members, two per side, just behind the front wheels and just in front of the rear wheels. Ensure that the head of the jack is fully engaged with the spigot on the car. In many cases the jacking points will be rotten, and great care should be taken in case the car slips whilst partially raised.

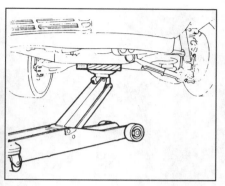

▲ RAI5. You can raise one front wheel by jacking directly under the suspension lower spring pan, or both front wheels by jacking directly under the front crossmember (shown here).

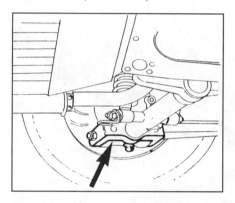

▲ RAI6. You can raise the suspension on one side by putting the head of the jack under the wishbone outer fork.

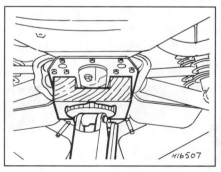

▲ RAI7. You can raise both rear wheels by jacking directly under the final drive plate.

IMPORTANT NOTE: Unless you have a jack with a built-in protective cover, always use a strong piece of wood on the jack saddle to prevent damage when jacking your XJ6 directly on to the crossmembers, etc.

TROLLEY JACKS

▲ RAI8. This is SIP's Omega 3-tonne Pro jack. Clearly, its Safe Working Load gives plenty of leeway and it has a large (140mm – approx. 5.5 in) saddle so there's little danger of it slipping. Where you are jacking on parts that might be damaged superficially, you can use the rubber protective cover provided, and its small extra 'Fast Lift' handle is very useful, getting the jack arm to the jacking point quickly. Its versatility is complete with a min/max lift height of 133mm/483mm giving a lift span of 350mm. Being of the professional style, the long main handle turns cog gears to release the pressure, thus obviating the need for constantly removing a handle to turn the valve manually.

USING A TROLLEY JACK

Leave the vehicle out of gear and with the handbrake off until you have reached the required height. This allows the vehicle to move as the jack 'rolls' into place. Exercise EXTREME caution during this procedure and ensure that no-one could be hurt if the car suddenly slips off the jack. Reapply the brake, put the vehicle in gear and chock the wheels remaining on the ground.

Always use axle stands as well as the jack to support the weight of the vehicle. Once the vehicle is safely at the right height, remove the ignition keys. If you need to run the engine for any reason, make sure you put the transmission in neutral.

▶ *RAI9. Having removed the wheel, it's a good idea to put it under the car as a belt and braces measure.*

RAISING HINTS AND TIPS

- If you're removing the wheels, don't forget to slacken off the wheel nuts BEFORE the car has been raised.
- Torque up the nuts when the car is back with all four wheels firmly on the ground.
- Never use ramps, jacks or axle stands on a soft surface, such as Tarmac.

THE NBN CHASSIS TILTER

▲ *NBN1. Possibly the ultimate XJ6 restoration tool is the NBN Chassis Tilter, which is almost as useful as a four-post ramp in your garage. We used it for much of the work on our Series 3 project car at Phil Blundell's workshops. It comes ready to assemble, with the basic set-up being the same for most cars, the difference being the fittings at each end which fit on to the bumper mountings.*

▲ *NBN3. ... and tightened securely into place.*

▲ *NBN2. The rear adaptor was offered up to the bumper studs ...*

▲ *NBN4. The tilting mechanism was fixed to the bumper brackets.*

▲ NBN5. This is the front assembly all ready for action.

▲ NBN6. Once the front and rear adaptors have been fitted correctly, the whole car can be lifted by turning the large nut on the end of each tilt assembly. Phil found it easier to use a socket in a pneumatic wrench. With the tilting mechanism at the required height, the car can be pushed around to the needed angle. Steel pegs (with safety clamps) are used to hold the car at the angle selected. It made working under the car much easier, especially if underbody welding is called for. We used this device for much of the restoration and repair work and reckon that the NBN Chassis Tilter should be at the top of any restorer's wish list.

TOOLS AND EQUIPMENT

Using quality tools is one of the cornerstones of successful maintenance and restoration. Good quality tools are seldom cheap (though the Sykes-Pickavant Speedline range is designed to bring quality to those on a limited budget), but good tools are often worth far more than their purchase price. The ability to complete a job in minutes with the right tools, rather than hours with the wrong ones, is best appreciated at the end of a long, arduous day in the middle of a winter restoration job. 'Sunday market specials' are often manufacturers' rejects and likely to break or fail under pressure. A good warranty is a sign that manufacturers have faith in their products; S-P's Blue Chip Guarantee is a lifetime guarantee of quality – provided that the tools have been used for their correct purpose!

SPECIAL TOOLS

Where a tool is required for a specific job but will not be used again for years, it will often make no financial sense to buy it. This is where the owners' club can help, with most having a tool hire facility of the most common 'one-off' items. Hiring the tool(s) you require for, say, a week, will allow you to do the job properly and without breaking the bank. Moreover, it will remove the temptation to 'make do' with incorrect tools which, at best, could lead to vehicle or component damage and, at worst, to personal injury.

AND AFTERWARDS ...

Hurling your tools, dirty and oil-stained, in the general direction of your tool box is a recipe for trouble. The next time you need them, you'll have to spend precious time searching and, if they've not been cleaned, they will gradually function more and more inefficiently. So, after the rigours of whatever job you've just completed, wind down with a little therapeutic tool care. Wipe them over with a rag and put them back in their places. This way they'll last much longer and give better service. Remember the adage – look after your tools, and they'll look after you.

▲ T1. Essential for serious engine-out work and/or rebuilds, is an engine stand. Clarke's CES750 model can handle a unit weighing up to 750 lb (340kg) and once mounted, the engine can easily be turned through 360 degrees. There is a smaller model, the CES500, rated at 500 lb (227kg). (Courtesy Clarke International Limited)

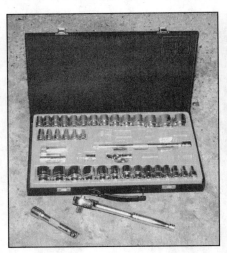

▲ T3. A socket set is an essential part of restoration and maintenance. A ⅜ in drive set is generally suitable for most applications, but for some fasteners you'll need ½ in drive to cope with the torque. The Jaguar is a mix of imperial and metric sizes (and some equivalents) so it pays to have a selection of both – as in this steel-boxed Sykes-Pickavant set.

▲ T4. There are three basic types of spanners; open-ended, ring and combination. A combination spanner set is particularly useful and probably the best place to start. There are open-ended and ring variants of the same size on the same spanner. The S-P mounting board shows silhouettes of each spanner, which enables the user to see at-a-glance if any are missing.

SPANNER JAW GAP COMPARISONS

Actual size	Nearest metric size (mm)	Metric size in inches (in.)	AF size
0.248	7	0.276	4BA
0.320	8	0.315	2BA
0.440	11	0.413	7⁄16 in
0.500	13	0.510	½ in
0.560	14	0.550	9⁄16 in
0.630	16	0.630	⅝ in
0.690	18	0.710	11⁄16 in
0.760	19	0.750	¾ in
0.820	21	0.830	13⁄16 in
0.880	22	0.870	⅞ in
0.940	24	0.945	15⁄16 in
1.000	26	1.020	1 in

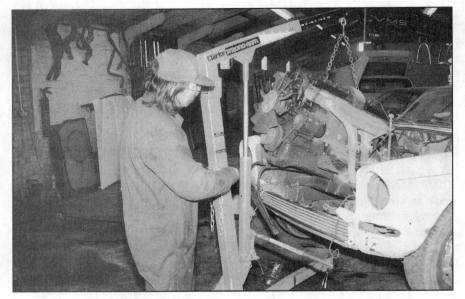

▲ T2. And to get the engine out in the first place, you'll need a heavy-duty engine crane. Quality is important here, as it is usual to remove the XJ6 engine and gearbox as a single unit. Clarke's Strong-Arm range comes in a variety of capacities and lifting heights, ranging from 500kg to a full 2 tonnes. The folding type is particularly useful for the DIY mechanic as it takes up far less space than conventional cranes.

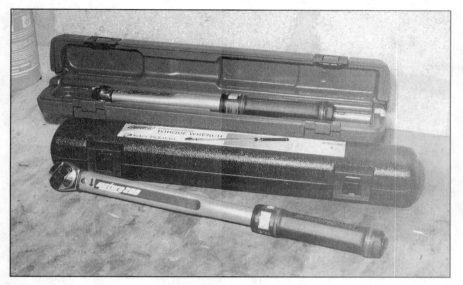

▲ T8. Like screwdrivers, it's important to use the right pliers for the task in hand. A standard pair and a long-nose pair should be seen as a minimum, though for specialised use such as circlip removal, you'll need circlip pliers. This particular S-P kit includes a range of 'jaws' for different sizes of internal and external circlips.

▲ T5. It can be dangerous to over- or under-tighten nuts and bolts, and for this reason you'll see torque figures given throughout this book. Use a quality torque wrench to ensure this doesn't happen. Seen here are two S-P Motorq wrenches, ⅜ in and ½ in drive, which come with the all-important hard plastic cases – a torque wrench is a precision instrument and should be treated as such. Twisting the end of the wrench locks the device so that accidental changes cannot be made. To avoid placing too much strain on the wrench, when you've finished using it, wind the adjuster right back to its lowest setting, but NOT below it.

IMPORTANT: A torque wrench should never be used as a 'breaker bar' for loosening particularly tight fasteners.

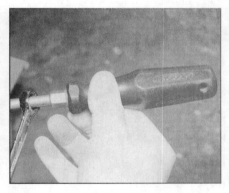

▲ T9. Almost all aspects of Jaguar restoration and maintenance will require the use of a puller at some point. It is possible to buy individual pullers, but S-P's Multi-puller Pack saves money in the long run by combining in different ways to make five different types of puller.

▲ T6. Buying screwdrivers in a set like this is one way to ensure you've always got the right 'driver for the job. Using the wrong one is a recipe for disaster. Remember that there is a definite difference between Pozidriv and Philips head screws. On most cars made after 1970, the screws will be Pozidriv. If there's absolutely no choice, a Philips screwdriver will just about fit a Pozidriv head but NOT the other way round.

▲ T7. Some 'drivers, like this one from Teng, have hex head shanks, meaning that a spanner (preferably a ring, as here) can be used to apply the turning force. Note also the hole in the end of the handle, designed to accept a tommy bar, again to enable more turning force to be applied.

▲ T10. By helping you do your own maintenance and restoration, your tools are saving you money and time. It pays to take care of them, and a quality tool box is a worthwhile investment. For portability, choose a cantilever box and …

▲ T11. … for garage-based storage, choose a chest. The S-P units shown here can be purchased separately. This is a two-drawer base unit and top section with more drawers and a pull-out tote box in the lid.

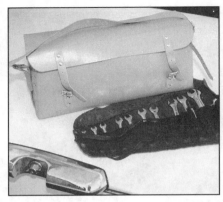

▲ T12. Oxton Classic Accessories produce a range of tough and stylish leather tool cases, ideally suited to your Jaguar, not least because they won't damage the trim if they fall over. There are various sizes available in black or tan and there's also a neat tool roll.

POWER TOOLS

SAFETY: Always take great care when using power tools. Read the notes about safety and mains electricity and wear goggles and gloves when using drills and wire brushes, etc. If using a mains-powered device outside with an extension lead, make sure no-one can fall over it and that it is not vulnerable to rain water or moisture in any way.

▲ P1. The use of power tools will make your Jaguar life much easier, especially if you don't have access to air tools. A mains-powered drill should be seen as a first step, with a cordless model close behind. Each can be used with a wire brush to clean up rusty surfaces. Always use a dot punch before you use a drill bit on metal, to prevent the bit from skidding.

▲ P2. For working on components off the car, a bench grinder is ideal. This 6 in disc model is one of Clarke's range of 240v bench-mounted grinders and comes with spark arresters, tool rests and a dust extraction facility on each wheel. Importantly, all have eye shields which should ALWAYS be in place when you're working. (Courtesy Clarke International Limited)

GARAGE HEATERS

▲ P3. A major problem with restoring your XJ6 in the UK is heat – or more usually, the lack of it. A garage/workshop attached to a house will generally be warmer, but for many months of the year, the ambient temperatures are likely to be near the lower end of the thermometer. Apart from the unpleasantness of being cold, there's the real danger that jobs are going to be rushed, and rushing is seldom consistent with doing something properly. So it's important to be warm enough.The Fireball 40 produces 10kW of heat and is reckoned suitable for a space of around 8,000 cu ft. The mid-range Fireball 80 model produces 23kW of heat and has been designed for spaces of around 20,000 cu ft. (Courtesy SIP (Industrial Products) Limited)

▲ P4. This is the mighty Fireball 120, capable of pushing out some 35kW of heat and designed for larger garages and workshops (around 30,000 cu ft) – or people who get very cold, very easily! All Fireball models feature a turbo fan which gives maximum heat spread and efficiency. All are virtually maintenance-free and come complete with hose, regulator and a 12-month warranty.

SAFETY: Always follow the safety rules included with any new heater.

HIGH-PRESSURE WASHING

▲ P5. Even if you lovingly clean your XJ6 on a regular basis, it's important to remember that the underside needs cleaning, too. Road dirt (and other substances!) accumulate in all those nooks and crannies and acts as a poultice holding moisture on to the car. Eventually this will rot through the steel. Winter driving means rock salt on the roads and under your car. This stuff is incredibly corrosive, and if you do much winter driving, you should make blasting the underneath clean a weekly task. The SIP Lunarstorm has a 2.2 hp motor boosting standard water pressure to 1500 psi (8 bar) which will shift the most

stubborn mud. It runs off mains electricity and a standard pressure water supply. Always let your car air-dry before putting it in the garage. With optional accessories, the Lunarstorm can also be used as a sand blaster. (Courtesy SIP (Industrial Products) Limited)

PNEUMATIC TOOLS

Once upon a time, the use of a compressor and air tools was the prerogative of the garage professional. However, the cost of going pneumatic has come down dramatically and prices are now well within the reach of most DIY motorists, all of whom will benefit. Anyone contemplating a full or part-restoration project will benefit even more. An air pressure of between 3.4 and 6.8 bar (50-100psi) is sufficient to operate most tools, with 6.2 bar (90 psi) being the most common requirement.

Lubricate all pneumatic tools on a regular basis by squirting a few drops of oil either down the air connection or into a special oil hole. Air contains moisture and this will collect inside the mechanism and cause rust problems. Oil daily or before every use.

SAFETY: Always follow the safety guidelines with any compressor or tools. Wear protective gear such as gloves, and goggles where appropriate.

▲ AIR1. Choose your compressor carefully. Clarke have a vast range of compressors from small DIY units to heavy duty industrial models. Though it may be tempting to go for the cheapest, think about future possibilities to avoid being 'penny wise and pound foolish'.

The Raider Air 50 is a very popular mid-range compressor and ideal for most aspects of Jaguar restoration. Its 3 hp motor produces 150 psi and it has a large (50 litre) tank, meaning that the motor is not always cutting in and out. In terms of safety, it has a hefty thermal overload with reset. Note here, the 'curly' air lead, probably the best bet for the cluttered DIY garage, where it will coil back on itself out of the way when not being used.

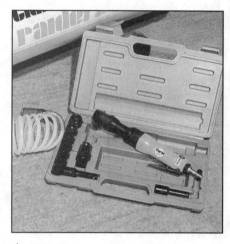

▲ AIR2. Once you have the compressor, tools can be added almost ad infinitum. Unlike electric tools, switching from one to the other is simply a matter of unplugging, say, the ratchet and replacing it with the metal shear. Whereas using three electric tools would require three cables (and probably an extension lead), using three air tools requires just the one hose.This is Clarke's ½ in drive socket set along with the metal shear – essential for the easy and effective cutting away of rotten metal. As well as a wide variety of spraying equipment, other tools in the Clarke range include high-speed saws, buffers, sanders, grinders, staple guns, impact wrenches and drills.

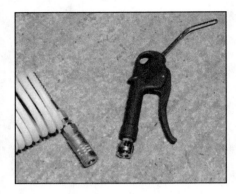

▲ AIR3. Sykes-Pickavant's air-blow gun has a multitude of uses and is ideal for blowing off swarf from newly drilled holes, drying off parts that have been cleaned using solvents, blasting carburettor venturi through, easing out brake calliper pistons, etc. In most cases it is essential to wear goggles to prevent airborne detritus getting into your eyes.

▼ AIR4. Most accessory shops, including Halfords, sell accessories such as air-pressure gauges. This one is an SIP version. By utilising your compressor, you'll never have an excuse for running with uneven tyre pressures. It's clearly vital that your tyre pressures should always be correct, and the small price of such a gauge will be more than offset in terms of extra tyre wear and replacement costs. The large handle and large wheels make it easy to move from one part of the garage to another, or outside if you can't get your XJ6 in your garage.

GARAGE SECURITY

The security of your XJ6 is something to which you should pay great attention, but it's becoming increasingly important to consider your tools and equipment, too. A compressor, welder and tool cabinet full of tools would make a good haul for any thief!

The typical garage door lock is of use mainly for stopping the door blowing open, for even to an amateur thief it represents a delay of mere seconds. It's wise to replace it with a more serious lock. Several companies offer separate lock/bolt mechanisms which are fitted into the concrete base of the garage and are bolted to the bottom of the door. These make it hard work for the thief and, in general, getting around this kind of lock is likely to take too much time to be worth the effort.

If you've got glass windows in your garage/workshop, cover them when you're not working in there, so that prying eyes can't see the contents. If the windows are even medium sized, then it's worth fixing some iron bars across them to prevent unauthorised entry.

The major problem with the theft of tools and equipment is that, if recovered, the police usually have no way of knowing whose they are. Equally, for most of us, it's hard to prove, say, a tool box, is ours. Datatag is a way of marking your equipment (and, indeed, parts of the car itself) in order to aid the police in identification and, better still, to deter the thief from stealing it in the first place.

▲ TS1. There are two methods of marking; the first is to chemically etch a stencilled number on to the equipment – it works on plastics, bare metal and glass. This leaves a clearly visible number which is difficult to remove without causing very obvious damage and creating suspicion. The number is logged with the Datatag IBM computer.

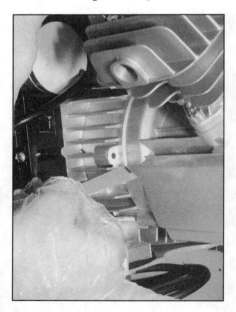

▲ TS2. The second way is to fit tiny electronic transponder tags to the equipment. There are various styles, two about the size of a pound coin, one looking like an electronic grain of rice and one the size of a credit card. They are unaffected by heat, cold and fluids, including petrol and oil.

▲ *TS3. When a hand-held scanner is run over an area where a tag is located, it beeps and displays the reference number. This number, like the stencil, is logged with Datatag and cross-referencing will show immediately who the legal owner is.*

BUYING SPARES

The most obvious place to buy spare parts is from a franchised Jaguar dealer. Though their prices are generally somewhat higher than those of specialist concerns, you can always be sure that you are buying the right quality part for your XJ6, and with a guarantee. It is also a fact that some parts are available at what seems like bargain basement prices (and on occasion, dealers have sales to clear out old and more unusual parts) so

it's always worth checking your local dealer. Almost all parts, mechanical, suspension and bodywork, are still available.

As well as the franchised dealers, there are many reputable specialists who can supply a wide variety of maintenance and accessory items either cheaper or in a wider variety. Companies such as SNG Barratt have an enviable reputation for providing quality service and body parts at reasonable prices with an excellent computerised parts location and mail order service.

It must be emphasised, however, that certain items should always be purchased on a quality, rather than price, basis, regardless of the source, notably safety items such as tyres, braking, suspension and steering components. Your XJ6 is a large, performance motor car and requires the best you can fit in all these departments – your life depends on it.

Naturally, as the earlier models get older and less prolific, it's reasonable to expect that the availability of genuine spares will decrease. However, the large number of specialists should ensure that most XJ6s can still be kept on the road at reasonable cost. Wiser owners will make a point of snapping up more unusual bits and pieces and storing them away – just in case. Getting out to one or more of the dozens of Jaguar 'events' held every year across the country can often be worth it just for

the opportunity to pick up such items.

In choosing a supplier, or someone to work on your car, a good reputation is worth a thousand adverts. Word of mouth from a contented customer (or two) is best, or perhaps a recommendation from a specialist magazine or one of the Jaguar Clubs or Registers.

BUYING SECOND-HAND
Some parts lend themselves to buying second-hand, notably interior trim, body panels, exterior chrome items, etc. Mechanical and electrical items are more difficult to recommend, because without testing, it is often impossible to judge their worth. And items such as alternators need to be tested under load in order to be sure that they are operating correctly.

It could not be advised that braking, steering or suspension items be purchased used. Second-hand wheels and tyres are often advertised and can sometimes be bargains – but you must be very knowledgeable in order to pick out faults which would make a wheel dangerous to use (cracks in the rim, etc.) or tyre problems which could be disastrous, such as sidewall damage, splits, cracks or imbedded objects, like nails, in the tread.

As a rule of thumb, buying used suspension and braking items is for the real experts only. And you should never buy second-hand seat belts.

Chapter 3

Buying an XJ6

The Jaguar XJ6 is a large, luxury, performance car and one where regular maintenance and, on occasion, a friendly bank manager are essential ingredients to its general well-being. By now, many XJ6s have fallen into the hands of owners who simply cannot afford to keep them in as good condition as they should and, as a result, many cars for sale are positively dangerous! This thought should be uppermost in your mind when checking over any car – unless you are literally buying it to restore before driving.

Something else to think about! Insurance for most owners is unlikely to cause too much heartache, as long as a limited-mileage Classic Car policy is obtainable. So, the main cost, in addition to general servicing and occasional items, such as tyres, is likely to be fuel – the XJ6 sips it at a prodigious rate, and doesn't respond awfully well to economy driving techniques. Moreover, most drivers are of the opinion that if economy is required, then you should choose a Mini! So, petrol costs – currently around £3 a gallon – must form part of the overall pre-purchase equation.

Unlike many 'luxury' cars, the XJ6 can be DIY-serviced by a competent enthusiast. Some specialist tools are required for certain jobs (they're usually available on hire from the clubs) and certain aspects have to be left to experts – air-conditioning, for example. It has to be remembered that the XJ6 is a lot of car and, as such, needs a commensurate amount of servicing. If you can't give it the attention it needs, then someone else must, in order to keep it safe. Consider this aspect very carefully before setting out, cash in hand.

BUYER BEWARE

The UK is the car-theft capital of the world and it has been elevated to the status of a highly efficient business. It's an unfortunate fact, but you must assume the car to be 'dodgy' until you can prove otherwise.

Do NOT buy any XJ6 until you have seen the V5 (log book). Without it, you cannot check the validity of chassis and engine numbers or any claims about the number of previous owners. Because it also shows the address of the previous owner, it means that you can contact him/her before you buy to check mileage, history, etc. There may be a good reason why the owner hasn't got it (it's been lost, the dog's eaten it, it's been through the washer), but these are also excuses used by thieves and your only option is to trust no-one. If the seller is genuine, he will have applied for the V5 and, if the rest of the car checks out, you can return when he has got it. Be suspicious of different ignition/door locks and keys. In many cases there are legitimate reasons – a lock may have failed or the car may have been stolen and the locks damaged. Assume the worst – you can't lose.

Ringing is the term used by thieves when they give a car another identity. Typically, they buy a written-off XJ6 legitimately from insurers and remove the chassis plate. They then steal an XJ6 of the same colour and specification, transfer the plate and amend the chassis number. They will either leave the original engine, or install the 'new' one,

grinding off the engine number and stamping in the new one. To all intents and purposes, the stolen car becomes perfectly legal. However, if you buy a ringer and it is discovered (and an increasing number are) you will lose the car to its original owner/insurance company, and the cash you paid for the car. If you've borrowed money to finance it, you're still liable for the balance. It's a terrifying business and one which makes purchasing your XJ6 even more tricky than it normally is.

A phone call to HPI Equifax (01722 422422) and a debit on your credit card of around £30 could save you many thousands of pounds. Equifax has access to details you can't get at; for example, whether the car has been written off – something which should be, but isn't, included on the V5. Some cars involved in accidents are easily repairable using, perhaps, second-hand parts or non-official labour, but insurance companies must get quotes for repair using franchised dealerships and new official parts. The result is that many cars are written off, bought either by salvage companies or individuals and repaired to a safe standard. BUT, as we have seen, many written-off cars are used for nefarious purposes and you should assume the worst until you know otherwise.

The company can also check if the vehicle is on the Police stolen vehicle register and if there is finance owing against it – better still, they can check the last details on previous registration numbers, a very important aspect with an XJ6, as 'private plates' are very much *de rigueur*.

CHASSIS NUMBER

This is stamped into a panel on the front bulkhead in the engine bay. Check that you can read the number and that it is the same as that on the V5 document. The numbers should be PERFECTLY level – if you can't put a straight edge under them, they are instantly suspect, and the car could be a ringer. Also, there's a security mark, typically an asterisk at each end of the number, and this cannot be reproduced by thieves. If these are missing DO NOT buy the car. Equally, some thieves try to get round this by grinding out and re-stamping the number in-between the security marks; this means there'll be a 'step' in the metalwork – look carefully for this.

ENGINE NUMBER

This is stamped into the back of the engine block near the flywheel housing. Again, use a rag to clean up the area and ensure it matches the number on the V5. Look for signs of grinding or numbers that aren't straight. If the owner has changed the engine at any time (quite possible) he should have notified the DVLC and Swansea and had the number changed on the V5. OK, he might have forgotten, but it makes the car suspect and should put you on your guard.

WHERE TO START

If you have any doubts about your ability to judge a good car, or think you've spotted a good one but have some nagging doubts, you are well advised to seek assistance. There are three main sources of 'experts'.

First of all, the three major clubs have amassed a wealth of knowledge and experience. By joining one (or all!) you can make the best of the buying help available. Apart from the fact that they all have magazines which have 'for sale' sections, many of the cars will be known to club officials and they will be able to offer more precise opinions on them.

Second, many of the Jaguar specialists will be able to offer a 'check-over' service for a (relatively) small fee.

Certainly, it will seem minuscule if they find that the car you were going to buy needs thousands spending on it!

Finally, of course, there are the major motoring organisations, such as the AA and RAC, who offer a similar vehicle checking service for a fee which is cheaper if you are a member. Relying on the advice of 'a bloke down the pub' is not recommended – unless you drink at the same place as Tom Walkinshaw!

Taking along a knowledgeable friend is a good idea, but only if he (or she) is truly up to speed on things Jaguar, rather than just generally.

Do not start your buying procedure by driving the car – it may not be your cup of tea and, in fact, there may be faults that make it dangerous. Start by using your eyes, ears and notepad. Look for signs of neglect – cheap and/or oddly worn tyres, dirty and oily engine bay, cluttered and dirty interior, etc. An enthusiast will almost always keep receipts, so any claims of money spent should be easy to substantiate, even if the dealer servicing stamps ceased years before.

Buying an XJ6 is a serious business, not least because it involves parting with your hard-earned cash! An XJ6 is rarely purchased for workaday reasons – Ford and Vauxhall make plenty of suitable vehicles for that purpose! The XJ6 is bought to fulfil dreams, to waft along country lanes in typically English style, to swallow hundreds of motorway miles without batting a headlamp, to indulge in typically aromatic walnut and leather Old-English motoring. Make a prudent purchase and you'll be rewarded with all that and more; but buy badly, and you'll rue the day you saw the ad and be disaffected towards Jaguars forever.

Despite the excellence of the product and the innovative design features, Series XJ6 build-quality was never the best in the world. This is particularly true during the mid-seventies, when quality control appeared to have been missed out altogether on some cars. As such, you should be looking especially hard at these cars, not only for the usual problems caused by old age, but also for problems which may have been built-in on the production line. Conversely, as Sir

John Egan stamped his authority on things, the company got its corporate act together, and life got considerably better as the '80s progressed – but it's still no excuse for not checking everything thoroughly!

Because the XJ6 has yet to reach the dizzy heights of Mk2 'Classicdom', even relatively young cars can be obtained at quite incredibly cheap prices. This tempts many buyers to dispense with the more stringent checks they would apply if buying a more expensive vehicle. Don't succumb to the same way of thinking – a bad buy could easily cost you many times the asking price trying to get it right. It's much better to buy well in the first place. Don't forget, the XJ6 was Jaguar's best-selling saloon range so there's always plenty of choice.

A full service history, especially one from a Jaguar main dealer, makes any Jaguar worth considerably more, but finding such old cars with an FSH is extremely rare. At best, you're more likely to find a car with some initial history (the first owner of any XJ6 is likely to have been well-off and/or a company purchaser) followed by gaps after 4/5 years. However, even if the current owner has been doing his own servicing and maintenance, he should still have plenty of receipts, and they are what you should look for – quite simply, evidence that the car has had its fair share of TLC.

With even the youngest XJ6 being over 10 years old and the earliest models being over 30, the odometer mileage reading should be treated as being 'miles out' unless there is conclusive proof that it is correct. Apart from the fact that the car could easily have already been around the clock once, at any given figure, the mechanical speedometer/odometer is very easy to 'clock', i.e. amend the mileage to a new, lower, figure. It may be that the present owner or even the one before have not touched it, and it could have been clocked years ago. Nevertheless, it is important to judge each car on its merits, not its mileage.

Invest in a clipboard. Pin to it a sheet of paper divided into sections as listed in this chapter. By arriving with a clipboard, the seller will immediately be put on the defensive and will probably be less likely to make wild claims for the car – after all, you are writing it down! It also shows him that you are serious about the car.

Before you go to view, make a note of the major parts that might need replacement – check the menu ads from specialist companies such as SNG Barratt and jot down the prices of, say, brake discs, springs, dampers, steering rack, power steering pump, etc. Being able to put a value on anything you think requires replacement is worth a lot.

As you make the various checks, write down your thoughts in the relevant section. Don't drive the car until you've done your preliminary checks. This is for two reasons; first, you may find enough to put you off the car and so you'll save your time and the seller's. More important, you may find something that makes the car positively dangerous to drive.

WHICH MODEL?

There are three 'Series' XJ6 cars to choose from, with two engine sizes in each Series. Different specifications within those groupings mean that there is, theoretically, plenty of choice, though the nature of the typical Jaguar buyer means that, for example, most XJ6s were ordered with auto 'boxes, leather trim and, latterly, air-conditioning. It follows, therefore, that unlike many more mundane forms of transport, the luxury model is the norm, whilst searching out such things as an XJ6 with a manual gearbox or cloth trim is the tricky bit. Don't forget that cars over 25 years old get a 'perk' – free road tax! Perhaps this could influence your choice of model? The tax disc must still be displayed in the usual way and an annual application still has to be made, to ensure that the car carries a valid MoT and is insured.

Over the years there were literally thousands of small changes – many made 'on the run' at production line level as feedback was received from customers. The main changes are listed in Chapter 1.

Buying a truly concours/restored/original car is a different matter, and price will depend on how much the seller wants to sell and how much you want to buy. More than ever, you should seek the advice of your club with regard to any such vehicles – very often, they will be known to the committee, and more likely than not, any truly exceptional car will have been featured in club publications. This does NOT make the car any more valuable, but it does help you build up a picture of its true condition and may give valuable evidence as to what was done to it, when and by whom – all vital stuff when you're buying a really special XJ6.

SERIES 1
Now unarguably under the heading of 'classic', the Series I cars will undoubtedly soon be up there with the Mk2 Jaguars. As the last Series 1 cars were produced in 1973 (and the first in 1968) all are around 30 years old and there are many obvious problems. Rust, of course, is the most obvious, though as yet, only the front wings are likely to cause supply problems. Mechanical problems can generally be solved fairly easily, as most parts are still available. One problem which may not be so obvious is that of deteriorating electrics; looms that have been *in situ* for that length of time are going to be the worse for wear, especially after four or five owners have fitted and refitted their stereo equipment!

SERIES 2
The Series 2 cars were first shown at the Frankfurt Motor Show at the end of 1973. Externally, they are instantly recognisable because of the raised bumper height. The first 12,000 or so were produced with the same wheelbase as the Series 1, with the LWB XJL running alongside it. After that, the LWB became the norm and added a valuable 4 in of length at the rear of the car, to the benefit of rear-seat passengers. The 2.8 engine was not available and the 4.2 litre cars were joined by a 3.4 litre model, aimed primarily at the fleet markets. As the '70s progressed and the British Leyland conglomerate got deeper

and deeper in trouble and debt, Jaguar build quality suffered. It wasn't sorted properly until the early 1980s, so take a great deal of care when buying any Series 2.

SERIES 3
The Series 3 models were introduced in 1979 with a raised rear roofline to give more head room. These are the most modern Jaguars and the ones which benefited from the huge turnaround in Jaguar build-quality, but pre-Egan cars ('79 and '80) deserve extra investigation – those after he joined in 1981 were a definite improvement. The two engine sizes remained 3.4 and 4.2 litres, with the latter being fitted with the more efficient Lucas-Bosch L-Jetronic fuel-injection; because of this, both engine sizes produced similar mpg figures when driven in a similar manner. The 3.4 models only got leather trim if specified as a cost-option when new, whereas all 4.2 cars had hide. Overall, there's a general feeling that the 4.2 litre car is a better buy – with around 200 bhp on tap, it's no sluggard and the fuel-injection means that it can often reach 20 mpg in the right hands (or rather, feet). It also included electric windows (tinted, naturally), central locking, electric aerial and radio/cassette deck as standard. In keeping with motoring tradition, the specifications of both cars increased dramatically as the XJ6 neared the end of its production life and for pure value, the later the car the better the bargain. Indeed, the Series 3 is regarded by many as the best bet for practical day-to-day Jaguar motoring; on the one hand, they are young enough for rust not to have got too serious a hold, but old enough to be interesting. However, as with all classic cars, logic does not always play too much of a part when it comes to choosing!

DAIMLER AND SOVEREIGN
Jaguar took the Daimler company over in 1963 and used the name to adorn up-market versions of the XJ6 through most of its lifespan. It's an example of badge-engineering and doesn't make them worth much more than the equivalent

Jaguar. Sovereign models, however, were considerably better-specced than their 'plain' counterparts, and will often fetch much more because of it.

DECISION TIME

So which model? The answer is simple – visit club events, check out the pros and cons of each, check out your bank balance and then, as it's your money, it's your choice!

▲ BUY1. It's a good move to go to at least one Jaguar meeting – the various clubs organise dozens every year. You'll be able to see XJ6s of most years and in conditions ranging from concours to questionable. Moreover, you'll find the owners more than willing to discuss their cars – there are few better places to pick up a few pointers. Don't forget to check out the car park, too.

BODYWORK, ELECTRICS AND INTERIOR

Without doubt, rust is the main enemy of any XJ6 – serious rot can render an otherwise good car a complete liability. Check all the obvious rusting places, namely wings (front and rear) bonnet, boot, sills, wheel arches, the base of the 'C' pillars and, perhaps not quite so obvious, the area at the base of the windscreen 'A' pillars – rot there can cause structural problems and, in addition, can allow water down into the bulkhead area. The resulting rust there can virtually write-off the car. It's

important to use your magnet around these areas, as many sellers apply filler here to disguise the problem.

The huge forward tilting bonnet relies on two hinges. Though they and the pins are substantial, they are positioned out of the way at the front of the car and seldom get greased. The result is that eventually, they shear. The box section where the hinges mount is a notorious rust spot – look carefully.

The front crossmember sits directly underneath the radiator and so gets a battering from stones and road water from underneath and leaking engine coolant from the top. Not surprisingly, it often rots, but is available on the aftermarket from companies such as SNG Barratt, though some skill is required to cut out the old and weld in the new.

The large sills are prone to rot from all directions. Press firmly along the sill with your fingers (wear gloves!) and expect the sill to give way at some point, most often on the outside. Check for the use of plastic filler or glassfibre by using a magnet. It's common to find welded patches where holes have been discovered at MoT time. Some welders are better than others, and as the car relies on the sills for a great deal of its structural integrity, do not skimp on this section. Don't miss the sections at the ends of the sill, front and rear; at the front they take a real hammering from stones thrown up by the wheels and, of course, mud and dirt tends to stick to that area, forming a rust-inducing poultice. At the rear, the mud sticks again in a mirror-image position, and rust

is a foregone conclusion unless serious anti-rust measures have been taken. It is possible to patch these areas, but again, skill with a welder is a prerequisite.

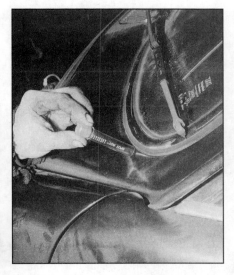

▲ BUY2. All XJ6s are prone to body rot, so a magnet should always be to hand. Rot can occur at the base of the windscreen pillars and this can dangerously weaken the whole structure.

▲ BUY3. The front wings corrode badly, particularly around the headlamps. Check inside the rims and the outside, too. Prospective owners would probably draw the line at this kind of behaviour(!) but your magnet could well reveal that much of the wing was filler, in which case, this kind of picture could be waiting for you. New front wings are readily available and not difficult to fit, but they're a bargaining point.

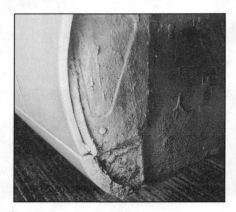

▲ *BUY4. This kind of overspray is something to look for all over the car, especially on the tyres/wheels, under the arches (as here), on engine components in the bonnet – a possible indication of a front-end smash – or in the boot area, pointing to a bump up the rear. Always check the ends of the sills with your magnet. No result probably means that …*

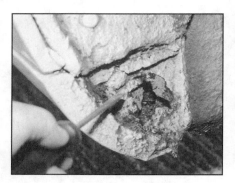

▲ *BUY5. … what should be solid steel is actually solid rust! XJ6s are prone to rusting at both ends of the sill and …*

▲ *BUY6. … on the outside, too. This area of rot seems fairly localised, but even gentle tapping with an MoT hammer reveals a considerable hole.*

▲ *BUY7. It's a similar story along the length of the sill. The importance of having solid sills cannot be emphasised too much because the XJ6 gains much of its structural rigidity from them.*

▲ *BUY8. It is also common for the inner sills to rot as well. Obviously, unless the outer sill is literally well-holed, it is impossible to check the inner sills – but you can make a reasonable judgement from the state of the outer sills. Small holes like this can be patched, but much larger areas of rot will require a complete inner sill.*

▲ *BUY9. Another common rusting point is the front crossmember. It is attacked by water, road dirt and stone chips from underneath and often a leaking radiator*

from above and so this kind of holing is the result. Apart from being dangerous, this is also an MoT failure point, so check it well.

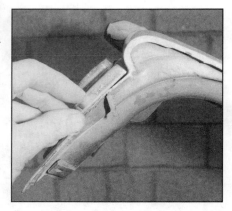

▲ *BUY10. The boot lid is double skinned and prone to collecting water – with the obvious results. As you can see here, the edge of this boot lid has started to fray quite badly – watch your fingers when encountering this kind of rot.*

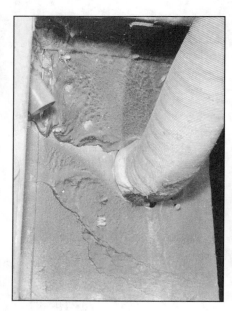

▲ *BUY11. Lifting the front wing on this late '70s car reveals the typical inattention to detail that gained Jaguar such a bad reputation at that time. The underseal has been applied, but in great globules in some places and not at all in others!*

DOORS

The standard XJ6 doors are large (even more so on the coupé!) and so naturally enough, worn hinge pins are common. Check easily by opening the door and then holding it at its outer edge and attempting to move it up and down. If there is play, you'll need to replace the hinges – a time-consuming process. Don't forget to check the rear doors, too. In many cases, these are used far less frequently and on occasions, can actually seize solid!

Check along the outside of the door for rust problems, particularly along its lower half. Check underneath for total rusting out where damp inside the door has rotted its way through. Door locks can fail, but all parts are still available.

WINGS

According to SNG Barratt, about the only thing not readily available for the Series 1 cars are front wings. This is more than a pity, as the front wings are almost certain to have some rot on them. What you have to look for is a well-looked-after car that has either (a) never had any rot on the front wings or (b) a well-looked-after car that has had new wings fitted at some point and that are still sound. The other alternative is to look out for a scrap or write-off Series 1 with good wings worth removing – the problem here is that you're not on your own in this quest!

FLOORS

Lift the carpets throughout the car and check carefully for signs of rot and/or bodged repairs. The floor was fluted and these ridges tend to hold water, which is held down by the stuck-in-place sound-deadening. The front footwells, which take a hammering from road dirt and stones thrown up by the front wheels on the underneath, suffer the most. In addition, windscreen rubber leaks are common and result in water draining into the front footwells and the inevitable corrosion. If you can, lift up the rear seat squab and check underneath – this is a common corrosion area and you can often come across some 'interesting' welded solutions! Replacing a complete (or even part) floor panel is a serious undertaking, and where corrosion is particularly bad it may be worth looking elsewhere for your XJ6.

Complete outer and inner sill sections, wheel arches, front wings, doors, replacement front crossmembers and just about all body parts are still available, either from Jaguar dealers or, more realistically, from specialists such as SNG Barratt. However, nothing is for nothing, and all parts needing replacement should be tallied up and taken into account when considering the purchase price.

CHROME

Check all chrome items, first to ensure they are there(!) and, second, for signs of heavy rust-pitting. Variable build quality over the years means that some cars have virtually mint condition chrome compared with others of a similar vintage. Most chrome parts are available as new/pattern spares, though there are some pieces not available on earlier models.

The rear bumpers are quite notorious for the speed of corrosion – early bumpers were single piece and replacement is more expensive than the three-section versions, where each can be bought separately.

ELECTRICS

There are no obvious problem areas here. Clearly, all lights should be operational when you try the car. Any non-functioning lights may simply require a replacement bulb, but their lack of light could point to more serious wiring faults – dig out a bulb and try them, first. The headlamps were originally sealed beam, and so failure means that the whole lamp has to be replaced. However, sealed beam lights were never the best in the world and, unless you are totally set on originality, you should budget to fit quartz halogen replacements as soon as you can, especially if you intend to use the XJ6's performance to the full during the hours of darkness.

Always make sure that all the electrical 'gadgets' work – electric windows, mirrors, sunroof, etc. New replacement motors can be quite pricey and, because of that, second-hand parts can be hard to find. Try the heater in all its modes, from full-hot to full-cold on both screen and interior. In particular, try the air-conditioning (where fitted), as problems with this mean professional attention – air-conditioning is categorically NOT a DIY item. Some drivers disconnect the drive to the air-conditioning pump during the winter, in order to save fuel, but the system needs to be used on a regular basis and this can often do more harm than good.

INTERIOR

As with other areas of the car, the condition of the interior trim can give some indication of how the car has been treated; you should be able to sniff the luxurious waft of leather the instant you open the door, and the wood trim should fairly gleam with a rich lustre.

Most interiors are leather-covered and, as a rule, last well. But even hard-wearing leather needs some maintenance – applications of a mild but effective cleaner/conditioner, such as Gliptone, will do wonders. Where the leather is simply dirty with ingrained years of dirt, it is usually possible to bring it back to life. It is also possible to re-colour it, if required. If leather has been ignored over a period of time, it is common for the stitching to split. This can be repaired, but it's not an easy DIY task. Where leather seats and trim are beyond hope, retrimming or fitting new trim is largely a matter of choosing the right professional – there are several who specialise in Jaguar trim – but it will be far from cheap. The seats are hard-wearing, but excessive use can lead to damaged springs. All parts of the seat are available but, again, are rarely cheap.

The door trims are basically leather (occasionally cloth) trim card panels and regularly warp with the damp which gets to them because successive owners don't bother to replace the plastic membrane stuck to the inside of the door panel. Even if the leather is in good condition, it is virtually impossible to straighten a damp-damaged card.

The carpets wear quite well, although the quality used varied wildly over the years. Damp again can be a problem, particularly in the front footwells. Carpet sets are available from a number of sources.

The wooden trim is unlikely to show many signs of damage other than old age, and, more likely, damp. Where the car has had a leak or two and/or has been left for long periods in an unventilated garage, the veneer can start to peel. Replacements are available, but they're quite expensive. Faded wooden trim can often be brought back to life by careful use of proprietary wood cleaners. A common problem area is the headlining around the rear window, which fades and falls from the effect of bright sunlight over the years.

Sunroofs (only available officially on Series 3 cars because of the raised roofline) are known for letting in rain as well as the sunshine. A leaky sunroof can quickly damage and stain carpets and seats, and can interfere with electrical switchgear if the leak is bad enough. By definition, any sunroof fitted to a Series 1 or 2 car has to be an aftermarket fitment. Does it look right and in keeping with the car? Has it been fitted well?

▲ BUY12. Inside the car, the condition of the seating and trim in general will give you some idea of how the car has been treated. Expect leather (the most common trim option) to be a little worn, but if it has been cleaned regularly and treated well, it should have just an attractive patina of age rather than look ready for the scrap heap. A little dirt and general cracking will usually respond well to specialist treatment (such as that from Gliptone) but rips and tears and general mistreatment may require replacement – new leather trim is NOT cheap! This driver's seat needs a little stitching and a

good clean, but isn't bad overall. The sagging could be solved by replacing the rubber diaphragm. Expect rear seats to be in better condition than the front seats. If they're not, it indicates that the car has been used a great deal with 4/5 occupants. Apart from being unusual (has this been a staff car, or even a taxi?) it means that there will always have been more strain on engine, gearbox and suspension components. Don't worry about the condition of the seat belts – unless the owner has invoices to prove it, you should always budget to replace them with new.

▲ BUY13. Aftermarket speakers are typical of the kind of 'uprates' XJ6s tend to receive as they get older. The quality of product and how well it is fitted will also give some indication as to how the car has been treated. It also means that the radio/cassette deck and associated wiring may well have been 'amended'. How well, though? The home-made aluminium cover plate at top indicates an owner who may have bodged other items elsewhere.

▲ BUY14. Always lift the carpets to check the condition of the floor. Even if it is undersealed underneath, it could be rusting its way down. The carpets often rot because of water leaks, and the sound-deadening material goes hard and brittle, and cracks. The strengthening ribs in the floor were filled with sound-deadening strips which tend to hold any moisture on to the steel floor pan – with inevitable results.

▼ BUY15. Check the front floors and carpets, too. This carpet reveals an awful lot of brown stuff underneath it, and when removed you can see that corrosion has really got a hold. Floor panels are available but it's a tricky job to replace them.

▲ *BUY16. If you can remove the rear seat, then do so, because water collects here, too. As you can see, some amateur welding and patching has taken place.*

ENGINE, EXHAUST, EMISSIONS, AIR-CONDITIONING AND TRANSMISSION

The XK six-cylinder engine, as fitted to so many Jaguars, and all XJ models, is a legend in its own time. It follows that an inherently bad engine wouldn't have lasted 10 years, much less 40, and so there's plenty to commend it. As long as an engine is serviced regularly with particular attention to its oil and filter, it could easily romp along to 150,000 miles or more without needing serious work. However, regular servicing often goes by the board as XJs get older, and this can hack tens of thousands of miles off the engine's working life. You should be aware of what to look for, what to listen for and the costs of putting right what is obviously wrong.

Coolant, too, is immensely important and needs changing regularly. The main problems relate to the fact that not enough anti-freeze is used, which leads to internal corrosion and overheating.

A cracked block between the cylinders is a common problem which affects almost all Jaguar models up to the 1982 Series 3 cars, which had a slot between each bore to allow for some expansion. A block cracked in this way used to have to be scrapped but, thanks to techniques developed by companies such as VSE, it is now possible to save most blocks.

ENGINE BAY

Checking the engine starts with your eyes; if the engine bay is oil-stained and covered in a thick layer of grime, it's probably time to walk away. Even if the price is decidedly right, you'll probably be in for a total rebuild. Conscientious owners take at least some measure of pride in the engine compartment, wiping it over every time they check the oil and water, etc. Moreover, a good owner will always be on the lookout for frayed cables, worn hoses and body rot or cracks. If everything is covered in dirt, how can he do this? The answer is that he can't, which means that all kinds of horrors could be waiting for you.

And, of course, a good engine will keep at least most of its oil circulation around its innards. Heavy oil deposits could be something as simple as a sadly neglected cam cover gasket, but it could be something far worse. Investigate ANY oil leaks very carefully and allow for their correction when it comes to negotiating the price.

▼ *BUY17. Start by taking in the general picture – this engine bay is probably fairly honest, not being very clean, but equally, not covered in 3mm of oil and grime! Worrying aspects would be the substitute washer bottle (top left) and, more important, the water rust around the pressure cap (at front of engine). Check the oil level and the oil condition by opening the filler cap and looking down at the cam. It should be clean and there should be no sign of the white mayonnaise which indicates water in oil and a probable head gasket leak. Check that there is no sign of brake fluid leakage and that the brake servo pipes are not cracked or split.*

▲ BUY18. Checking the chassis number is an essential part of buying a car. It's here on a plate on the chassis bulkhead. Look carefully for signs of tampering and make sure that the security marks (asterisks) are still there. Compare with the V5 (logbook) – if the seller doesn't have it, don't buy the car! There's also a plate on the nearside (RHD) inner front wing.

▲ BUY19. This became an official VIN (vehicle identification number) plate with effect from 1980 when European regulations came into force. This shows the various weight capabilities, the chassis number and the paint and trim codes relating to the car.

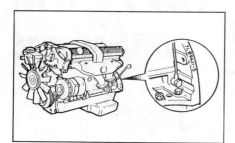

▲ BUY20. Check that the engine number, found at the back of the engine block near the flywheel housing,

matches that on the V5. Look for signs of tampering or a previous number having been ground away, indicating that the engine is from a stolen vehicle.

COMPRESSION TESTING

If the seller will allow it, checking the compression figures is a good measure of any engine. Use a quality tester and take care not to strip the plug threads in that alloy head. Remove all the plugs (don't let debris get into the holes) and remove the '–' lead from the coil. Insert the tester and turn over the engine with the accelerator flat to the floor. Turn for around 10 seconds (it's also a good check of battery condition!) and note the final reading. When new, it should be between 160-180 psi (11-13 bar) and obviously you have to accept some wear which should relate directly to the age/mileage of the engine. Repeat with the other cylinders and compare the readings. They should be within 10 psi of each other. Any readings wildly adrift means trouble of some sort. If the readings are low, pour in a teaspoonful or light oil and repeat the tests; if the readings improve, it points to bore and piston ring wear. If they don't, it indicates possible valve/seal problems.

OIL

Check the oil level; if it is too low or high, this is a worry straight away – either could be trouble, and an enthusiastic owner always makes sure that the level is correct (between the upper and lower marks on the dipstick).

Remove the oil filler cap and check around its top and just inside the cam cover; you're looking for the tell-tale 'mayonnaise' of oil and water that spells trouble. It means that water is getting into the engine, and as the XK engine is prone to cylinder head gasket leaks, this is very likely.

Even if there is no water there, you can still learn a lot. If the top of the cap is covered in a thick sludge of dirty oil, it means that the all-important regular oil changes have been sporadic, to say the least. Even worse, cheap oil could have been used.

Check also inside the cam cover and

along the top of the head. With a cold engine and quality oil that has been changed regularly, you should be able to see everything clearly, with just a thin film of clean, quality oil clinging to the metal.

The importance of using good oil and changing it more often, rather than less often, cannot be over emphasised. Dirty oil is bad news and may be your cue to walk away.

OIL PRESSURE

Before starting the engine (but with the ignition on) check that the oil pressure gauge is reading zero. Start the engine – you'll probably hear some cam chain rattle, but all XK engines do this, and it should quieten down fairly quickly. If the rattle remains, it suggests a new chain is required – the noisier it is, the more imminent the change. All things being equal, it's not the end of the world, but it is a negotiating point. Rumbling from the bottom end of the engine is more serious as it points to possible big-end and/or crankshaft problems. This means taking the engine out and lots of time and money.

When the engine has reached operating temperature, a healthy engine should be showing an oil pressure of at least 30 psi. If it's less than this, it points to the possibility of some serious engine wear. If there's no reading it could be a faulty gauge, but it could just as easily be a faulty oil pump – again this could be really bad news, so don't be fobbed off.

Check for signs of blue smoke from the exhaust. This is increasingly important as exhaust emissions are part of the annual MoT test and an inefficient/badly worn engine could result in a 'fail'.

FUEL

The automatic enrichment device (used instead of a choke) fitted to later carburettor engines, can fail. The engine will still start and run, but mpg can get down into single figures! The AED is a sealed unit and replacement is the only solution.

Service items, such as the fan belt, water pump, alternator, etc., aren't great areas of concern. Whilst replacement costs money, almost all parts are available off the shelf from main electrical dealers, Jaguar specialists and even the high street giants, Halfords.

When it comes to serious engine rebuilding, the XK engine can be worked on by the committed amateur (given a reasonable level of time, ability and equipment) or by specialists, such as VSE, who turned an ugly duckling 4.2 litre engine into a true swan for this book. They mix many years experience of building, racing and rallying XKs with the facility to handle all aspects in-house to produce superb quality work at an incredibly reasonable price.

EXHAUST

Many Jaguar enthusiasts who use their cars on a regular basis opt for stainless steel as the ideal exhaust material – we found it to be so with the Falcon system fitted to our project car. Though not initially cheap, neither is the regular replacement of standard steel exhaust parts, and it will soon pay for itself. Viewing a car with a stainless exhaust is generally encouraging, as it shows that the owner was thinking more of the car than his wallet and that this logic may (but not necessarily) have carried further through his XJ6 ownership.

Most exhausts, though, are good old, rot-prone mild steel. The Jaguar system is complex and expensive, so don't skimp here. As with all mild steel systems, they tend to rot from back to front, with the rearmost boxes running cooler than those at the front and collecting more condensation. Check all the boxes and pipes very carefully, though.

EMISSIONS

What comes out of any Jaguar engine has always been important – a heavily smoking XK is not good news. However, with MoT emissions testing getting ever tougher, it's more important than ever that some attention should be paid to this aspect of engine performance.

AIR-CONDITIONING

Air-conditioning is a very desirable extra, despite the fact that it can adversely affect the mpg. However, check that the pump and the rest of the system is operating correctly, as replacements are expensive. Moreover, you should never attempt to remove, replace or maintain any part of the system yourself – it is highly dangerous. This means that on top of replacement parts, there will also be the cost of skilled labour to sort it out. Later air-conditioning systems were much better than the early type.

TRANSMISSION

If you are viewing an automatic car, check the gearbox oil level. It should be between the two marks on the dipstick. Moreover, the oil on the stick should be very clean. If it is dirty, or has black bits and pieces in it, it almost certainly means trouble. Don't drive the car if the auto 'box fluid level is too low.

Look for signs of oil leakage around the half shafts, in particular check that the rear brake discs are not covered in oil. The halfshaft oil seals can leak, and replacing them means the removal of the rear suspension and axle – involved and expensive!

In general, the Type 65 and 66 Borg-Warner auto transmissions are hardy units and usually only fail at high mileages or through extreme neglect. Earlier 'boxes can be more fragile and not so good to use.

A faulty gearbox isn't the end of the world – as you will see in Chapter 9, companies such as Graham Whitehouse Autos can rebuild Jaguar auto (and manual) boxes and torque converters to be better than new, and at present no 'boxes are problematical in terms of spares and service items. But it's a cost that has to be worked into the purchase of the car, so do your sums before buying.

According to Jaguar transmission expert, Graham Whitehouse, the 'boxes for the Series 2 and Series 3 cars are interchangeable. As the Series 3 box is better, a backward swap makes sense. However, take great care to ensure that, if you are buying a Series 3, someone has not already performed the swap the other way round (say, as a panic measure because of failure of the original gearbox). The gearbox type numbers can be found on a plate on the side of the gearbox – you'll have to get under the car to look at it, so take the usual safety precautions.

BRAKES, STEERING, SUSPENSION, WHEELS AND TYRES

BRAKES

Whichever model you opt for, you'll be buying a large and heavy car – typically tipping the scales at 1600/1800 kg. This means that the brakes must be perfect, with no excuses. Check the discs to ensure that they are the correct thickness and that they do not show signs of scoring. The pads should have plenty of 'meat' left on them – check if you can that they do not contain asbestos. If you can't confirm that, make a note to change them for non-asbestos pads as soon as possible. (See Chapter 8 for further details about brakes and asbestos.)

Checking the rear brakes is not easy, but it is essential. Ideally, they should be checked on a 4/2-post lift, but if you don't know a friendly garage owner, you'll have to resort to using ramps or a jack and axle stands. Take all the usual precautions to avoid injury.

Whilst checking the rear brakes, check the inboard handbrake discs/callipers as well – they often seize solid. Make sure that both are operational – it's an MoT failure point as well as being dangerous.

Under the bonnet, check around the master cylinder and pipes for signs of leaks. Check the condition of the fluid (nice and clear) and that the level is correct. Check the servo by pressing the brake pedal down hard (ignition off) and then turning on the ignition – the pedal should go down substantially as the servo cuts in. If the pedal remains 'hard', the servo is probably shot – an expensive and professional job.

STEERING

Power steering components are not cheap, so don't skimp here. Look in the engine bay at the pump and its associated pipework. Look for signs of serious leakage and check that the fluid reservoir is up to its mark.

SUSPENSION

Clearly, all suspension components must be in good condition in order that the car does not become a danger on the road. Start by making simple and obvious tests; stand back and look at the car on level ground. It should sit square and not droop to one side. Such drooping indicates tired springs (never replace a single spring; always in axle sets and preferably all around). Press down on each corner of the car and let go – the car should rebound once. If it bounces up and down many times, it points to worn or leaking dampers. As previously, dampers should never be replaced singly.

The dampers have a hard time, supporting all that weight and controlling all that torque, so check them carefully. Look for signs of oil leakage and that the mounting rubbers don't look old, cracked and perished. Don't forget that dampers that don't leak may just not have any oil left in them, having already leaked it all out! Like springs, dampers should always be replaced in axle sets – that's two at the front and four at the rear! Also at the rear, remember that replacing the springs/dampers means removing the complete sub-assembly.

Check the springs to ensure that they are locating correctly and that they are not cracked. For the latter, check particularly at their highest and lowest points – it's hard to see there, but a good torch and some determination should do the trick.

At the front, jack up the car and check for movement in the bottom ball joints. The wheel should barely move at all – maybe 20/30 thou. When you have a wheel with ¼ in of movement, replacement (both sides) is required. A clue as to the condition of these ball joints is to check the tread on the inside of the front tyres. Uneven and extra wear there will confirm your suspicions.

RUBBER BUSHES

Under the general heading of suspension come rubber bushes. There are lots of them (on sub-frames, anti-roll bars, etc.) and they are prone to wearing out quite quickly, particularly on the torque-laden 4.2 litre cars. Most bushes aren't that expensive, but replacing them all soon adds up to a large bill. Check carefully the metalastik front and rear subframe mounting bushes for signs of damage or play. If they are seriously worn, the MoT tester will issue a 'fail', and at the rear, replacement means dropping the entire suspension subframe – not an easy task. The rear bump stops are often missing altogether, though these are much easier to replace, even if (as on our project car) part of the original mounting plate has rusted into place. Once more, these aren't expensive so why hasn't the original owner already done it?

WHEELS

The standard steel wheels are usually badly rusted but covered up by the wheel trims. Surface rust is a cosmetic problem, but it could damage the wheel so that it becomes dangerous, so remove any trims where possible and examine carefully. Alloy wheels are naturally prone to being bumped and scuffed around town and, although unsightly, this sort of damage is usually superficial. Check carefully for signs of heavy damage which could result in a bent and dangerous wheel. Baked on brake dust can often prove virtually impossible to remove and, whilst it won't affect performance or safety, it will detract from the overall appearance of the car, and looking good is a big part of the Jaguar ethos. As is shown later in the book, companies such as Pristine, can bring scuffed and dirty wheels back to life much cheaper than buying new wheels, but a badly cracked or bent wheel MUST be discarded.

Don't forget to check the spare wheel and tyre.

TYRES

Any XJ6 is a big, heavy car capable of dramatic performance which requires tyres capable of handling these factors. By definition, they're not cheap, but neither is your life and it depends very much on having quality rubberware on your Jaguar. If your potential purchase is sitting on remoulds, mix-'n'-match sets or tyres you've never heard of, it could be that the owner has been working to a slender budget. If he's cut corners here, where else has quality been sacrificed? Check the condition of the tyres – look for a good depth of tread and at the side walls to make sure there are no splits, cuts or bulges. Make sure that the tread has not worn unevenly, which points to possible problems with the track and/or suspension, etc. – and more expensive still!

▲ BUY21. Nice shiny wheel trims can hide a multitude of sins. Apart from a really ropy steel wheel (which clearly has never had any attention and could be cracked), any oil or bearing grease leaks could be covered up. If possible, jack up the front wheels and test for wheel bearing or other play by holding the wheel at top and bottom and rocking slightly. Repeat, holding the wheel at both sides.

▲ BUY22. In the UK, the awful climate and use of rock salt on the roads in winter, makes it hard work to keep alloy wheels in good condition. This is typical of how most alloys corrode as a result of moisture getting under the original lacquer. Expect a fair number of kerbing scuffs, but check carefully for signs of heavy damage, which could render the car unsafe.

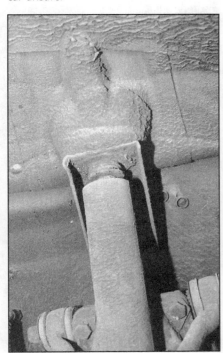

▲ BUY23. Don't be afraid to get a little dirty. Get down on the floor and check the front damper mounting points – this can rust away and make the car dangerous.

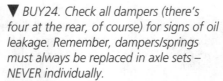

▼ BUY24. Check all dampers (there's four at the rear, of course) for signs of oil leakage. Remember, dampers/springs must always be replaced in axle sets – NEVER individually.

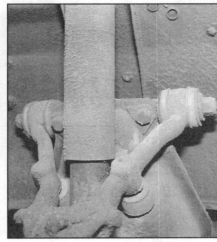

▼ BUY25. There are plenty of rubber bushes underneath any XJ6 and they take a real hammering, especially with the torque of the 4.2 litre cars. Seen here are two of the top/bottom wishbone bushes. Play in this kind of bush can usually be checked by using a pry bar.

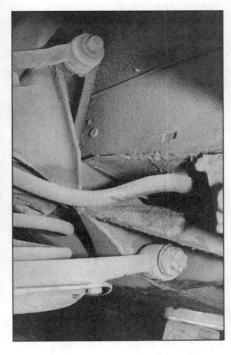

▲ BUY26. Check the disc condition, thickness and also the condition of the pads BEFORE you drive any XJ6. Look for signs of brake fluid leakage. Note the top wishbone bush grease nipple in this photo – there are many around the car and you should make sure you know where they are so you can check them. Do they look as if they've been greased recently or are they covered in several years worth of road dirt and sludge?

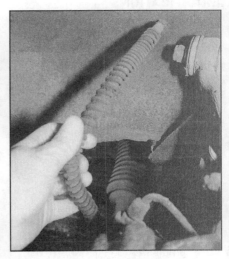

▲ BUY27. Don't forget to check the condition of the steel brake pipes and the flexible brake hoses. Check flexible hoses by bending them back hard and looking for hairline cracks. Have an assistant press the brake pedal hard while you look at the hose to make sure it doesn't bulge under the pressure – if it does, it is dangerous and needs replacing – quickly! Look all around the brakes for signs of fluid leakage.

ACCESSORIES, MODIFICATIONS AND INSURANCE

ACCESSORIES

Some owners just can't abide a car to be standard, and so it is adorned with various accessories. Some are tasteful, some are not, but the overriding point is that they should be well-fitted or, better still, able to be removed if required. Treat electrical accessories with some suspicion, as most DIY fitters have little grasp of how mobile electrics should be wired; expect to find live, unsheathed wires, wires passing through ungrommeted holes (with the possibility of chafing and short circuits) and wiring strung everywhere in an unplanned fashion.

With very few exceptions (hard-to-find, period Jaguar items, for example), accessories make little or no difference to the price.

MODIFICATIONS

Modifications must be treated with some suspicion. First of all, is the modification worthwhile? Swapping sealed beam for halogen headlamps, for example, is sensible and the sign of the driver who likes to be able to see at night. Bodykits and other addenda are definitely an acquired taste. Purists argue that they detract from the timeless elegance built into the XJ6. Others argue that over the years, all Jaguars have been modified to some extent (view TWR's hugely body-kitted, over-engined, massively powerful specials, for example) and that it is they who are carrying on the true tradition. Whilst arguments rage to and fro, only *you* can decide which way to spend your cash. The important thing is that any modifications should have been done properly and safely; body kits should be securely mounted, holes drilled should have been rustproofed, paintwork should be high quality and wiring should be carried out in a professional manner – it's easy to set fire to a car at any time. Aftermarket alloy wheels should be of the right type for the car and fitted using

the correct size bolts – often, original bolts are utilised and when the wheel is much bigger than standard, these could be much too short. Remember that bigger wheels and tyres place more strain on the suspension, steering, bearings, etc., and that the tyres will cost more to replace.

INSURANCE

Most XJ6s are now old enough to be insured under a Classic Car Policy. These are most often available from specialist brokers who are well aware that anyone enthusiastic enough to run an older car on a regular basis, is probably going to look after it (both in terms of maintenance and driving) and thus be a better risk. Most limit the mileage from between 1500-7500 miles. Most owners opt from the mid-range 3000 or 5000 mile options. If your car is worth more than the 'book' price, you should consider getting an agreed value policy – quite simply, you and your insurers agree a specific value for the car before the policy is taken out. You'll need to prove that it is worth what you say by producing receipts and photographs showing its condition.

Given that the average value of, say, a 20-year-old XJ6 is virtually nothing (to an insurance company), a good, well-cared for example should definitely be agreed value.

Don't forget that your insurance company needs to know of ANY modifications made to your car, no matter how insignificant they may seem. Switching to aftermarket alloys and low-profile tyres may not seem important, but they may make the car more attractive to the thief, i.e., they could increase the insurance risk. More obviously, engine uprates and suspension modifications should be detailed to your insurers; very often, they will ask for a roadworthiness certificate from an independent engineer – at your expense.

You are well advised to have a quality alarm/immobiliser fitted, and if you opt for a Thatcham-approved device (see Chapter 11), then you may well be eligible for an insurance discount – even if your car is modified.

IMPORTANT NOTE: Remember that all insurance policies are taken out purely on a trust basis – your insurers trust you to tell them the whole truth and ALL material facts. The time they will question you is if you claim. If they find anything they believe to be material to the claim, they may have a case for refusing to pay. So make sure you disclose everything about yourself and the car at the time of issue.

ROAD TESTING

Having ascertained that this is a car you might be interested in, and that it is safe, then it's road-test time. Don't forget to check your insurance before driving someone else's car. Most insurers' comprehensive policies cover the driver (NOT any named drivers) to drive another vehicle but with only *third party* cover. This means that if you drive the seller's car and damage it, YOU, not your insurers, are liable for the cost.

It's a good idea to drive a good XJ6 *before* you try one that's for sale, because the difference between even an average XJ6 and most other cars is quite marked. Club members will often be willing to expound on the finer points of what should be and what definitely *shouldn't* be. It's vital to avoid being taken in by the opulence of wood, leather and almost total silence as you hush along the road. When you've done a good deal, you can savour your piece of motoring history, but now is the time for clear-headedness.

The ride should be as smooth as silk, with no undue banging and crashing. Despite its size and luxury nature, the XJ6 has suspension with a decidedly sporting heritage (notably the E-type) and should roll around much less than its peers. Don't forget that suspension trouble means replacing SIX dampers and springs. If the car feels 'lively' at the back end, it's probably worn bushes (in the radius arms, for example) and/or worn fulcrum bearings.

Check for front wheel wobble – it could be just a spot of wheel-balancing required (though such simple things should have been sorted by a conscientious owner, especially prior to a sale), but the same effect can be caused by worn universal joints at the rear of the car – an expensive problem to rectify.

The 4.2 litre engine should hustle the car along quietly and quickly, spinning smoothly through its rev-range. The smaller engined cars won't be quite so quick off the mark, and unless you desperately want one, the 2.8 litre Series 1 cars are probably best left alone. The oil pressure remains an important monitor of engine condition – it should not drop below 30 psi at idling speeds and should be around 40 psi at 3,000 rpm. Check your rear view mirror regularly as you accelerate and decelerate sharply; if you see great clouds of blue smoke, it points to the need for an engine rebuild in the not too distant future.

Any automatic transmission should slur its changes almost imperceptibly, though remember that the later cars have better 'boxes, the Type 65/66 Borg-Warners being the best. Engage 'drive' with your foot on the brake – it should engage the gear smoothly and quietly; a clunk accompanied by a jerking movement is bad news. Make sure the kick-down works correctly and that there is no sign of slipping – the bands on the automatic transmission should be checked and tightened regularly, but many owners ignore it simply because it means rolling around under the car.

The XJ6 manual gearbox was never the sweetest in the world and gained few friends throughout its life. It should engage its gears cleanly (though it will probably feel a bit notchy). Make sure you try all the gears, including reverse, and accelerate hard in each gear to

ensure there is no trace of clutch clip. Expect synchromesh to be worn, particularly on 1st and 2nd, but really bad graunching is a prelude to gearbox-out work and lots of expense. From the end of the '70s the British Leyland Rover five-speed manual was used. Never the best in the world, it at least has the advantage that there were lots of them made, so spares or even complete used 'boxes are quite common.

Stopping the XJ6 should be simply a question of resting your foot on the pedal and watching the speed disappear, totally without drama. Any snatch or jerking probably indicates warped discs.

The power steering was always very light – there should be only a slight resistance felt. If it is noisy, particularly on full lock, it indicates either a PAS belt in need of tightening or, more seriously, a pump on the way out. Check by looking into the PAS reservoir immediately after driving. If the fluid is frothing as if it's just been in the blender, then there's an expensive replacement due anytime now.

Your test drive should take around half an hour, making sure you take in a variety of road surfaces and types; tight twisty bends, smooth tarmac sections, quick dual carriageway or motorway, and steady in-traffic motoring. Always keep an eye on the water temperature gauge. As mentioned, the XK engine often blows head gaskets, which can lead to overheating. Also, the radiator and cooling system in general is often ignored for years at a time.

On your return, allow the engine to cool for 20 minutes or so, then carefully remove the pressure cap from the header tank. Make sure that the coolant level is still correct.

DOING THE DEAL

This is the really tricky bit. Once more, this is where you can make your club membership pay for itself. Contact the club before you buy to get a ball-park figure for the age/model XJ6 you're thinking of – some buyers deliberately price their cars much higher than they should be in order to seem magnanimous when it comes to negotiation.

By the time you've finished your checks you should have a nice collection of ticks, crosses and cryptic notes. It's good to let the seller see you scribbling, though not wise to let him see *what* it is. It may be that your list contains far more work/expense than you want to get involved with. If that is so, don't be afraid to walk away – the XJ6 is Jaguar's most prolific car ever, so they're far from thin on the ground. If you think you can live with or rectify its faults, make your counter offer, based on deductions required to put things right. If the seller queries your thinking, list the problems. Often, the seller will 'suddenly remember' that he has a set of new dampers in the back of the garage, or a spare headlamp in a box in the corner. Haggling is a part of car-buying life and you shouldn't be afraid to offer less than is required or ask for more than is offered – if you don't risk a 'no', you won't get a 'yes'! Once again, if you are not totally happy with the deal – DO NOT BUY! It's important to remember that the heady days of the '80s are gone. In almost every case it is, quite simply, a buyer's market.

Chapter 4

Bodywork

– When fitting new rubber seals, use washing up liquid or WD40 to make them easier to slide into place.
– When dealing with nuts and bolts which are likely to be heavily rusted (almost all of them!), try to plan ahead; clean them up with a wire brush and give them a good soaking in releasing agent the day before you want to remove them.
– Many bolts will only come free if you drill them out – allow for this and plan to replace at least some of them.
– Removing riveted body panels requires a quality sharp drill bit of the right size. Because they are small, they will break on a regular basis, so you'll need some spares.
– Buy a quality rivet gun and practice on a scrap panel before progressing to your car – riveting isn't hard, but neither is messing up your easily-marked bodywork.
– Don't skip over any areas of rusted steel. Use an anti-rust agent, primer and some form of protective paint finish (or underseal, etc.).
– Always remember – look after your tools and they will look after you! Clean them and put them away after every job; you'll feel good about it, especially next time out.

TOOLS AND TECHNIQUES
As said before, it will pay you to buy good quality tools as they will help you in every task you do. When dealing with bodywork and sheet metal in general, a good pair of tin snips is essential. For more serious work, an electric nibbler makes life easier. Sykes-Pickavant has an excellent range of body tools available, such as dollies and hammers (either singly or in sets), bending tools and jogglers (for putting an indented edge in repair panels for flush-fitting).

When applying turning effort to any nut or bolt (whether with a socket or spanner) consider what will happen if the tool slips; skinned knuckles are painful to say the least, and when you're dealing with large areas of rotting, jagged metal, such an error can be extremely dangerous.

Not using the right tool for the job is a common mistake; a crosshead screw needs a crosshead screwdriver. Use a socket on nuts and bolts; failing that, a ring spanner, then an open-ended spanner and, as a last resort, an adjustable wrench. The more you can grip a fastener, the more likely it is to yield without drama.

SAFETY
(Thanks to Sykes-Pickavant for providing these basic safety rules relating to the use of pulling and extracting tools.)
– **Always read specific instructions which come with any tool or kit.**
– **The tool must be fitted squarely on to the workpiece.**
– **Excessive pressure must not be used.**
– **Care should be taken to prevent damage or injury from the sudden release of the pressure generated by the tool.**
– **The tool and workpiece should be covered during the operation.**

– **The operator should guard against injury from flying debris caused by failure of the tool or workpiece.**
– **Where possible, a retaining nut should be left on the end of the workpiece to prevent the tool being projected upon sudden release of pressure.**

THE 'NUTS AND BOLTS' OF FASTENERS

▲ *BTT1. You won't get far in sorting out XJ6 bodywork without an impact screwdriver. Many fasteners will have rusted solid and others will have been deliberately tightened to a high torque figure on the production line. This S-P model comes in a steel case with a selection of screwdriver bits. It's a ½ in drive and can also be used as an impact socket wrench, BUT ONLY with suitable sockets, as shown here – standard sockets may shatter and injure the user.*

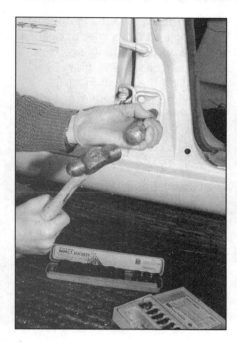

▲ BTT2. Removing the door hinge bolts is a typical use for an impact 'driver. By definition, a large steel hammer has to be used and with considerable force, so concentration is required to prevent the all too obvious injuries that may befall your hand!

▲ BTT3. Rusted-solid nuts, bolts and self-tapping screws are likely to be your biggest enemy, so when you do get them out (or when you replace them) always coat the threads with a hefty dollop of copper grease. That way, when you come to remove them again, they will come out as they should – easily. When you've removed a bolt, always take the trouble to clean it up properly before replacing it. Use a wire brush to get rust and dirt from the threads and then …

▲ BTT4. … apply some copper grease. Note the short cut here – make a large enough hole in the top of the tin and use a modeller's paintbrush to apply it. If you use it from a tube, squeeze it directly on to the brush so you can get it where it's required without wasting any.

▲ BTT5. Screw the nut up and down the threads a few times until it has a smooth passage. If it's easy on the workbench, it will be easy when you're working upside down under the car trying to fit it in an awkward position.

REMOVING BROKEN FASTENERS

Always try the simple methods first. Soak a difficult fastener in penetrating oil for as long as you can – preferably overnight. If there's some of the fastener sticking out of the hole, you may be able to grasp it with locking pliers or a pipe spanner. Failing that, saw a slot in its centre to take a large screwdriver blade or file it down so that a spanner can be used. If the fastener is suitably positioned (i.e. NOT next to the fuel tank!), heating it with a gas torch (if

you've been using penetrating oil recently, beware that this could 'fire' as a flame is applied) will often free off the rust. Wear protective gloves and goggles and remember that the workpiece will remain hot for some while after the source of heat has been removed.

▲ BTT6. The S-P stud-extractor is fitted over the broken or seized stud and a ½ in drive ratchet used to turn the elliptical knurled section. As it turns, it 'grabs' the stud and applies a turning force not possible by gripping it with, say, pliers or by using two nuts. As seen in Chapter 6, it can also be used to replace studs (in that case on a cylinder head) without damaging the threads.

▲ BTT7. Sometimes it's possible to 'shock' a fastener free – either tap it or use a punch to do it. (Note: brute force isn't required here – just a short, sharp shock.) Always use a purpose-made punch, such as those featured in this multi-size kit. These are designed to take the kind of forces you'll be using. Even when using punches, protect your eyes against flying pieces of fastener or rusty bodywork.

▲ BTT8. Subtlety is usually the best way to approach problems on your XJ6, but sometimes a little more brawn is required – with a little brain, too, of course. Make sure you use the right hammer for the job. Shown here is a ball-pein version together with a selection of plastic mallets. You need to be able to choose the right hammer to administer all kinds of force, from a short, sharp tap, to a hefty wallop. Always wear goggles in case of sparks or flying pieces of metal, etc.

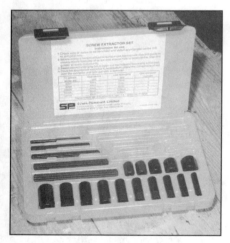

▲ BTT9. If all else fails, you'll need stud extractors, such as those in this straight-fluted S-P kit. First, check the size of screw to be removed and select the appropriate pilot drill. Where the screw is broken off flush or below the surface, use an appropriate size guide to closely match the diameter of the screw and ensure that the hole drilled is dead centre. Then select the correct enlarging drill to open out the hole, leaving only a thin wall. Drive the appropriate extractor into the hole bottom, place the nut over the top of the extractor and use a spanner to remove both it and the troublesome screw.

To extract screw dia	Use centre drill	Use enlarging drill	Use extractor No.
6	4	4	1
8	4	5	2
10	5	6	3
12	5	7.5	4
14	6	8.5	5

▲ BTT10. Nuts can often be as recalcitrant as studs and bolts. Again, try the same principles – plenty of penetrating oil to start with, followed by the 'shock' treatment and/or heat (if you've been using penetrating oil recently, beware that this could 'fire' as a flame is applied). If possible, file rounded flats down to suit a smaller-sized spanner. On occasion, a hammer and chisel can be used to force the nut round the thread. If there is room, you can grind it off (with the usual safety caveats) but ultimately it may require the serious force supplied by a hydraulic nut splitter. This Sykes-Pickavant kit (with two sizes of splitter), comes in a strong steel case and takes no prisoners! Care is needed when using it because, by definition, it's a powerful tool indeed – always wear gloves and goggles to protect your eyes.

USEFUL TIP: If you've had problems removing a stud, it's wise to clean up the hole using a suitably sized tap. This should be done very carefully, especially if the hole is in soft aluminium. This procedure can often save a thread, even if it is partially stripped.

POWER TOOLS

▲ BTT11. One of the most useful tools available to the home restorer is a mini angle grinder, such as this one from Clarke International. Most take 4 ½ in diameter discs and can be used for a variety of tasks, including grinding off seized nuts and bolts and welds and, with a change of disc, sanding down paintwork. ALWAYS wear gloves and protect your eyes from the dangerous sparks. Remember that the sparks you see are the bits of (usually) metal that you're removing. Consider where they will end up, and take steps to protect any good paintwork in the vicinity. Thoughtless grinding can ruin a windscreen. (Courtesy Clarke International Limited)

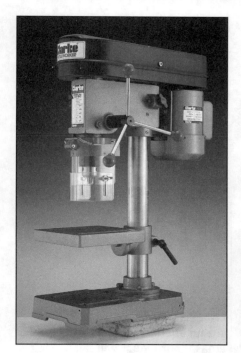

▲ BTT12. For accurate hole-drilling off the car, a bench drill is ideal when you're making new body parts, etc., which require holes for bolts to pass through into existing holes on the car. (Courtesy Clarke International Limited)

BODYWORK BASICS

▲ BB1. Almost all body parts are available for all XJ6 models, but having invested in your bodywork tools, there'll probably be some things you want to tackle yourself. In many cases, fabricating and welding-in your own patch repair is much simpler (and cheaper) than replacing a whole panel, especially if most of the area is good

metal and the patch is only a small one. Mild steel sheet (flat bar, etc.) is available to the general public from companies who supply commercial enterprises. You can buy it in various size sheets, the one shown here being approximately 6 ft x 3 ft, which is about the limit for easy handling in the workshop.

SAFETY: When dealing with mild steel sheet, always wear strong gloves to prevent the sharp edges cutting your hands.

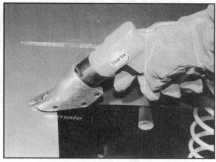

▲ BB2. Probably the easiest way to cut this kind of sheet is to use an air-fed shear, like this Clarke model. It cuts through the steel like the proverbial knife through butter, but don't forget that it cuts out a channel about 6mm (¼ in) wide, so you need to allow for that when marking out. Note the gloves – essential to prevent nasty cuts from the sharp edges of the sheet steel. If you've got the space, leave the sheet as it comes and cut off the pieces to size as you need them.

▲ BB3. For cutting more complex shapes or working in confined spaces on the car, you'll need either tin snips or shears, like the S-P version shown here.

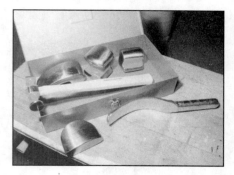

▲ BB4. Fabricating metalwork requires special tools and, if you're new to the subject, S-P's Starter Kit comprising panelwork hammer and various spoons and dollies is ideal. It's packaged in a strong steel case.

WELDING

Unless you have lottery-luck, you're likely to find several areas on your XJ6 that require welding. Once the preserve of the professional, welding has now been brought within the realms of the DIY enthusiast by companies such as Clarke International who have an impressive range of electric arc/brazing, MIG, TIG and spot welding machines suitable for all welding tasks. Naturally, the instructions and information supplied with the equipment should be studied and followed to the letter. Also it's a good idea to get some form of tuition, for example, at a night-school course run by the local education authority.

Always wear thick strong gloves and, ideally, wear a leather apron – it's fairly common for amateurs to set their clothing on fire! Failing that, a flame retardant overall is useful. Don't start welding unless you have a dry powder (CO_2/BCF type) fire extinguisher to hand. Do NOT use a water extinguisher on welding fires.

NEVER weld without protecting your eyes with either a hand-held shield or, a little more expensive but more versatile, fold-down mask. The UV light given off during the welding process is very damaging to eyes – human and pets – so as well as protecting your own eyes, clear the immediate area of flammable materials and warn any onlookers to look away.

It is also recommended that *The Car Bodywork Manual*, published by Haynes, is purchased and used to complement this book. It picks the brains of specialists from a variety of fields, and covers arc, MIG and 'gas' welding, panel beating and accident repair, rust repair and treatment, paint spraying, glass-fibre work, filler, lead loading, interiors and much more besides.

Practice makes perfect, and welding is no exception. It pays to take some time to learn how to use your welding equipment properly – preferably on scrap metal, rather than your pride and joy!

SAFETY: The temperatures involved in any form of welding are huge and thus there is an ever-present danger of fire or explosion. Never weld near petrol tanks, even if empty – the fumes are as dangerous as the liquid itself. Remember also that there are lots of other flammable items in your XJ6. It always pays to have a helper standing by and watching out for the first signs of flames that you won't be able to see from behind your darkened shield or visor.

When carrying out MIG or arc welding on your Jaguar ALWAYS disconnect the alternator. Because the chassis is used to pass the electric current, leaving the alternator connected could damage it beyond repair. For total safety, we would always recommend removing the battery altogether and storing it remotely from the welding operations, i.e. in another building. As an alternative, you could use a special isolating device which connects across the battery; these are quite expensive, but it does save removing the battery, and on later cars with complex ECUs and/or coded radios, etc., this could be an advantage.

BUYING EQUIPMENT

Buying new welding equipment is easy enough, and flicking through the Clarke catalogue reveals that it is far from expensive (especially when you pull back the initial cost in terms of cash saved in paying someone else to do the bodywork repairs). Always buy recognised quality products, where your safety has been a prime consideration (with the fitment of thermal cut-outs, etc.). Make sure that the welder you buy is powerful enough to handle the jobs you want to tackle – ask your supplier what is recommended. A good warranty and back-up service from the seller is very important.

Buying used welding gear of any description should NOT be attempted unless you are an expert in the subject; it is extremely easy to buy equipment which is dangerous.

GAS WELDING

Thanks to the growth in the home restoration market of the last few years, suppliers of gas welding gear are now selling some excellent equipment, obtainable from national companies like BOC who market the 'Portapak' range of equipment by Murex.

Two types of gas welding equipment are available. The type supplied by BOC uses mini oxy-acetylene bottles hired for a period of a few years at a time and refilled at quite low cost as and when necessary. Cheaper systems use refillable oxygen bottles but with disposable gas canisters. Both types are effective, although the latter is more difficult to use and far more expensive in terms of running costs. Gas welding remains the most versatile technique of all, but has a few drawbacks in that a higher level of skill is required (why not enrol in one of the many welding classes run by local authorities?) and in that, if using acetylene, the gas bottles are less safe to store and use. (Also, check local by-laws regarding gas bottle storage.) Moreover, novice gas-welded panels are almost certain to buckle and distort and will take a lot more work to be made to fit properly and to allow a smooth and ripple-free paint finish.

ELECTRIC WELDING – ARC WELDING

Arc welding is an efficient means of welding thicker metal, but can be rather too fierce for thinner steel body panels. Special arc rod holders which operate in a pulse current delivery mode are available. Carbon arc attachments can also be obtained quite cheaply to enable brazing work to be carried out, ideal for repairing and even replacing unstressed panels. The brazing attachment can also be used as a source of heat to help shift stubborn bolts and to bend exhaust pipes and so on. A further advantage of this equipment compared with other welding gear is that it is the most inexpensive while being quite versatile.

SAFETY: Brazed joints are NOT strong enough for major structural areas. Your Jaguar will fail its MoT test if any are found.

▲ *WEL1. This is a selection of three of Clarke's vast arc welder range. It ranges from a DIY potterer to a huge 'let's build a suspension bridge' serious machine. Because they are all fan-cooled, they can be used for longer periods of time. As with all DIY-style machinery, they work off 230v single phase mains power and have safety thermal cut-outs to protect against accidental overload. (Courtesy Clarke International Limited)*

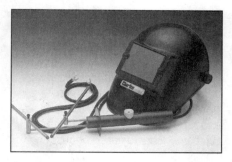

▲ WEL2. All arc welders can be used to braze, simply by using this special kit. In many cases, brazing is a better way to achieve the result you require, but it must not be used for MoT test repairs – it isn't strong enough. (Courtesy Clarke International Limited)

▲ WEL3. This heavy duty kit is desirable if you are using arc welders over 170A output. (Courtesy Clarke International Limited)

ELECTRIC WELDING – MIG WELDING

MIG welding equipment is now well within the reach of most DIY restorers, which is good because it's probably the best all-round method there is. Like arc welding, MIG welding can be used for chassis rails, etc., but it is just as effective on thin body panels.

For the DIY welder, MIG equipment often comes with disposable canisters of inert gas (argon, carbon dioxide or a mixture of the two). This can be very expensive and it is usually cheaper in the long run to hire mini-professional gas cylinders (these require gas cylinder valves, which are fairly cheap to buy).

The transformer in the machine passes current to the MIG welding torch which has a continuous metal wire fed through it. An arc is generated, causing the wire to melt simultaneously with the metal workpiece (your bodywork, patch repair, etc.). This produces a molten pool which creates the weld. The gas is fed into the torch during the entire welding process to act as a shielding agent, preventing contamination of the weld, the gas also creates a much cleaner weld with no residue. Because the wire in the torch is being fed continuously, an uninterrupted weld can be made – unlike arc welding, where the electrode burns out relatively quickly. On the downside, the MIG welder cannot usually be used as a source of heat in the same way that an arc welder brazing attachment can.

You can use different gases with your Clarke MIG welder, depending on the work you're doing.

75% Argon, 25% CO_2	Thin sheet metal, mild steel (the type of gas usually supplied with the machine)
100% Argon	Aluminium, stainless steel
100% CO_2	Mild steel

▲ WEL4. For many of the practical sections we used the Clarke Turbo MIG 150TE, an excellent mid-range choice for the DIY restorer, having plenty of power (150A) and capable of handling most tasks. It works off a standard 230v mains supply and features thermal overload protection, reel of 0.6mm wire and hand-held welding mask – note the mask at the right of this shot is a flip-down shield from Halfords which leaves both hands free to work with.

▲ WEL5. The pack also includes a small gas bottle which locates neatly on the rear of the machine. The Clarke welder has six settings, so that the device can be set-up exactly for the material thickness in question and the wire size being used. This has to be balanced with the correct wire feed – too fast or too slow will mean a bad weld. Getting the initial settings wrong is the main DIY welding failure point. The various settings are listed in the comprehensive handbook.

▲ WEL6. The wire is supplied ready-wound on to spools which fit on to a spindle inside the machine. When the initial spool has been used, it can be replaced with either a 0.8kg mini-spool or a hefty 5kg spool. It is vital that the wire is cut cleanly and that there are no barbs which could snag on the liner.

Mild steel is the type of wire that most DIY welders will use. It is suitable for different thicknesses of metal, as follows:

0.6 mm	Suitable for thin metals up to 3mm
0.8 mm	Suitable for thicker metals up to 6mm

One of the key points of using a MIG welder is to get the machine set-up correctly, and this starts by loading up the new reel – this is a 0.8kg reel of 0.6mm mild steel wire. It should be slotted on to the spool holder and the wire threaded through the guide tube and …

▲ WEL7. … over the correct-sized groove in the wire roller. Note that the plastic pressure knob has been released at this point. Keep some tension on the wire so that it doesn't unwind all over the place, but not too much, otherwise it will jam the machine. Once the wire is in the liner, the pressure knob can be put into position and tightened – too tight will crush the wire and damage the wire feed motor; too loose will mean that the wire cannot be pulled to the torch by the motor.

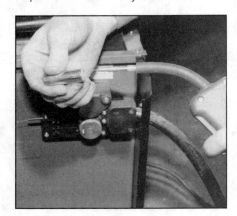

▲ WEL8. Remove the torch shroud (at left) and contact tip (seen here fitted to end of torch) and pull the trigger on the torch to feed the wire through. When it protrudes from the torch, replace the contact tip and shroud. The amount of

wire protruding from the torch is called the 'stick-out' (sometimes incorrectly called the 'arc length') and should be between 5mm and 10mm. Whenever you're welding you'll need to keep a set of wire snips handy to make sure that the wire is always at the right length and to snip off the end when a 'ball' forms at the end. Never allow the liner to the torch (which carries the gas to the tip, the electrical feed and the wire itself) to get kinked, otherwise the wire could snag inside.

▶ WEL9. Having set your welder correctly for the thickness of plate in question, make sure that the workpiece is firmly secured. Use clamps where necessary and clamp the welder earth lead to it. Start with the nozzle at an angle of around 45 degrees, with the wire protruding around 5-10mm from the nozzle and around 10mm from the workpiece. Make sure that you put your mask in position BEFORE you make contact.

There are two basic MIG welding techniques. Fig A shows forehand welding, where the welding gun is directed toward the progress of welding and Fig B show's backhand welding, where the gun is directed opposite to the progress of welding. This is sometimes called the 'pull technique'. A good weld will be accompanied by a sharp crackling sound. If the wire speed setting is too high, the wire can 'bounce' off the workpiece, or the workpiece could be burned through. On the other hand, if the speed is too low, the

crackling will become more of a spluttering and the wire will probably burn back into the nozzle, resulting, of course, in no weld at all.

When you're trying a long weld, it's advisable to make a series of 'tack' welds, i.e. small blobs of weld, along its length first, then join then up with a number of longer welds. (Courtesy Clarke International Limited)

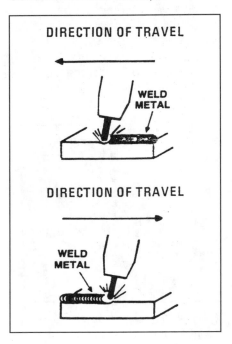

▼ WEL10. There are many types of joints to be made, including; butt, single-V, double-V, single bevel, double bevel and corner, examples of which are shown in this diagram. (Courtesy Clarke International Limited)

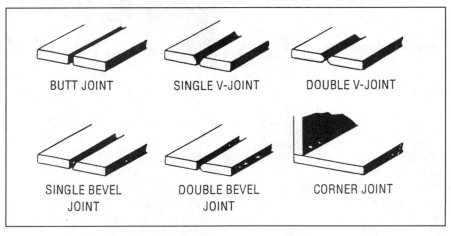

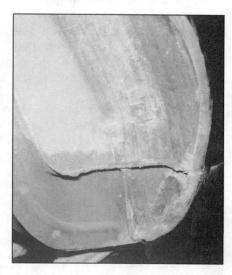

▲ WEL11. When joining thin sheets of metal (below approx 22 SWG), it's advisable to use an edge setter (or 'joggler'), such as this one from Sykes-Pickavant, to form a lap joint, as shown …

REMOVING AND REPLACING A ROTTEN SILL AND REAR WHEEL ARCH

The welding and bodywork removal sections of this chapter were carried out using the expertise of Colin Wood, of CE Wood Welding Services. My thanks to him for using his years of experience to show not only how the job should be done, but how it should be done *safely*.

As for many of the practical sections, the Jaguar in question is perfectly placed for access, being supported by the NBN Chassis Tilter.

▲ SA2. The sills are frequently holed at either end, too. This damage is usually disguised by underseal/road dirt/filler. The sills contribute more than on most cars to the car's structural strength and are, of course, MoT failure items.

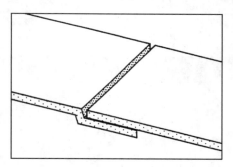

▲ WEL12. … which creates a definite lip which can be slotted under the bodywork in order to make a flush finished panel repair. This is a DIY style (and DIY priced) hand-held edge setter, but you can get much larger versions, though they are for professional use and consequently much dearer. (Courtesy Clarke International)

SPOT WELDING

Spot welding is a technique used by most manufacturers when making thousands of vehicles on a production run, and Jaguar is no exception. But its use in vehicle restoration is limited because of the cost of the equipment, especially as a wide range of 'arms' would be required to enable all the welds to be made properly. The technique of spot-welding is not something easily acquired and, in general, it is recommended that arc or, better still, MIG welding should be preferred.

▲ SA1. The first job is to assess the amount of corrosion. Often, what appears to be a small area of rotten metal can turn out to be a nasty gaping hole. XJ6 sills are notorious for rotting through.

▼ SA3. The rear wheel arch is also favourite food for the rust bug. This one showed signs of fraying around the edges, but as we found out later, all is not what it appears.

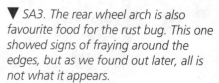

▶ SA4. We'd obtained a new factory sill panel from SNG Barratt, who can supply just about any panel for any model. This is the full sill, which assumes serious rust along the top of the sill but …

▼ SA5. … we removed the scratch plates to find that on this car, they were quite sound. Whilst it's always best to do any job properly, and skimping should be avoided, cutting away good metal to replace it with more good metal is pointless and just makes more work! Before he started work, Colin covered the interior with a selection of thick curtains (old ones, of course!).

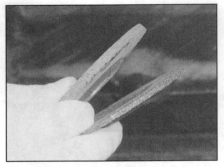

▲ SA7. Note the difference between grinding and cutting discs. At top is a grinding disc, designed for grinding metal to shape – it can be seen that the cutting disc is much thinner so that it can pass easily through the metal. A grinding disc can sometimes 'snag' if used to cut through large sections of metal (as here) and a cutting disc could break if used to grind metal down. Always unplug the grinder while changing discs – it's very easy to switch it on inadvertently, with obvious unpleasant results.

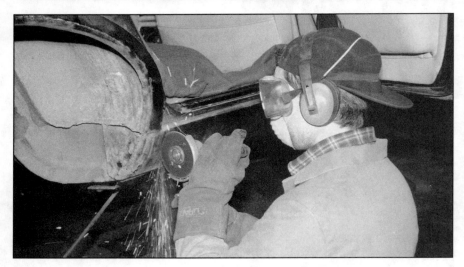

▲ SA6. Colin started by cutting away the rotten old sill. Note the safety precautions; very heavy duty gloves, mask, goggles, heavy leather boots and strong flame-retardant overalls, buttoned right up. The baseball cap isn't being worn the wrong way round as a fashion statement – it keeps dust and debris from landing on his head or getting down his neck! If you're using an angle grinder, ALWAYS put the guard in position. He started at the rear, making a vertical cut and then cut his way along the bottom of the sill, keeping it as straight as possible.

▲ SA8. The SNG Barratt panel and what was left of the rotten section Colin cut away.

SA9. He cleaned up the lower fixing edge of the sill all the way along. This gets rid of excess rust and provides a good surface for the new sill.

SA10. Removal of the outer sill had revealed that the inner sill was starting to suffer, too. This is common and if it's bad enough, a new inner sill panel will be required which will call for the car to be braced in order to keep it in shape. The rot here was restricted to a small area towards the rear of the car.

SA11. A little more work with the grinder and cutting disc and Colin had a very nasty piece of jagged, rusty metal in is hand. Now you know why heavy-duty gloves are essential.

SA12. Because it was a flat area, Colin easily cut a suitably-sized piece of mild steel and then showed the worth of the Clarke 150TE Turbo MIG welder (shown earlier) by …

SA13. … making a perfect repair. This shows the patch just after the welding process had been completed. Note that it is a seam weld – i.e., there are no breaks in the weld at any point. This is important, as tack welds on such important areas are not only unsafe, but they will also cause MoT failures. Any weld should be cleaned up using the grinding wheel in the grinder, in order to present a smooth face to the world.

MAKING A PATCH REPAIR

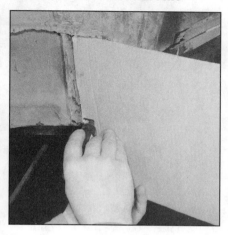

SA14. To make a suitable patch for repairing the sill ends, Colin started by making a template, using a piece of stiff cardboard to mark out the rough shape of the patch required along the bottom edge and then where the vertical line should be.

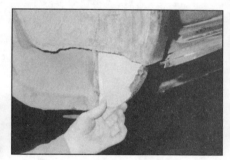

SA15. Cut to size and trimmed a few times with scissors, he ended up with a patch that fitted perfectly. It wouldn't pass an MoT, though!

SA16. He then transferred the template to a piece of mild steel sheet and measured the ½ in overlap required all the way round. He used a scriber to mark the position of the template on the sheet and then …

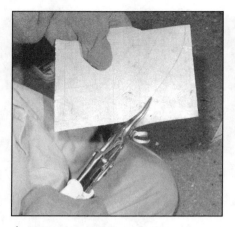

SA17. ... used tin snips to cut the sheet to size. Note the use of strong gloves to prevent cutting his hands.

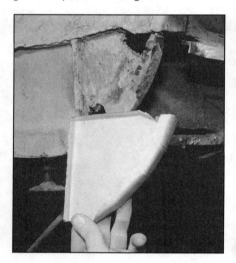

SA18. In order to get the metal overlap to bend, it's necessary to make incisions in from the edge of the template. With a little patience, you can end up with a perfect patch like this. Compare it with the horrible corroded area above it.

SA19. Having cut away all of that, he welded the patch in place to provide a suitable rear anchor point for the new sill section.

SA20. Colin then welded on the new sill, using the same techniques already shown. For the most part DIY welders will use a MIG welder and end up with a weld looking like this. All welds should be ground flush.

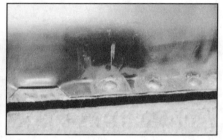

SA21. The original sill was spot-welded at the factory, and, of course, Colin had that facility. For demonstration purposes, he spot-welded this section of the sill. The welds still needed ...

SA22. ... grinding off as before. For the DIY restorer, the extra cost of spot welding equipment is usually prohibitive.

SA23. A definite improvement over the original, wouldn't you say?

REAR WHEEL ARCH

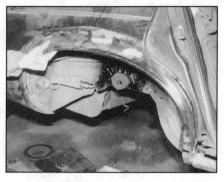

RW1. A rotten rear wheel arch is a common enough problem for SNG Barratt to have repair panels sitting on the shelf. It's shaped to be a perfect fit with the car's original body lines. Note that the top edge of the panel extends high to allow for really bad rot. You can trim the panel to suit your requirements.

RW2. Colin ran the grinding wheel along the top lip of the arch in order to check the extent of the damage. It's common to find lots of filler along this area and, as the white dust up the wing reveals, this was no exception. Always wear a mask to prevent breathing the filler dust.

▲ RW3. The rust was severe in places and travelling up to 1.25 in from the edge of the arch. As ever, you can't weld to rust, so Colin had to cut back until …

▲ RW4. … he could find a smooth line of solid steel. The rear wing area is double-skinned, and he trimmed carefully in the hope that the underside was in better condition than the top section. Unfortunately, it wasn't.

▲ RW5. Once more, Colin's skill came into play and he seam welded and ground the new arch section into place.

REPLACING/ REPAIRING A FRONT CROSSMEMBER

▲ CR1. One of the most common points for rot at the front of the car is the crossmember. It leads a hard life, taking punishment from its underside (rainwater, road dirt, stone chips, etc.) and from above from a leaking radiator. This is a structural item and so is of concern from a safety point of view and a MoT failure point. This kind of nasty damage is typical. One of the main problems is 'out of sight, out of mind' in that few owners think to apply any form of rust-prevention. Sometimes, the damaged area can be patched, though you must be justifiably confident in your welding abilities. Use a grinder to cut out the rotten metal and then measure the area of damage to make a template, as shown previously. Cut your patch to suit and weld it in – note that this must be seam-welded, i.e. the weld must be continuous all the way around the patch, NOT tack-welded at intervals. This is both a safety and MoT requirement.

▶ CR2. If the rot is too bad, or if you just want a long-lasting solution to the problem, SNG Barratt can supply suitable replacement crossmembers for all XJ6 models. Clearly, the original will need cutting out and it's essential that the car is braced in such a way that it can't go 'out of true' whilst the new crossmember is being welded in place.

It's a wise move to apply Waxoyl to the centre of the crossmember to prevent an early repeat of this problem!

REMOVING THE BONNET AND GRILLE

Removing the XJ6 bonnet is not particularly difficult, and for serious engine work it makes life much easier – for engine removal it is essential. However, it is a very large and very heavy piece of metal and you will need an assistant to steady it as the check strap is released and to carry it to safety once all the fastenings have been removed. Don't be tempted to try it alone; at best you'll damage the bonnet, car or workshop, and at worst you could damage yourself into the bargain.

▲ BN1. This diagram shows the positioning of the items to be released.
KEY
1. Wiring cable connectors
2. Check strap bolts
3. Hinge bolts

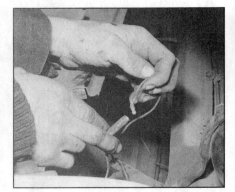

▲ BN2. Phil started by removing the battery earth lead and disconnecting all wiring from the car to the headlamps and sidelamps (where applicable).

▲ BN3. He unbolted the check strap – at this point, it is essential to have a helper standing by so that the bonnet or hinges can't be strained.

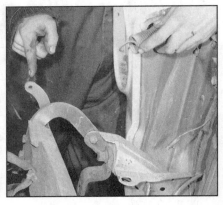

▲ BN4. This photo shows where the very strong counterbalance spring fixes to the bonnet – there's one at each side. We cannot emphasise how strong these springs are, and it's vital to keep your fingers well clear.

▲ BN5. Having removed them, Phil was able to enlist the aid of welder, Colin Wood, to ease the bonnet over …

▲ BN6. … and on to a padded kitchen stool – every garage should have one! Whatever you use to support the bonnet at this point should be substantial and not likely to dent or scratch the paintwork.

▲ BN7. Access to the fixing bolts (two or three) is much easier – Phil chose to removed the bonnet/hinge bolts rather than removing the hinge altogether. These are always very tight and if you've invested in some Clarke air tools, now is the time to make them work for a living! Phil used his impact wrench to make light work of it. Again, Colin was taking the weight of the bonnet to prevent damage to the hinges. Once removed, it should be placed carefully where it can't be damaged and where it won't fall on anyone! During replacement, it is just as important to have at least one helper to prevent bonnet, vehicle or personal damage.

▲ BN8. The bonnet can stay in situ to remove the grille. This is secured by a number (which varies) of nuts on studs fitted into the rear of the grille and protruding through the bonnet front, as shown here. As ever, if the grille has been in position since it left the factory, you'll need to use lots of WD40 before trying to remove the nuts – take your time and ease them free to avoid shearing the studs.

HEADLAMPS, SIDE LAMPS AND INDICATORS

HEADLAMP CONDITION

When checking your headlamps, make sure that the lamps are secured firmly – use firm hand pressure to make sure that the mountings are not loose or rusty. Look for cracks in the lenses, often caused by stone chips. These are not necessarily reasons for an MoT failure, but such cracks can let in water and/or cause condensation within the lamp. Where this happens, the condensation can build up and cause the beam pattern to be altered so that it is illegal and fails the test. The long-term result will be that

the reflector surface of the headlamp will corrode and, again, the beam pattern will be adversely affected. Depending on your car, replacement will involve purchasing a whole sealed beam unit or just the damaged item. It is possible to buy lamps from breakers' yards, though you should make a thorough check that you are not buying another lamp with exactly the same problems you already have. Naturally, correct (matched) wattage bulbs should be fitted and working.

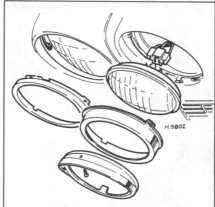

▲ HL1. This diagram shows the basic headlamp components. Expect most of the small screws to be well-rusted and possibly problematical.

▲ HL2. Phil started on the dipped beam (outer lamps) by removing the single screw securing the chromed embellisher rim. Because it's a slotted screw, it is often chewed-up, so take care to take your time and use the right-sized screwdriver. This simply pulls out, though there are a pair of lugs at its lower edge.

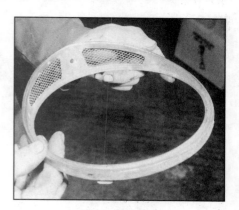

▲ HL3. From the Series 2 cars, the top of the rim has a mesh grille through which air was passed into the car.

▲ HL4. He then removed the three screws holding the sealed beam unit in place and …

▲ HL5. … removed the chrome securing ring and headlamp – after the three-pin electrical connector had been unplugged from the rear of the lamp. If you're intending to re-use the unit, don't touch the beam-setting screws, otherwise you'll have to go through the process of setting up the beam again.

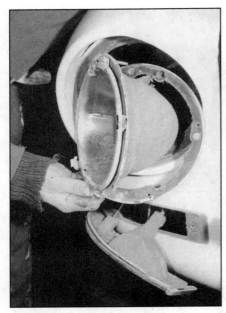

▲ HL6. Phil unscrewed the four fasteners which held the headlamp bowl, and eased it carefully out of the wing. It has to be done steadily in order not to damage the gasket, seen here. The removal procedure for the inner (main beam) lamps is almost identical.

HEADLAMP ALIGNMENT

Having your headlamps pointing exactly where they should is an obvious safety requirement and part of the annual MoT test. In a four-headlamp system, as on all XJ6 models, the outer pair is required to provide the *dipped* beam. Because of the wording of the MoT test (in that only the *obligatory* lamps are checked) inner lamps which provide a main beam only are not checked. In fact, neither are any fog or spot lamps, other than to check that they are securely mounted and not likely to cause a hazard to other road users.

At test-time they will be tested on a professional beam-setter and, ideally, that's where they should be set-up – most garages will charge very little to point your lights in the right direction.

REMOVING INDICATOR/SIDE LAMP ASSEMBLY

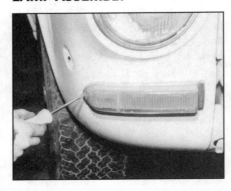

▲ HL7. Prior to the Series 3 models, the front side lamp and indicator lamp were included in the same assembly fitted to the front wing below the headlamp. The cover can be removed by unscrewing the single crosshead screw (the number varied between models) at the outer edge ...

▲ HL8. ... and then pulling the lens away.

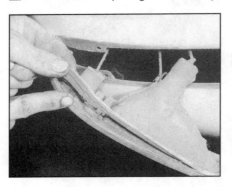

▲ HL9. The assembly housing is secured by two self-tapping screws. The gasket is likely to be hard and damaged in places, so replace it. The bulbs are often rusted into their holders – so wear thick gloves in case the bulbs break in your hands. When re-fitting the bulbs and electrical wiring, spray liberally with WD40 to protect against further moisture damage.

REMOVING REAR TAIL LAMP CLUSTER

▲ HL10. This is similar to the front unit. Three crosshead screws secure the outer lens and underneath, there's a gasket which you can expect to need replacement. The same applies to the gasket between the wing and the lamp holder. The latter is secured by three more crosshead screws in similar positions to those on the outside.

The reflector is tricky to remove. In its back are two threaded studs which pass through the wing and are secured by two small nuts. These are accessed from inside the rear wing and, apart from being tricky to get at, are likely to be covered in road dirt and well-rusted. Getting a reflector off without shearing off a stud is difficult indeed, so be prepared to buy a new reflector – or two!

WIRING AND GROMMETS

When replacing headlamp/sidelamp components, always make sure that wiring connectors are sound by giving them a reasonably sharp tug. Replace any connectors that are loose. Ensure that where wiring passes through holes in bodywork there is a grommet in position. If not, the wiring could chafe, resulting in a short circuit or even a fire.

REMOVING FRONT AND REAR BUMPERS

FRONT BUMPER REMOVAL

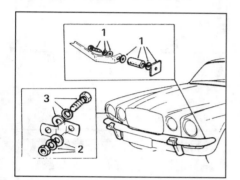

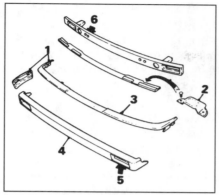

▲ BM1. Removing the wing demands prior removal of the bumper, or you may be removing the bumper for remedial work. The ends of the bumper are secured by bolts accessed from inside the wheel arches. Note that there's a flat washer and rubber spacer between the bumper and the wings. There are three nuts securing the front of the bumper to the bonnet hinge brackets and then a further bolt securing the underriders to the brackets. When these have been removed, the bumper can be eased away from its position – it's not heavy but it is unwieldy so it will need supporting at both ends to prevent damaging the bumper or anything else. Make sure you collect all the flat/spring washers.
KEY
1. Bumper outer location.
2. Bumper/bonnet hinge location.
3. Underrider/bonnet hinge location.
  Badly pitted chrome will mean a new bumper or professional re-chroming. It's a good idea to de-rust the back of the bumper – use an anti-rust agent and then paint/spray with Hammerite smooth finish. Clean up all rusted threads on the fasteners and use copper grease on them before replacing. If they're particularly bad, replace as a matter of course.

▲ BM2. Removing the front bumper from the Series 3 cars is made a little more difficult by the fitment of indicators into the centre section and the inclusion of the rubber finishers.
KEY
1. Chrome finisher and side bracket
2. Plastic covers
3. Finisher
4. Rubber finisher
5. Lamp unit
6. Bumper beam

REAR BUMPER

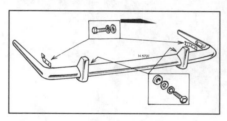

▲ BM3. This shows the single-piece rear bumper as fitted to early models, now something of a rarity, as Jaguar soon started to fit …

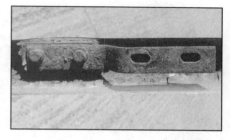

▲ BM5. This is a side mounting in typical condition – not very good! The bracket itself is well-rusted and, more important, the bolts holding the bracket to the bumper will be tricky to remove. Note the condition of the inside of the bumper – again a victim of rust.

▲ BM6. The side pieces join the rear centre section neatly behind the overriders. The large flat section shown here is the mounting point for the bumper to the car.

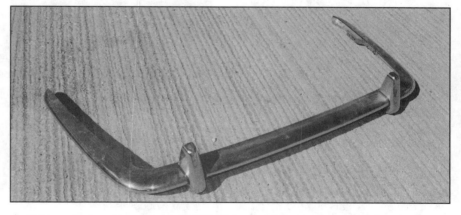

▲ BM4. … 3-piece bumpers to the XJ6. This meant that in the event of a minor bump, it would often be much cheaper from an insurance aspect, as only the damaged section would have to be replaced. If required, it can still be taken off all-of-a-piece, as here with this Series 2 bumper.

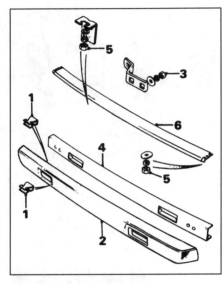

▲ BM.7. The Series 3 cars are more complex because of the rubber finishers required to meet American safety standards. This is the centre section and ...
KEY
1. Clip
2. Rubber finisher
3. Fixing nuts
4. Bumper beam
5. Fixing nuts
6. Blade

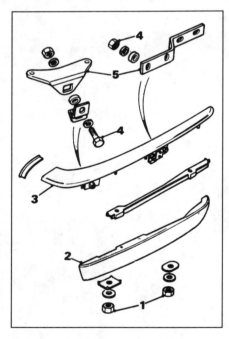

▲ BM8. ... this is the side section. Don't forget that Series 3 cars had fog lamps mounted in the centre section which have to be removed first of all. The side sections can only be removed after the centre section. Because of their

positions, almost all fasteners are likely to be well-corroded. Apply lots of releasing agent and use a little patience to prevent them shearing off. Use new fasteners or clean up the originals and apply copper grease on the rebuild.
KEY
1. Fixing nuts
2. Rubber finisher
3. Blade
4. Fixing nuts
5. Mounting brackets

REMOVING THE BOOT LID

Because there are electrical cables running from the car into the boot lid itself, it is advisable to remove the battery earth strap before starting work. The boot lid is a large and heavy piece of metal. To avoid straining the lid, hinges or yourself, a helper is essential.

▲ LID1. Disconnect the plastic tie wraps securing the cables and unplug the wiring connectors. The lid is secured to the brackets by two bolts at either side, each with a spring washer and flat washer. Remove the bolts at one side and then, with your helper taking the strain, remove those at the opposite side. Lift the boot lid carefully away. Make sure you have a suitable surface (bubble wrap or cardboard packing) on which to rest the lid in order to avoid paintwork damage.

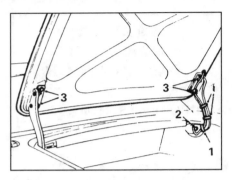

▲ LID2. This diagram shows the positioning of the bolts, tie wraps and nuts/bolts.

REMOVING FRONT AND REAR DOORS

All four doors are very heavy, especially if the door furniture, window glass, etc., is left in situ. Always have a helper on hand to prevent straining the hinges or yourself.

FRONT DOORS

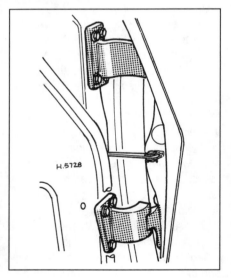

▲ DR1. The Series 1 cars had simpler hinge mechanisms than later cars. This diagram shows that it is just a pair of hinges with a check strap. Start by removing the split pin and clevis pin from the check strap. Open the door as wide as possible and place a support under its furthermost edge – use an old rag to prevent paintwork damage. Have your helper hold the door at that point to prevent it twisting to one side as the six hinge-to-door bolts are removed.

HINGES

The hinges are secured to the door by three bolts each, but before removal mark the positions of the hinges so that they can be replaced in exactly the right places. Access to the bolts requires the wing to be separated from the lower sill/valence. Remove the under-wing panel and the bolts that secure the lower edge of the wing to the sill and the rear of the wing to the body pillar. Carefully prise the wing from the body pillar using two wooden wedges to give enough space to get the spanner on to the hinge bolt heads. Undo the bolts, supporting the door as already suggested.

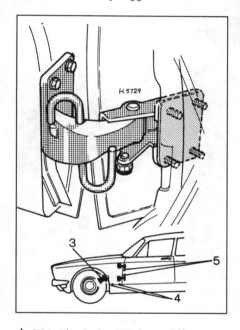

▲ DR2. The Series 2/3 doors differ slightly in that the hinges are held to both door and pillar by four (rather than three) bolts. Also, the check strap is replaced by a spring. Removal procedure is essentially that described in the previous caption.
KEY
3. Under wing access panel.
4. Wing to sill bolts.
5. Wing to body pillar bolts.

▲ DR3. This photo shows the hinge/spring mechanism and the positions of the hinges and bolts (the front wing has been entirely removed for clarity). Replacement is a reversal of the removal procedure. If you're fitting new hinge components, do not tighten the bolts completely until you have adjusted the door correctly. In extreme cases, it may be necessary to use misalignment shims under the hinge plate to get the door to shut precisely. Make sure that the door lock striker plate allows positive and accurate closure.

REAR DOORS

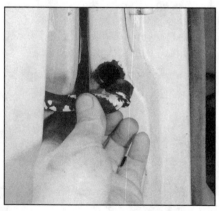

▲ DR4. Where there are electrics passing into the rear door, disconnect the battery earth lead and the wiring, then remove the flexible grommet between the door and 'B' pillar.

▲ DR5. When removing the rear doors, it's easier to take off the hinges with the door, simply because there's more straightforward access to the securing bolts. Don't forget to mark the exact positions of the hinges. Unlike the front doors, if you remove the hinge bolts while the door is shut, there's no need for support – until you come to actually lift the door off.

▲ DR6. On this door, the interior trim panel has already been removed. Always replace the plastic sheeting – if you don't, it allows moisture to get on to the trim panel and damage it and/or moisture to get into the car and damage the carpets or leatherwork.

REPLACING

If you've removed the hinges with the door (and replaced them accurately), the door can be put into position so that the lock engages and the hinge holes line-up perfectly.

REMOVING THE FRONT WING

Though XJ6 front wings rust away with alarming rapidity, there are bolt-on units and relatively off-the-shelf from companies such as SNG Barratt and they are relatively simple to swap. Spray the fasteners with plenty of WD40 or equivalent, ideally the day before removal starts. Be prepared for at least one fastener to seize or snap. This may mean drilling out a seized bolt or even doing a spot of re-tapping, so allow some 'emergency' time.

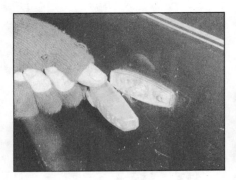

▲ WN1. Before starting work, Phil unplugged the wiring to the headlamp, side lamp and indicator. Don't forget that on Series 3 cars, there's a wing-mounted side repeater lamp to remove, also. Two screws hold the lens cover in place, and when removed the two screws holding the base to the wing can be accessed. They are quite small and easy to snap if they're even slightly rusted in situ.

▲ WN2. Phil treated all the fasteners to a healthy dose of WD40, letting it soak in as long as possible and reapplying throughout the procedure. This is the rear stone protector panel which is secured by …

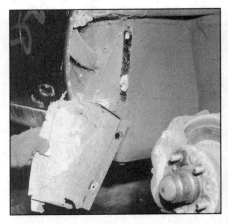

▲ WN3. … bolts around its perimeter. It's almost certain that at least one of them will seize and snap, so be prepared. Having removed all the bolts, you can see that rot has started to attack the edges of the panel. It would be possible to weld patches around the affected areas, though a new panel would be a simpler option.

▲ WN4. Phil removed the two rear wing mounting lower bolts and the two accessed from the A-pillar (the top one is shown here with the spanner on).

▲ WN5. He moved to the front of the wing and removed the remaining five bolts and …

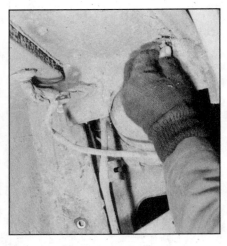

▲ WN6. … the self-tapping screws securing it to the top stone panel.

▼ WN7. Then, it was outside the car to remove the series of bolts which run along the top of the wing, which meant that the wing could be lifted away.

▲ WN8. Even if your wings don't need replacing, there's no doubt that it makes working at the front of the car much, much easier. Access for the brakes, suspension and steering components is much improved, not to mention de-rusting and applying underseal.

▲ WN9. Barrats supplied the new wing (at right!) to replace that rusty specimen Phil had just removed. Fitting the new wing is a reversal of the removal process. Phil used new nuts and bolts where appropriate, cleaning-up and applying copper grease elsewhere.

FUEL TANK REMOVAL

SAFETY NOTE: Never attempt to solder or weld a damaged fuel tank – petrol fumes are as lethal as the liquid itself. Such repairs should be carried out only by professionals who will steam the tank clean for several hours before attempting to work on it. If a tank is badly damaged and/or corroded, a replacement tank is probably the best solution, from a specialist such as SNG Barratt. If you buy a second-hand tank, make sure that it is structurally sound and that the interior is totally free of dirt and rust.

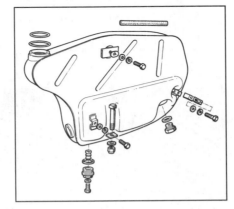

▲ FT1. All models featured twin fuel tanks positioned in each of the rear wings. This diagram shows the fuel tank attachment details for earlier cars.

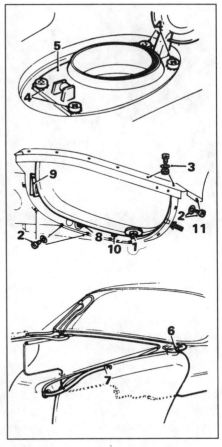

▲ FT2. This diagram shows the fuel tank attachment details on later models (post '78).
KEY
1. Drain plug
2. Cover securing screws
3. Cover securing nuts and bolts
4. Filler neck securing screws
5. Filler neck
6. Vent pipe
7. Vent pipe
8. Fuel pipe connector
9. Rubber wedge
10. Hanger bolt
11. Gauge sender unit

Don't start removing the tanks until they have been totally drained of fuel and left to stand for several hours (preferably 24 hours) with the drain taps and fillers open. This will vent most of the flammable fumes to the atmosphere – make sure the area is very well ventilated.

▲ FT3. Open the filler cap to prevent air locks and to speed up the draining process and then remove the drain plug from the tank. Note here that Phil has a suitable container AND a large funnel ready and waiting to catch the fuel as it emerges. Raise the funnel as close as possible to the tank to reduce the amount splashing – our car is higher than normal because it's on the NBN Chassis Tilter. On early cars it is necessary to remove the complete rear bumper; on later models with three-piece bumpers, only the side piece(s) needs to be removed. The fuel filter, overflow flexible hose and fuel pump feed from the union at the base of the tank should be disconnected. Take note of the differences between early and late models when it comes to fixing points and, of course, items like the in-tank fuel pump, the pipes and electrical connections which will have to be removed.

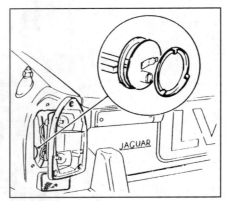

▲ FT5. … the sender on later models is much easier to access, being positioned directly behind the rear lamp clusters. Remove the cluster as described elsewhere in this chapter (just six crosshead screws to undo).

▲ FT6. This is the nearside (RHD) fuel tank from a Series 2 car. It's not in bad condition and would clean up well – DO

NOT use any form of wire brush to clean off the rust unless the tank has been totally drained of fuel and vapour. It should be treated to anti-rust treatment and particular attention paid to the seams. You can see the various fitting positions.

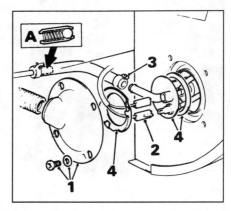

▲ FT7. Details of the fuel pumps are shown in this diagram. If faulty, this kind of pump cannot be repaired. The internal fuel pumps were AC Delco models, reference 0363 (LH) and 0364 (RH).
KEY
A. Non-return valve
1. Cover plate and fastenings
2. Electrical connector
3. Fuel hose
4. Pump and sealing washers.

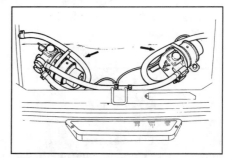

▲ FT8. Early models featured twin SU AUF301 fuel pumps mounted under the boot floor, behind the spare wheel.

TORQUE FIGURES

	lb/ft	kg/m
Drain plug on fuel tank (large)	28	38
Drain plug on fuel tank (small)	25	34
Fuel pipe banjo union bolts	25	34

▲ FT4. Pull off the two wires to the fuel gauge sender using masking tape around the wires to mark their positions. The fuel sender was originally positioned at the front of the tank, and accessed from under the car, just to the rear of the rear wheel where it was protected by a small cover plate. However …

WINDSCREEN REMOVAL, WIPERS, WIPER MOTOR AND WASHER MOTOR

REPLACING THE WINDSCREEN
SAFETY: Early model windscreen removal/replacement is within the range of most DIY restorers, given that strong gloves and protective goggles are worn. (Later cars with bonded screens must be removed and replaced by a professional.) Early models were fitted with toughened glass, which shatters into many pieces when struck. Laminated glass, as fitted to later models and/or as an option, will still craze over but stay in one piece – this is much safer to deal with.

Use an old sheet or similar to protect the paintwork on the outside of the car, and another inside lest the screen should shatter.

CHECKING THE WINDSCREEN SURROUND RUBBER
Minor leaks caused by a worn out or damaged windscreen rubber can usually be cured by squeezing a proprietary liquid sealant into the problem area. To check, apply chalk powder to the inside of the rubber and have an assistant spray water on to the screen. The ingress of water should be easy to see in the chalk.

▲ WS1. Remove the windscreen wiper arms before starting. The chrome finisher surround is a two-piece item which should be prised carefully from the rubber moulding along with …

▲ WS2. … the top and bottom chrome sections which cover the joins.

▲ WS3. Then remove the rubber insert completely. Run a thin-bladed tool around the screen to break the seal between the rubber and the aperture flange.

▲ WS4. Strike the glass carefully with the flat of the hand from inside the car – gloves must be worn – starting in a corner and working towards the bottom of the screen. Examine the windscreen rubber for signs that small pieces of glass have become embedded – if so, replace the rubber. Carefully examine the windscreen flange to ensure that it is without bumps – if so, they should be pressed or filed flat before the screen is replaced.

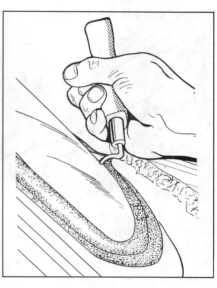

▲ WS5. Place the sealing rubber in the window aperture with the flat side towards the rear of the car and the join at the bottom, in order to prevent water getting in. Lay the screen in place and start by getting the bottom edge into the seal. You'll need a special tool (shown here) and when the screen is in all the way round and sitting 'square', replace the sealing strip, with the rounded edge to the outside. Again this ideally requires a special tool.

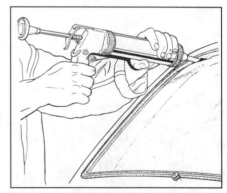

▲ WS6. Use a trigger type holder to squeeze sealing compound between the metal windscreen flange and the rubber seal. Work all around the screen, getting an even amount of compound throughout. Then repeat the process but with the nozzle between the glass and the rubber seal. Use a plastic or copper nozzle to ensure that the glass is not scratched. Remove any excess sealing compound using white spirit, because thinners can easily damage paintwork.

WINDSCREEN WIPER MOTOR

▲ WS7. For access to the windscreen wiper motor, the battery (and box with cover, where appropriate) has to be removed. Take off the two battery cables (starting with the earth) and then …

▲ WS8. … undo the battery box securing screws and ease the clamp arms out of the way. Don't forget the breather hose from the rear of the box. Ease the box out first – it's a tight fit, so you'll have to waggle it carefully – and then the battery.

▲ WS9. The wiper motor assembly is in the nearside (RHD) wing. Remove the wiper arms from the spindles and unscrew the large nut which connects the driving cable conduit to the wiper motor, and withdraw the electrical plug connector from the socket in the motor.

Removing the two setscrews and clamp strap will free the motor so that it can be withdrawn along with the drive cable, which has to be pulled carefully down the conduit guide.

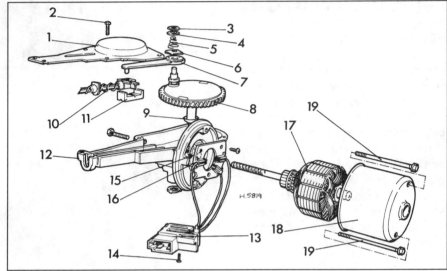

▲ WS10. It is possible to check out and, in some cases, repair a worn wiper motor, though replacement motors are available from SNG Barratt and the time taken to effect repairs would have to be balanced with any overall cost savings. This diagram shows the component parts. Dismantling should be undertaken with some care, noting where each nut, bolt, washer and circlip goes. In particular, items like the gearbox cover have a spring underneath which can release its pressure and associated fastenings all over your workshop!

KEY
1. Gearbox cover
3. Circlip
2. Screw
4. Washer
5. Spring
6. Friction plate
7. Crank arm
8. Gear
9. Dished washer
10. Cable rack
11. Slider block
12. Gearbox
13. Limit switch
14. Screws
15. Bush
16. Brush gear
17. Armature
18. Yoke
19. Tie bolts

► WS11. If your washer jets fail to work, open the bonnet and listen for the sound of the pump as an assistant operates the washer control inside the car. The pump is fixed to the front bulkhead at the rear of the engine bay. If there's no sign of life (it should make quite a loud humming sound), use your meter or test lamp to ensure that the wiring to the pump is getting there. If cleaning up the contacts fails to make it work, the pump has failed – a common occurrence. Pull off the electrical leads and the pipes and unscrew the fasteners at the bulkhead. Replace with a new/used pump – it's always a good idea to apply 12v to the

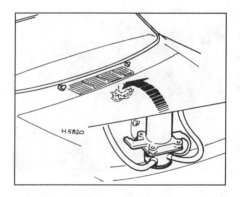

pump while it's out of the car to test its operation. Refit the pump, wiring and pipes, easing the way of the latter by spraying WD40 inside the pipes.

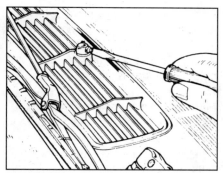

▲ WS12. If the pump is buzzing but there's nothing at the washer nozzles, check first that the washer bottle has some mixture in it. If it has, it points to a blockage in pipework and/or a blocked nozzle – use a pin to unblock it. Sometimes, corrosion caused by the water can rust the nozzles solid and they have to be replaced. Make sure the jets are hitting the screen correctly by adjusting the nozzles as shown here.

DEALING WITH RUST

Even if you've only studied a few of the 'horror' photos in this section, you'll be aware that, despite its up-market image, the Jaguar XJ6 is extremely susceptible to the dreaded tin worm. Follow the techniques shown here to ensure you don't end up paying a small fortune for repairs that really shouldn't have been necessary.

BATTERY BOX BLUES

▲ RP1. Just about anything made of steel will rust. Though it may not be an MoT failure, it will look unsightly and,

ultimately, when it rots away you'll have to pay out for a new item. This Series 2 fan-cooled battery box is typical of the condition they're likely to be in – i.e. rough! The golden rule is the same as for putting on paint – anti-rust treatment is 90 per cent preparation. As ever when you're renovating anything, it's important to take it down to its component parts – cleaning or painting around the fan housing, for example, would be silly. The rust underneath would soon spread back to the main box. Moreover, if you painted over the fan you'd fill up the crosshead screw tops and they'd be even more difficult to remove next time.

▲ RP2. The fan housing is secured by seven self-tapping screws. They're only short but apply plenty of releasing agent as they're likely to be well-rusted. If you chew up the head, you'll have to drill them out with a small pilot bit.

▲ RP3. Don't forget to remove the wiring. This is the bi-metallic strip which plugs in inside the box and switches the fan on when required.

▲ RP4. It's important to remove all rust and flaking paint. Use a wire brush (don't forget the goggles to prevent it 'flaking' into your eyes) to start with and then a rotary wire brush in a hand drill to really make a job of it.

▲ RP5. Apply an anti-rust treatment. We used Jenolite, here, a chemical developed originally for use on Ministry of Defence vehicles. As with most anti-rust compounds, it does extremely nasty things to corrosion, but it can do that to you, too! Protect your eyes and your skin from accidental splashes. According to the makers, it has a phosphoric acid base which bonds chemically with the rust and converts it into a harmless iron phosphate compound. So now you know! It had to dry (around 15 minutes) before we could apply a second coat which was wiped off straight away.

▲ RP6. We then used a special anti-rust primer, in this case another Jenolite product called Double Act which contains rust inhibitors and resins. Double Act is claimed to neutralise rust and protect against its return through a unique 'active' formulation. We finished off with a coat of RE-paint, another product designed for covering previously rusted metal. Because the overall finish wasn't permanently on display, we brushed it on to get …

▲ RP7. … an excellent finish. When you're painting or using primer, the temperature should be around 20°C (68°F). If it's lower than that, drying time will be extended and you'll run into problems with moisture – either in the air or in the form of condensation. A domestic fan heater (with the usual garage electric products' safety precautions) can be used to raise the temperature accordingly – but remember it could stir up the dust.

UNDER THE CAR

Thoroughly clean the underside of your XJ6 a few days before you start rustproofing, otherwise you'll have to hack your way through acres of dried-on mud to get to the metal. Tap all metal surfaces to ensure that they are solid; if not, you'll have to cut away the rotten metal ready for repair. It's good advice to clean your Jaguar on a regular basis, particularly underneath, because where mud gets lodged in the numerous 'traps', it holds moisture on to the steel panels so that it can quietly get on with the business of making holes in your car! Moreover, remember that in winter, the rock salt used on UK roads is incredibly corrosive. When you see the white deposits along the lower edges of the car, consider that the underneath will have suffered much more. A regular blast with a pressure washer will help keep corrosion to a minimum. When you've washed your car, it's best to leave it to air dry, rather than put it straight away into the garage. Certainly, it will need to dry for several days before you apply anti-rust wax to the underneath of the car.

▲ RP8. Rustproofing should be an on-going process and you should always be looking for areas where rust can get a hold – and doing something about it! Keep a small container (this is the author's own ex-margarine tub!) topped up with Waxoyl. When you're working on the car, particularly if it's underneath where most rust occurs, use an old paintbrush to apply the liquid wax to the surrounding areas. Top-up areas where

wax has already been applied but where it is being worn away – under the wheel arches for example. Spending 10 minutes doing this on a regular basis will pay huge dividends in the future.

Here are a few examples of where you could use your anti-rust 'margarine' to good effect:
– Flexible rubber brake pipes (Waxoyl has the effect of keeping them supple).
– Around all brake unions to prevent them seizing up.
– Around brake bleed nipples – replace the rubber caps afterwards.
– All metal brake and fuel lines.
– Around all nuts, bolts and all exposed threads under the car.
– Around the inner lip of the wheel arches.
– Component mounting points (damper location, bumper brackets, etc.).

SAFETY NOTE: Always keep anti-rust wax away from braking friction components. If using a spray applicator put plastic bags over braking components and secure them with elastic bands.

▲ RP9. Even having blasted the underside of the car, there will still be plenty of dirt and (probably) flaky rust and the nearer you get to metal, the more effective the rust-treatments will be. Here, Phil Blundell is using a small rotary wire brush to get into some awkward nooks and crannies before …

RP10. ... using the Jenolite anti-rust treatment as previously described. The section behind the front wing is a perfect breeding ground for rust as it is totally enclosed and left to its own devices. In this case, we had removed the wing for replacement, but if you're not doing that, it's a good idea to drill a hole in the covering panel and use an extension nozzle to spray in liquid wax. Don't forget to rust-proof the edges of the new hole and to seal it with a suitably sized rubber bung – Halfords sell them in multi-packs.

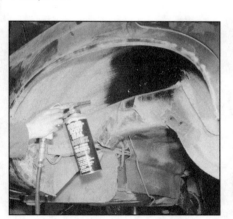

RP11. Waxoyl's Underbody Seal can be purchased in standard cans for brushing on (it's non-drip, you'll be pleased to hear!) or, if you have a compressor and gun, in Schultz format, for spraying on. Being a professional, Phil used his compressor for most jobs and so ...

RP12. ... applying it was a simple matter. The word 'underseal' has unfortunate connotations, as for decades the bitumen-based stuff was responsible for more rust than it stopped! Because it hardened as it aged, it then cracked and allowed water in-between the body and the underseal – rotten holes were the inevitable outcome. Underbody Seal contains powerful rust inhibitors, doesn't harden and remains flexible. It's been designed for application under wings, in door sills, and on chassis and fuel tanks.

It's said to reduce drumming and noise if applied in door panels and under the boot lid, etc. It must not be used on the sump, gearbox, exhaust system, cables or mechanical parts. Any excess can be removed with white spirit.

FURTHER PROTECTION

Some owners would leave it at that, and in truth your car would be heavily protected. However, you can never have too much rust protection. A layer of Waxoyl's original protective wax is a good idea for panels which don't take the battering that wheel arch and floor sections do. You can't always get to the metal you want to protect, notably in hollow cavities, such as sills and the insides of chassis members, etc. This is where you need to 'inject' the liquid wax using an applicator or your compressed-air equipment if you have it. Because of its very nature, wax will clog up at the drop of a hat, so it should be heavily diluted with white spirit – 50/50 or even more. It's a good idea to inject the wax on a warm day, as it will help it to 'flow' along into all the crevices. Though initially runny, the white spirit will soon evaporate, leaving only the coating of protective wax. Where there are no naturally occurring holes to inject the wax into, drill a small hole for the nozzle but make sure you thoroughly rustproof it and fit a rubber bung to prevent the ingress of water.

Chapter 5

Painting and Filling

ABRASIVES GUIDE

ALUMINIUM OXIDE

This is a synthetic long-life aggressive abrasive material which should only be used when preparing bodywork for the removal of rust or accident damage. The coarse grades allow for cleaning and keying the metal for fillers. All aluminium oxide papers should be used in grade sequence (starting with coarse and progressing to fine). Ideal for initial shaping of fillers, it can be either machine or hand held.

WET AND DRY

This is used where a high level of finishing is required. The abrasive lasts longer and gives a smoother finish when used wet with its specially formulated waterproof backing paper, to give a longer life and improved finish. Soak wet and dry abrasive paper for 10/15 minutes before sanding and use with plenty of water to lubricate and prevent clogging. Again, wet and dry should be used in grade sequence to ensure complete removal of scratches. It is ideal for fine-shaping fillers, erasing scratches and between-coat sanding.

FLEXIBLE SANDERS

Flexible foam sanders can be used wet or dry. Ideal for sanding paint, metal or fillers and particularly useful for contoured areas.

ABRASIVE PADS

Abrasive pads have been specially designed for removing light rust, cleaning metal and sanding primer. Manufactured from tough, non-woven material that will not rust or splinter like steel wool, abrasive pads will last a long time and can be rinsed clean for repeated use.

Metal	Aluminium Oxide			Wet and Dry		
	40/60g C	80g M	120g F	80/150g C	180/320g M	360/1200g F
Rust removal	•					
Flaking paint removal	•					
Surface rust removal		•				
Initial filler sanding		•				
Shaping of filler		•	•			
Removal of light scratches			•	•		
Final filler sanding				•	•	
Sanding of primer					•	•
Sanding between coats of paint						•

Plastic and Fibreglass	Aluminium Oxide			Wet and Dry		
	40/60g C	80g M	120g F	80/150g C	180/320g M	360/1200g F
Filler shaping	•					
Intermediate plastic/filler sanding		•				
Final plastic/filler sanding			•	•	•	

(C = coarse. M = medium. F = fine.)
This table and information kindly supplied courtesy Halfords Limited.

AEROSOL PAINT SPRAYING

SAFETY: The rules listed in the 'professional painting' section apply here equally – paint fumes are dangerous and flammable.

Over the years, with the advances made in aerosol technology and when correctly used, an extremely good finish can often be achieved. It can be used to touch-up small areas of paintwork damage or to respray specific parts of the car, as shown here. The lower the ambient temperature, the harder it is to spray successfully – around 15-20°C (59-68°F) is ideal. If you use external heating to assist with the paint-drying process, make sure it doesn't affect the finish (when using a fan heater, for example, by blowing up dust). Try to avoid spraying in damp conditions.

AEROSOL SAFETY TIPS

– Always spray in a well ventilated area and wear a protective mask.
– Work in short bursts and keep taking plenty of fresh air.
– Use thin plastic gloves to protect your hands when using paint, primers or thinners.
– Wear goggles when spraying (anything) to protect your eyes.
– Never allow smoking or naked flames in the immediate area.

SPRAYING HINTS AND TIPS

– Spray paint gets everywhere – mask off where you don't want it.
– If you can, remove items from the car to spray them.
– Clean is the name of the game – paint won't stick to a dirty or greasy surface.
– Use a special plastic primer to prevent the paint flaking off.
– Spray in a series of light coats, otherwise it will cause unsightly runs.
– Always allow the paint to dry thoroughly before handling it – then wear clean gloves.
– Allow plenty of time for the job, and remember – it's 90 per cent preparation.

– Always use a clear lacquer final coat on metallic paints – they're too soft without it.

MATCHING

As your paintwork is exposed to the elements, it changes colour – the older it is, the more it will differ from the brand new paint from the aerosol. If there is any great difference, visit your local paint shop and get a small quantity of paint made up specifically to match the exact colour of your car as it is **now**.

SPRAYING PART OF A BODY PANEL

▲ *GP1. Touch-up paint sprays can be obtained from Jaguar dealers, of course, or from specialists such as Auto K. The latter include a selection of very useful 'accessories' in the lid – two pieces of fine sand paper, a sachet of stopper (fine filler) and a small brush for touching up stone chips, etc. You'll also need some masking tape. Where existing paintwork is being sprayed, it's important to remove all traces of silicone – one of the main constituents of wax polish – use white spirit, then a mixture of warm water and washing up liquid. NEVER use wax car shampoo! Repeat until all the 'shine' has disappeared.*

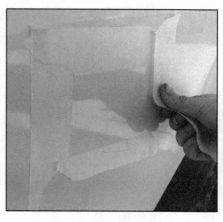

▲ *GP2. Apply masking tape in a square, as shown here, allowing around 2 in leeway around the damaged area.*

▲ *GP3. Sand down the affected area and good paintwork for an inch all around it. Don't use wet and dry paper if you're painting over a repaired area as it might get into the filler. If required, spray primer on, but not right up to the masking tape, to avoid a ridge. This is called 'feathering'. When dry, sand down again using a fine paper on a block – wet and dry is OK now because the filler is 'protected' by the primer.*

◄ *GP4. Once dry, the top coat can be applied using the spraying techniques described elsewhere. To help it blend, remove the masking tape and paper from the immediate area so that the overspray spreads on to the good paintwork. Allow a week for the paint to fully harden (longer in colder/wet weather) and blend into the original using a light cutting compound.*

TOUCHING UP SMALL DAMAGED AREAS

Stone chips are the main cause of small bodywork damaged areas. If there is a definite and visible 'step' where the paint has been chipped off, use stopper to bring the area level with the surrounding paintwork before spraying. For this, you can use a small 'stick' of touch-up paint or the aerosol of body colour you already used for the colour-coding operation. If you need to repair paintwork on a painted 'plastic' surface, you can use the technique here unless the damage has gone through to the bumper itself. In that case, you'll need to clean the area and apply plastic primer before the new paint.

▲ GP5. Spray a little of the paint into the can lid. Use a small brush to mix it thoroughly for around two minutes in order to totally remove all traces of the propellant. Apply it carefully to the damaged area. Allow it to dry and, if necessary, use a light cutting compound to blend the new paint to the old.

PUTTING ON PAINT

CELLULOSE AND TWO-PACK PAINTS

At the time of writing, the implications of the Environmental Protection Act make it likely that by 1998 almost all professional bodyshops will be using water-based paints. Ultimately, all paints will be electrostatically power-coated, thus removing all harmful emissions usually associated with putting on paint. At present, most professional paint spray shops use two-pack paints, and these

two factors have already resulted in a dearth of cellulose paint-suppliers. References to home-spraying and cellulose paints must be cross-referred to legislation (constantly being updated) in force at the time of reading.

FINISHES

Cellulose paint produces a reasonable finish, but it must be cut back well and polished to really shine. In order to keep it like that, you have to keep applying the 'elbow grease' on a regular basis.

The finish provided by a correctly applied two-pack paint is superb without the need for labour-intensive cutting and polishing. This is because the paint is pre-mixed with a hardener (hence 'two-pack') and when it sets it is hard enough not to need polishing for years. Breathing in two-pack paint is lethal because it contains isocyanate – a relation of cyanide! Anyone using two-pack paints MUST have an independent air-fed supply. This places limits on its use in the DIY market. Moreover, there must be suitable facilities for disposing of excess paint and thinners.

For those on a limited budget, it may be best to apply some division of labour. If you do the preparation yourself, you will be carrying out the lion's share of the work. Whilst few good paint shops will be satisfied with the standard you can provide (after all, they're professionals), the work involved in 'finishing off' your preparation will be nothing like that involved in doing the whole job – and nothing like the cost, either! Let the paint shop paint your car (or panels) using two-pack paint and you'll end up with a better, longer-lasting finish.

SAFETY: Working with paint and thinners can be highly dangerous and extremely unpleasant – to say the least! A suitable part of your painting budget MUST be spent on safety equipment. You'll need protective latex gloves (which will protect your hands but still allow some sensitivity), goggles and a charcoal-charged mask. These should be worn whenever you are working

with paint – that includes mixing and thinning, not just the spraying itself.

If you have an air-fed mask receiving air from your compressor, there's no use keeping the compressor where the spraying is being done. Position it outside your work area.

Obey all the safety rules when using compressed air – there are lots of potential dangers for the unwary and careless.

– Keep paint away from your eyes and wear barrier cream on your hands.
– Always wear the correct safety gear. Goggles and mask are minimum.
– Always check the recommendations for the particular paint and/or primer you're applying.
– Remember the fire risk that is always present when working with paint and thinners – avoid naked flames, electrical sparks and ban all smoking!
– Keep a fire extinguisher handy at all times.

TOOLS REQUIRED

▲ SPR1. If you are doing your own spraying, a compressor such as Clarke's Raider Air 50 model is ideal for DIY painting and other DIY jobs, with its powerful 3 hp motor, 50-litre tank and 150 psi capability. Ideally, you'll need a pressure of around 50 psi at the gun fluid tip which this compressor would produce easily. Anything much below 2 hp would be struggling to do this.

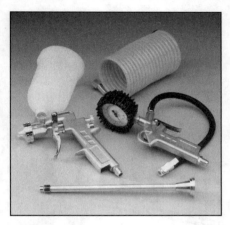

▲ SPR2. With accessories you can make more use of your compressor. This Hobbyair kit from SIP includes a five-metre coiled hose and equipment for spraying, washing, degreasing, blowing and tyre inflation, etc. (Courtesy SIP (Industrial Products) Limited)

PREPARATION

Putting on paint successfully is 90 per cent preparation and 10 per cent spraying. You should be absolutely meticulous in your preparation, whether it's a front wing or the whole car.

PAINTING OVER?

It can save time and effort to spray over the existing paintwork, but make sure that the old paint and the new are compatible. Try a small area beforehand – if they react and produce a 'wrinkly' effect, then they are not compatible and you will either have to (a) strip the original paint off altogether or (b) spray an isolator coat on to the original paintwork before applying the new paint.

PRIMING BARE METAL

Like the top coat, the primer will need mixing with thinners (though a different type) in the amount specified by the manufacturers. Apply a light coat of primer and, when it's dried, gently flat it down to reveal any 'low' areas. Apply three coats of primer, allowing sufficient time for it to 'go off' between coats. Because there are more 'solids' in primer, this will usually be longer than for the top coat.

LEARNING THE TECHNIQUES

Practice makes perfect – it's an old saying but true, especially when it comes to spraying. The important point is to practise on something that doesn't matter. When you've developed your technique sufficiently, only then should you progress to your Pride and Joy. As with welding, many local adult education authorities run practical classes in automotive paint preparation and spraying. If you're looking to do any serious spraying, such a course could only be a good thing.

SPRAYING TECHNIQUES

– Keep the spray gun at a right angle (90 degrees) to the workpiece at a distance of around 7-8 in (175-200mm).
– Start spraying 4 or 5 in before the edge of the panel and continue spraying for the same distance at the end of that pass.
– It's easy to let your concentration lapse as you move on a curved section. If you move your spray gun without bending your arm, it will trace an arc, which will result in an uneven paint finish – it will be thicker in the middle than at either side. Bend your wrist in order to keep the gun at an even distance from the workpiece and be prepared to move into a suitable position so you can keep this up, even on a large panel.
– You can't spray successfully at low temperatures – it should be at least 15/20°C (59/68°F). Much below this and the solvents used in the paint simply won't evaporate, which will lead to a poor paint finish.
– Take great care when trying to heat a garage or workshop in the winter – paint and its associated solvents are flammable.
– In searching for heat, make sure you don't also get humidity; moisture in the air will not help in your search for the perfect finish.
– Always move the gun at an even speed.
– Whether you're spraying primer or top coat, don't try to cover the panel in one pass or you'll end up with runs and a real mess on your hands. Cover it in a number of passes to ensure an even distribution of paint and no runs.

– Applied properly, a cellulose top coat won't look glossy immediately, a fact which causes many DIY sprayers to panic. It usually takes 2/3 minutes before the gloss appears.
– Apply three cellulose top coats. Allow approximately five minutes between each coat – check the manufacturers' recommendations.

USING FILLER

Using plastic/metal filler on heavily rusted panels isn't really advisable, and on some sections it could be positively dangerous. But when your XJ6 has been through 'trial by car park', you may find its sleek lines interrupted by one or two 'dings' in the doors and/or wings. When the damage is minor, it is possible to use filler to solve the problem. Filler won't stick well to the existing paint so remove it before you start.

SAFETY:

– **When working with filler and/or fibreglass always wear gloves to protect your skin.**
– **Work in a well-ventilated area and when sanding paintwork or filler wear a mask to prevent breathing in the dangerous particles.**
– **Fumes from filler, glassfibre and paint are flammable – impose a no-smoking rule and take care that there is nothing likely to cause sparks or naked flames.**

▲ FIL1. Use the right filler for the job in hand – shown here is Plastic Padding's metal filler, which contains aluminium. More conventional fillers are the renowned P38 (small dents and scratches) and P40 (larger holes) from David's Isopon. Clean the area with white spirit and then wash the whole panel down using washing up liquid in warm water. Do not use car shampoo, as this contains wax and the whole point is to remove it! The filler won't stick to paintwork, so you'll need to remove the existing paint from the area to be filled and for around one inch (25mm) all around it. Use a fine grade sandpaper – if you use an electrical sander, take care not to gouge chunks of metal and paint out. A Scotchbrite pad is an excellent way to provide a 'key' for the filler without being too harsh.

▲ FIL2. Using the right tools for the job is always a good idea. As well as the right grade of sandpaper (see earlier in this chapter) you can also benefit from using some of the many Surform tools, an abrasive sponge block (which allows you to put more pressure on but also follows the line you want), and Scotchbrite material, which is abrasive but not as harsh as some papers and more long-lasting.

▲ FIL3. The filler (metal or conventional plastic) is mixed with a hardener which makes it 'go off'. Adding too much hardener will make the filler set too quickly and be difficult to use; too little

will leave it soft for far too long. Use the plastic spatula supplied, or a plastic/metal domestic filling knife, to mix the filler. Don't use an offcut of a cardboard box, as the fibres from it may tend to get into the filler and prevent it from smoothing down properly.

▲ FIL4. Don't put too much filler on the damaged area, just enough to make it stand slightly proud – the higher it stands, the more you'll have to sand down! (Courtesy David's Isopon)

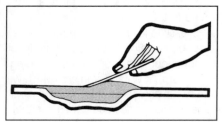

▲ FIL5. Alternatively, where a dent is particularly deep, apply the paste in two or more layers, allowing the paste to harden before adding the next layer. The final layer, as previously, should be just proud of the bodywork. (Courtesy David's Isopon)

▲ FIL6. When it's set hard, sand the filler down to the level of the surrounding bodywork. Wrap the sandpaper around a block of wood or buy a sanding block. Sand diagonally, alternating the direction as you go, don't take off too much of the adjacent paintwork. There will be small holes or ridges in the filled area so

mix up a little more filler and 'wipe' it over the original filler. Let it set and then sand it smooth. This procedure should be followed until the filled area is indistinguishable from the original body panel. (Courtesy David's Isopon)

▲ FIL7. Shut your eyes and run your fingers over it – if you can feel the repaired section, you've got some more work to do! When you're sanding down, never use wet and dry paper – if you get water on to the wet filler, the paint won't adhere to it, and it's a devil to get all the moisture out. When you've finished, use cellulose thinners (wear gloves) to clean your tools. If you leave the filler to set hard on them, it's very difficult to get it off again. (Courtesy David's Isopon)

HOLEY PROBLEMS

If you've a bodywork hole to fill (for example, where a previous owner had fitted a fog lamp bracket), then clean the back of the panel in question and brush on a layer of fibreglass resin. Cut a square of fibreglass matting or aluminium mesh (both available from DIY motoring shops) and stick it on behind the hole. When it is dry, apply metal body filler to the hole as described in the previous section.

TWO-PACK SPRAYING

According to Nigel Worker, spraying your Jaguar is easy – it's the hours of preparation required beforehand that make it hard work! At Beds Auto Panels, Nigel and his son Jeff showed how the task of respraying our 1983 4.2 litre XJ6 should be undertaken. Remember that this is professional spraying using highly dangerous two-pack spraying materials which are not for DIY use. Though initially costing more, the superb finish achieved is unlikely to be replicated by a DIY sprayer.

▲ TP1. Beds Auto Panels use only Standox paints, primers and thinners.

▲ TP2. The front wing was exactly as it came from SNG Barratt and still in its primer. Jeff used 500 grit paper in the dual action orbital sander and …

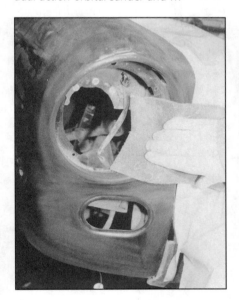

▲ TP3. … worked carefully around the edges and awkward sections with a hand-held Scotchbrite pad.

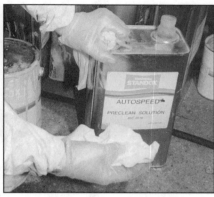

▲ TP4. He then used the compressor air line to blow off the excess dust and cleaned it with Standox Autospeed preclean solution.

▲ TP5. He wiped the wing over with a tack rag and blew it off yet again. Then it was ready for the primer which was …

▲ TP6. … Standox 1K Fullprimer, an etch type used where there is bare metal (it provides a key for the paint). Note the use of air-fed breathing gear – absolutely essential with both primer and top coats when using two-pack products.

▲ TP7. The colour chosen was Jaguar Racing Green, a metallic colour. All metallics are softer than flat colours and must have a clear lacquer coating applied. Because the colour was known, this had been made-up at Standox HQ – all Jeff had to do was stir it. However, Beds Auto Panels have the full Standox mixing facilities and can make any amount of any colour. Where they are spraying just part of the vehicle and it has to match the rest, an exact paint can be made-up to suit.

▲ TP8. Jeff sprayed the wing in a series of light passes.

▲ TP9. At the rear of the car a repair panel had been welded into the wing, but it was impossible to get it totally smooth. There's no point in painting it like that so …

▲ TP10. ... Nigel used Plastic Padding Type 100 lightweight two-part filler, and skilfully applied it to the basic contours of the wing edge. Don't forget that this means applying the filler in two planes – not as easy as it sounds!

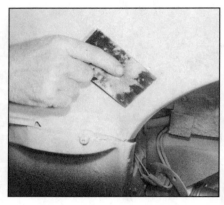

▲ TP13. Tiny imperfections in the filler surface were remedied by using stopper, a fine filler for this purpose.

▲ TP11. After 30 minutes the filler was dry enough for him to sand it down using 80 grit paper in the dual action sander.

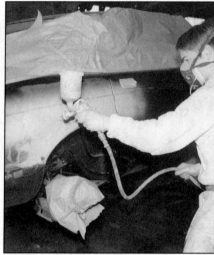

▲ TP14. Once it had been made perfectly smooth, it was blown off with the air line, pre-cleaned and wiped with a tack rag. 2K Fillerprimer was used because this is thicker than normal and gets into any fine scratch marks. After being left to go off overnight, it was sanded yet again with 500 grit paper – flat colours would be finished with 320 grit paper. To highlight any coverage problems ...

▲ TP15. ... Nigel sprayed a very light coating of black aerosol paint over the primer. This was then flatted back using 500 grit paper, with 800 grit wet-and-dry on the edges and corners. The air line, preclean and tack rag procedure was repeated before the top coat and lacquer were applied. Having spent time and money getting a great paint finish, you'll want to keep it that way. Putting your car in a garage will keep it reasonably safe from the elements, but even there the paintwork will still attract dust and moisture. Metex dust covers are made from a unique and durable cotton fabric that is soft and non-scratching. Moreover, air can flow through the cover preventing damp forming on the paintwork. Metex have been making protective car covers for years, and the good news for consumers is that they're now available from most Halfords stores.

▲ TP12. This was followed by 180 grit paper on a hand-held block. Note the use of a breathing mask because of the filler particles in the air.

Chapter 6

Under the Bonnet

REMOVING THE ENGINE AND GEARBOX

The engine was removed by Phil Blundell of PB Restorations. My thanks to him for his help with the production of this section.

LIFTING AND SAFETY

- **Because the engine and gearbox are removed as a single – very heavy – make sure your hoist has sufficient capacity.**
- **Never stand or work beneath an engine suspended on a hoist.**
- **Never try to lift an engine on your own.**
- **Drain all fluids from an engine before removing it.**

▲ ER1. If you are working on your engine while it is still in the car, it is always a good idea to prop the bonnet open – the springs can get weary on older cars. For engine removal, the bonnet should be removed (see Chapter 4), the oil and coolant drained and the

radiator removed (see elsewhere in this chapter). Remove the battery earth lead to prevent any accidental short circuits.

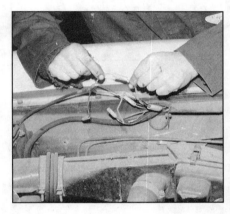

▲ ER2. All wiring from car to engine has to be disconnected and/or removed. Phil removed the protective cover from the loom which passes into the offside (RHD) wing for the headlamps, indicators, etc.

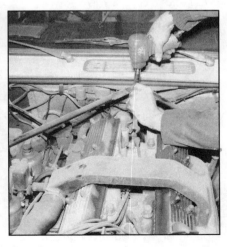

▲ ER3. The two cross-braces have to be removed – they are held by three bolts.

▲ ER4. Phil then unscrewed the jubilee clip on the air duct and unclipped the air cleaner cover to remove both, and the filter inside.

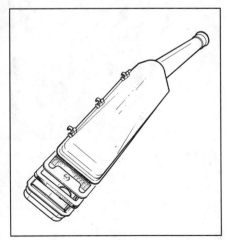

▲ ER5. This diagram shows the basic construction of the non-emission type of air cleaner assembly.

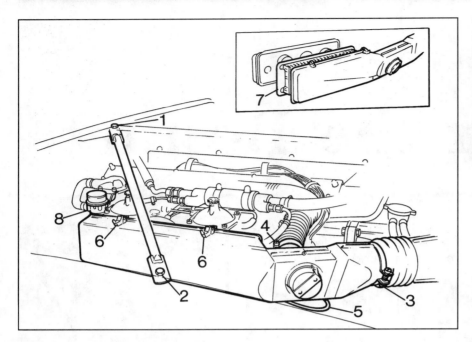

▲ ER10. The air cleaner is a different shape. The end unclips and comes off altogether, giving access to the circular air cleaner element inside.

▲ ER11. Though the manifold assembly and fuel rail can remain in place for the engine removal, the airflow meter has to come off. When removing fuel pipes and connections, it is important to take the usual precautions with regard to fire. Keep fuel off the bodywork and your skin.

▲ ER6. This diagram shows the emission control type air cleaner – as you can see, it differs only in detail from the non-emission version.

KEY
1. Inner end of stay
2. Outer end of stay
3. Flexible inlet pipe
4. Air duct
5. Vacuum pipe
6. Toggle clips
7. Filter element
8. Gulp valve

FUEL INJECTION MODELS

▲ ER8. Taking out a fuel-injection engine is almost the same as its carburettor'd cousin. There are, of necessity, a few more electrical and air/fuel connections.

▲ ER7. Phil then removed the air filter mounting plate. The two outer fixings are nuts and bolts; the two inner fixings are bolts which screw directly into the SU carburettors. There are two vacuum pipes from the bottom of the plate to remove. It's common to find the SU-to-plate gasket is damaged, so put a replacement on your shopping list.

▲ ER9. As previously, it's important to ensure that anything linking the engine to the body of the car is unplugged or disconnected. This is the multi-plug from the ECU (electronic control unit) to the all-important air-flow meter.

▲ ER12. Back on our Series 2, Phil removed the brake servo pipe, on the RH side of the carbs, alongside the distributor. The electrical multi-pin connectors to the engine have to be unplugged and tied back safely. Check the contacts for corrosion – spray with WD40 as a precaution.

▲ ER13. On an automatic gearbox car, the kick-down cable has to be removed from the accelerator linkage. It's secured by a clevis pin and an R-clip, once this is off. Then the cable bracket assembly can be released. By undoing the knurled nut on the kick-down cable, Phil was able to disconnect it from the bracket. He also released the throttle cable and disconnected the choke cable. (Some models have a start enrichment device.)

▲ ER14. The metal fuel line from the tanks culminates in a flexible rubber hose with filter connection to the carbs. Fuel can spill out, even after the fuel tap has been closed, so take care.

▲ ER15. Phil then removed the twin heater hoses from the nozzles on the engine compartment rear bulkhead.

▲ ER16. There are lots of individual wires to be removed as well, such as that to the oil sender at the bottom of the engine. There's also the lead from the starter motor solenoid and the HT and LT cables from the coil and, shown here, the earth cable on the bulkhead – there's one at each side.

▲ ER17. Phil unscrewed the bolt holding the steering pump supporting strap which is bolted into the water pump at one end and the power steering pump at the other. He adjusted the fan belt so it could be removed. A long bolt secures the power steering pump. It's possible to ease the pump back out of the way so that the engine can be extracted with the pump still in place. This means that there is no need to remove those tricky-to-refit crimped-on hose connections. If the pump is leaking, an exchange unit is the best option.

▲ ER18. There are two engine mountings, one at either side of the engine. The single bolt to the engine is hard to reach and probably rusted solid, so …

▲ ER19. … it's easier to remove the bracket itself. There are three bolts per bracket, the front two being captive, the rear being secured by a nut.

▲ ER20. He removed the connectors from the rear of the alternator and the easily-missed, chassis-to-engine earth wire at the back of the engine. The exhaust down pipe connections will probably be seized at the manifold, so it's simpler to release the downpipe clamp where it joins the exhaust system and remove the down pipe at the engine strip-down stage.

▲ ER21. Phil attached the Clarke engine hoist to the lugs on top of the cylinder head and eased it up slightly. This serves the purpose of easing the strain on the car a little, because he had to get under it (supported by twin axle stands and the Omega 3-ton jack) to remove the various gearbox connections. The jack was placed under the rear of the gearbox whilst Phil removed the four setscrews holding the sump-to-transmission stiffener plate (not fitted to all models). He then lowered the jack and removed the plate, replacing the jack afterwards to take the weight of the gearbox while …

▲ ER22. … he removed the gearbox at its rear mounting (shown here out of the car for clarity).

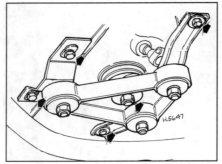

▲ ER23. Two different types of rear engine mounting were used, but the removal method is the same. This is the mounting for earlier cars and …

▲ ER24. … this the mounting used on later models. Easy to forget is the gearshift knob – you can't get the engine/gearbox out if it's left on! Phil disconnected the propeller shaft at its front flange and tied it securely out of the way and disconnected the speedometer cable. On manual transmission cars, it is necessary to unbolt the clutch slave cylinder from the clutch bellhousing and tie it up out of harm's way. However, there's no need to disconnect the clutch hydraulic lines. The leads to the overdrive switch (where applicable) should be disconnected.

AUTO TRANSMISSION REMINDERS

On cars with an automatic transmission, you will have several items to undo or remove over and above those cars with manual transmission, notably:
– The speed selector cable from the lever on the side of the transmission housing.
– The speed selector cable clamp from the torque converter housing.
– The vacuum pipes and electrical leads.
– Fluid cooler pipes.

▲ ER25. Phil lowered the rear of the engine/gearbox until the gear lever cleared the console grommet and then hoisted the assembly forward and up out of the engine bay. It has to be a steep angle to clear the front of the car.

▲ ER26. We cannot emphasise enough the fact that the gearbox/engine is extremely heavy – on no account try to lift the engine manually, as back or other injuries are almost guaranteed. Use a quality engine hoist, such as the Clarke model shown here. If you haven't got one, most hire shops will supply them on a daily or weekly rate.

AIR CONDITIONING AND FUEL COOLER SAFETY WARNING: The condenser has to be unbolted and withdrawn before the radiator can be removed. Do NOT disconnect any air-conditioning hoses. If disconnection is required, the system MUST be discharged by a Jaguar

dealer or air-conditioning specialist beforehand. Similarly, if you wish to remove the fuel cooler, it cannot be done before the refrigerant has been professionally discharged.

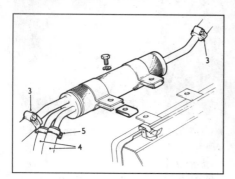

▲ ER27. If required, the air-conditioning compressor can be unbolted and pulled to one side of the engine bay where it can be secured (strap it back securely using strong cable ties). In the same vein, the fuel lines may be released from the fuel cooler, and the cooler itself unbolted and the assembly moved aside for access (within the obvious limits of the flexible hoses).

REMOVING THE GEARBOX FROM THE ENGINE

▲ ER28. Remove the oil pipes from the gearbox to the engine. Don't forget that the auto 'box dipstick is secured on this stud into the exhaust manifold.

▲ ER29. The starter motor is held by two long nuts/bolts which pass through the engine/gearbox flanges. There's a large gasket which should be replaced.

STARTER MOTOR TYPES
Early 2.8 litre engines:
  Lucas M45G inertia drive
Later 2.8 litre engines:
  Lucas 3M100 pre-engaged or inward/outward inertia type
All 3.4 litre engines:
  Lucas M45G pre-engaged
Early 4.2 litre engines:
  Lucas M45G pre-engaged
Later 4.2 litre engines:
  Lucas 3M100 pre-engaged or inward/outward inertia type

▲ ER30. The torque converter can now be seen through the hole left by the starter motor. There are four equally-spaced bolts on this. These feature two tab washers per bolt which have to be bent back before the bolts can be removed.

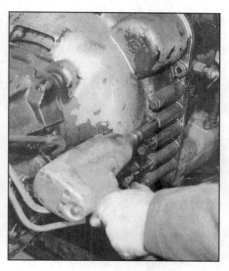

▲ ER31. Looking from the gearbox to the engine, there are three nuts/bolts on the lower right and left followed on each side by two bolts which go directly into the back of the engine. Note that the engine earth strap is fastened to one of the lower LH bolts. On the left, there are two bolts in a mirror image position of the holes left by having removed the starter motor. At the top there is a trio of bolts, although, as here, it is common to find that the very top one is missing. This indicates that the 'box has been removed previously with the engine in situ – and it is very difficult to reach that bolt on a reassembly!

ENGINE STRIPDOWN AND REBUILD

This section, dealing with the stripdown, investigation, repair, replacement and rebuild of the engine, was photographed at the premises of VSE Engineering Ltd. Tim Camp's highly professional operation, deals solely in the restoration of XK engines and sale of XK spares. Tim has raced and rallied many Jaguars, with tuned XKs of various hues providing the power. Between Tim and his crew, one very tired 4.2 litre engine was transformed from an oil and travel-stained caterpillar to a resplendent black and silver butterfly. My grateful thanks to them all, and for their words of wisdom, passed on to you now.

THE XJ6 ENGINE

All three Series were available with 4.2 litre engines. The Series 1 was also available with the underpowered and unpopular 2.8 litre version, and the Series 2 and 3 cars offered the alternative of a 3.4 litre motor.

BITS AND PIECES

When rebuilding your own engine, it is vital to make a point of storing all fasteners and components so you know where they are AND what they are. Make a note of sequences and the positioning of washers, etc. – it may seem obvious now, but in three months time when you're rebuilding the engine it may not be quite so simple. Taking photographs is a good way to aid your memory, or, better still, purloin the family video recorder which, when tripod mounted, is ideal as a visual and aural aid, as you can make verbal notes on the tape to explain any particularly intricate sections.

▲ ENG1. The VSE team – left to right they are Malcolm Standen, Russell Kemp, Doug Whittingham, Neil Arnold and Tim Camp.

▲ ENG2. With the engine at a good working height, Russ started by taking off the exhaust manifold heat shield. Two bolts hold this, a large one at the back with a copper washer underneath and a smaller one at the front which has a spring washer underneath.

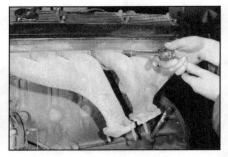

▲ ENG3. Removing the heat shield gives access to the exhaust manifold. Fitted to the lower rear stud is a 'steady' for the auto transmission filler/dipstick tube which has to be removed along with the rest of the manifold nuts. Most of these will be well-rusted and some easing agent will be needed. Take your time, because stripping threads on the studs will only add to your grief. If you're having trouble, ease the nut out a fraction of a turn, then back again, to work some of the accumulated rust free of the threads. Tap the manifold gently with a rubber mallet to break it free. The two three-cylinder manifold gaskets are always replaced. VSE also replaces the nuts and studs with stainless items.

◄ ENG4. Russ removed the engine-to-bellhousing brackets and the metal fuel pipe from its clip alongside the engine mounting. Remember, there will be fuel left in the system.

▲ ENG5. Russ removed the engine mounting – there is a flat and a spring washer underneath the nut – and then the three bolts holding the engine mounting bracket to the engine. Note that two of them are longer because part of the bracket is double-thickness metal.

▲ ENG6. Russ removed one of the bolts from the alternator adjusting rod. This steel bolt goes into the aluminium engine timing cover at the front of the engine and with the inevitable electrolytic reaction, it often seizes. He slackened the adjusting rod bolt where it fits on to the alternator mounting bolt. It's still quite a snug friction fit, so Russ could easily steady it with one hand while he removed the drive belt, before easing the alternator away. The drive belt is always replaced and the alternator is performance-tested. Drive belts, and even alternators, are easily available, even in high street stores like Halfords.

▲ ENG7. Four bolts hold the alternator mounting bracket. You can't remove the bracket and alternator as a single unit, as it hides one of the bolts. The top left-hand bolt requires the use of a ring spanner. Two bolts are short and two are slightly longer because the inner section of the bracket is double-skinned.

ALTERNATOR DETAILS

	Voltage	Output
Early (without air-conditioning)		
Lucas 11AC	12	43A
Lucas 18ACR	12	45A
Early (with air-conditioning)		
Butec	12	60A
Later		
Lucas 20ACR	12	66
Lucas 25ACR	13.5	66
Lucas A133	13.6/14.4	65 or 75
Motorola 9AR	14.0	70

1. Pump body
2. Spindle
3. Lock screw
4. Lock nut
5. Thrower
6. Seal
7. Impeller
8. Adaptor
9. Copper washer
10. Fan pulley
11. Stud
12. Gasket
13. Fan
14. Fluid coupling
15. Belt

▲ ENG8. This diagram shows the basic layout of the water pump and fan components.

▲ ENG9. To remove the water pump, Russ first took off the large hose which leads to the bottom of the radiator, and the three others, not forgetting the small one at the back of the pump that connects to a metal pipe that goes to the heater. Check the condition of all the hoses, bending them back and examining for hairline cracks. Five bolts secure the water pump. There are two studs at the top and one at the bottom. When you've removed them all, you can …

◄ ENG10. … pull the water pump off the block, complete with the fan assembly.

▲ ENG11. In order to remove the front pulley, Russ used a special VSE tool to lock up the flywheel.

▲ ENG12. He bent back the two tabs locking two of the four bolts holding the pulley to the damper before undoing the bolts. This is the single-piece locking tab washer – always replace it on rebuild.

▲ ENG13. It's usually necessary to tap the pulley gently with a rubber mallet to break the seal.

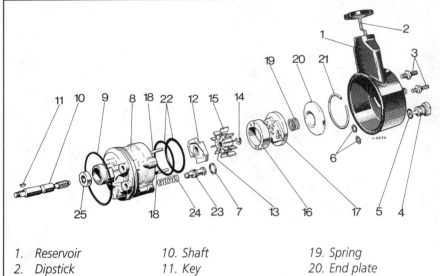

1. Reservoir	10. Shaft	19. Spring
2. Dipstick	11. Key	20. End plate
3. Stud	12. Thrust plate	21. Clip
4. Union	13. Rotor	22. O-ring
5. O-ing	14. Clip	23. Flow control valve
6. Seal	15. Pump rotor vanes	24. Spring
7. Seal	16. Pump ring	25. Oil seal
8. Pump body	17. Pressure plate	
9. O-ring	18. Pin	

▲ ENG16. This diagram shows an exploded view of a power steering pump.

▲ ENG14. With the nut removed, the damper should follow, but it often sticks. A conventional three-leg puller would pull the damper off the rubber inner, so …

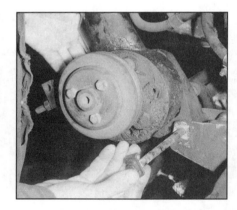

▶ ENG17. The pump is held by a single long bolt and nut, like the alternator. The bolt holding the stay to the water pump had already been removed (in the engine removal section). Russ supported the weight of the pump as he withdrew the bolt – note the locating plate on the end. There is a steel insert in the rearmost hole of the pump and mounting bracket and a steel collar which goes on the outside to aid the location of the bolt.

▶ ENG18. If you're not replacing them, mark your plug leads with 'Tipp-Ex' BEFORE removal! No. 6 cylinder is right at the front, and No. 1 at the back.

▲ ENG15. … VSE has a special puller which does the job quickly.
DIY overhaul of a power steering pump is possible, but it's more cost-efficient to obtain an exchange unit from a parts supplier, such as SNG Barratt. The tolerances worked to are very fine and generally beyond the realms of DIY instrumentation.

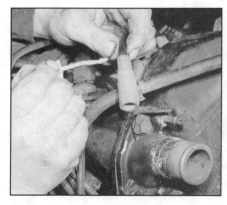

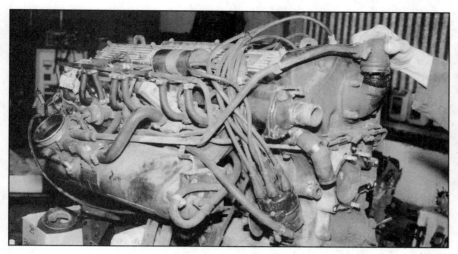

▲ *ENG19. The cylinder head breather pipe passes from the front of the engine into a rubber pipe on the inlet manifold. Removing it means that the plug leads can be taken off all at once, rather than separately.*

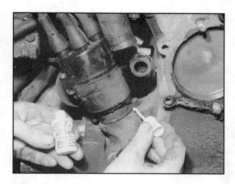

▲ *ENG20. The central HT lead was removed from the coil in preparation for the removal of the distributor. If you are re-using the distributor, use 'Tipp-Ex' to mark its exact position and save a lot of time setting up. A single bolt secures the distributor. Unplug the wiring from the front of the unit and remove the inlet manifold vacuum pipe, and waggle the distributor out of the block.*

DISTRIBUTOR TYPES AND INFORMATION
Contact Breaker Type

2.8 litre	Lucas 25D6-42175
3.4 litre	Lucas 45D6
4.2 litre (early)	Lucas 22D6-41060A
4.2 litre (late)	Lucas 45D6
Rotation (all models)	Anti-clockwise

Electronic
Some Series 2 and Series 3 cars were fitted with electronic ignition as follows:

Series 2	Lucas Opus
Series 3	Lucas Constant Energy

▼ *ENG21. This engine is fuel-injected, so there's a lot more 'gubbins' to remove before you can actually get at the inlet manifold. Ensure all electrical connections have been disconnected before you pull the manifold off. Russ removed the two brackets securing the steel section of pipe from water pump to heater, then he removed these two wires. One goes to the oil pressure gauge sender, the other goes to another sender at front of engine which cuts fuel supply if pressure drops too low. The latter can prevent the engine from starting and can be the cause of mysterious no-go problems.*

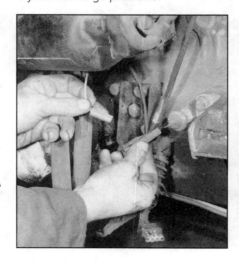

▲ *ENG22. Remove the two screws that hold the coil bracket, and ease it to one side. Then the three bolts that hold the three brackets from the top wiring loom running along the injector rail can be removed.*

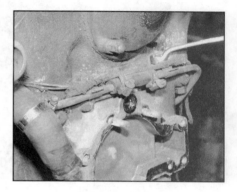

▲ *ENG23. At the front of the engine, the wiring loom to the alternator is held by four brackets, secured by two nuts. Remove these before the manifold, otherwise the loom will be damaged.*

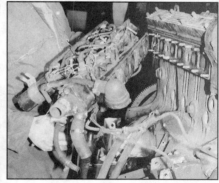

▲ *ENG24. The manifold is secured by 18 nuts and spring washers, which will probably require a tap from a rubber mallet. Don't damage the soft aluminium cylinder head.*

1. Cylinder block
2. Core plugs
3. Blanking plate
4. Gasket
5. Timing cover
6. Dowel
7. Core plug
9. Dipstick tube guide
10. Plug
11. Hexagon plug
12. Copper washer
13 Dowel
14. Stud
15. Stud
16. Dowel Stud
17. Rear oil seal cover
18. Dowel
19. Socket headed screw
20 Socket headed screw
21. Banjo bolt
22. Copper washer
23. Sealing ring
24. Filter gauze
25. Drain tap
26. Copper washer
27. Fibre washer
28. Crankshaft
29. Plug
30. Bush (Clutch pilot)
31. Thrust washer
32. Main bearings
33. Damper
34. Cone
35. Distance piece
36. Oil thrower
37. Crankshaft sprocket
38. Oil pump drive gear
39. Woodruff key
40. Pulley
41. Bolt
42. Lock washer
43. Bolt
44. Washer
45. Lock plate
46. Connecting rod
47. Big-end shell bearing
48. Flywheel
49. Dowel
50. Dowel
51. Setscrew
52. Lock plate
53. Piston
54. Top compression ring
55. Lower compressing ring
56. Oil control ring
57. Gudgeon pin
58. Circlip
59. Sump
60. Gasket
61. Crankshaft front oil seal
62. Crankshaft rear oil seal (part)
63. Drain plug
64. Copper washer
65. Baffle assembly
66. Oil pump pipe
67. O-ring
68. Stud
69. Hose
70. Hose clip
71. Dipstick
72. Ferrule
73. Ignition timing point
74. Engine mounting bracket
75. Engine mounting bracket
76. Flexible mounting pad
77. Washer

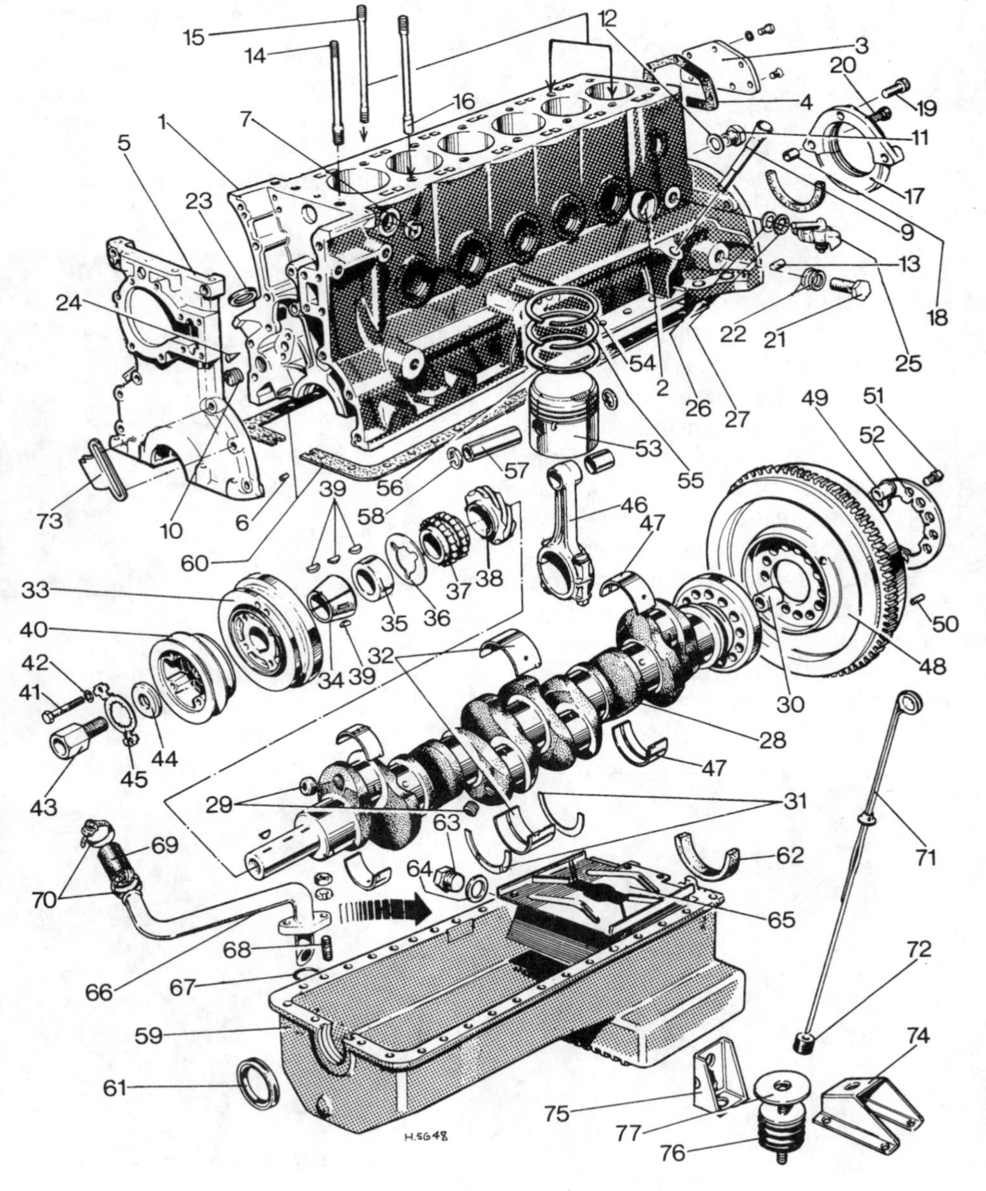

H.5648

▲ *ENG25. As you can see here, there's plenty of work still to do in order to get the XK unit down to its component parts!*

▲ ENG26. The flywheel is secured by 10 bolts, and locking tab washers (which cannot be re-used). The locking device is still in situ at the top left of the photo. Note the use of a long breaker bar.

▲ ENG27. Beneath the bolts is the single-piece lock plate, the inner sections of which form the tabs for the bolts. To the left in this photo is the packing plate – note the larger locating holes, at 12 and 6 o'clock. The flywheel/driveplate locating dowels fitted to Series 1 and 2 cars are not fitted to Series 3 models.

▲ ENG28. Russ used a socket, flat washer, threaded bolt and nut to wind it out from the threaded thimbles that go into the back of the crank, and the flywheel came gently away.

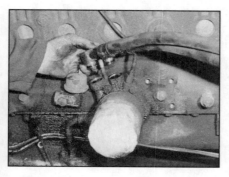

▲ ENG29. Russ removed the bellhousing bracket (two bolts), the other engine mount and the cast aluminium power steering bracket. The oil-cooler pipes are held on the block by a plate secured by a single nut. When removed the pipes will come off, as shown. There will be plenty of oil about, so be prepared for some spillage. Always plug the ends of the pipes before storing to prevent the ingress of dirt.

▲ ENG30. Russ removed the pipe from the filter housing, and plugged the holes to obviate accidents.

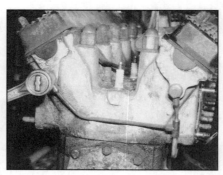

▲ ENG31. The pipe leads up the side of the block to the underside of the head where it is clipped into place. It continues around to the rear of the head where a T-piece and extensions carry oil to each camshaft. The pipe has to be released

from the clip, and then the bolts removed. As you can see here, the olive gland has a copper washer at each side of it, which should be replaced. The oil pressure sender is held by a single gland bolt which again has two copper washers.

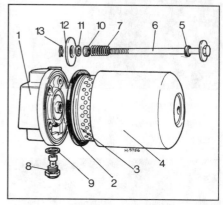

▲ ENG32. The oil filter was unscrewed and discarded. This diagram shows the various parts involved in a typical filter assembly.

KEY

1. Base	8. Relief valve
2. Sealing ring	9. Seal
3. Element	10. Felt washer
4. Canister	11. Washer
5. Sealing washer	12. Plate
6. Centre bolt	13. Spring clip
7. Spring	

▲ ENG33. The oil filter drain-back pipe, which carries the oil back down to the sump, is secured by two bolts. Russ removed them, and then the four bolts holding the filter housing to the block, so that the whole assembly could be removed as a piece. There's a rubber sealing washer on the pipe where it goes into the sump.

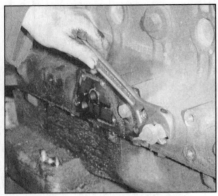

▲ ENG34. Russ used a large adjustable wrench to remove the front oil pressure switch.

▲ ENG35. The cylinder head breather is secured by four domed nuts with washers underneath. You should find two gaskets sandwiching a gauze filter. Often, both gaskets will have been replaced by a silicone 'bodge'.

▲ ENG36. Before removing the timing pointer, Russ cleaned up the area and marked its position by gently making a mark across the edge of the pointer and the timing cover. He then removed the two bolts and the pointer (these bolts are two of many holding the timing chest cover in place).

▲ ENG37. Each rocker cover is held by a single Torx bolt at the front, and by 10 domed nuts with copper washers underneath, removal of which allows the covers to be released – tap gently to free them from the gasket.

▲ ENG38. There's a notch at the front of each cam, seen in this photo at 12 o'clock. The cams should be aligned so that the lobes point outward like 'rabbit's ears'. When the head is removed it can be placed on a flat surface with the minimum of protrusion from the valves.

▲ ENG39. Each cam is held to its sprocket by four bolts, with a locking tab for each pair of bolts (earlier models had locking wire). Only two bolts can be removed at once. Turning the crank gave access to the remaining two bolts.

▲ ENG40. Don't forget the six nuts holding the front of the cylinder head in place. Two had already been removed (they secured the fuel pipe and alternator wiring loom) but there were still two at either side, together with suitable washers.

▲ ENG41. There are 14 domed nuts to be removed and to prevent head warpage, it's important that they are tackled in the right order – a reversal of the order for tightening them (see diagram elsewhere in this chapter). There should be just one washer underneath each nut, but studs stretch over time and it's common to find more than that on some studs. They also rust because they sit in the water jacket of the cylinder block, so wind them out slowly and carefully! When they've all been removed, the head can be lifted free – a tap with a rubber mallet will probably help.

▲ ENG42. Russ removed the cylinder head gasket, and used an elastic band to hold the cam sprocket assembly in one piece.

▲ ENG43. At this point, Malcolm Standen took over. He took off the sump, which is held by a series of bolts all the way around except at the front, which is four studs, nuts and washers. At either side of the rear seal housing, the bolts are much longer than the others. Note also the rear main oil seal Torx screws.

▲ ENG44. He used the engine hoist to raise the whole block assembly high enough to remove the sump, and then laid the engine on its RH side to avoid damaging the dipstick tube. Don't damage the pick-up pipes in the sump, and it mustn't rest on cam sprockets at the top.

▲ ENG45. Malcolm removed the various brackets which secure the oil pick-up pipes, and …

▲ ENG46. … laid them on the bench.

▲ ENG47. The oil pump is held by three bolts – two are shouldered and one is part threaded. VSE always replace the pump – it's a small item that can wreck an engine.

▲ ENG48. With the oil pump off, Malcolm then removed the pump drive assembly. This bronze bush comes off first, and the rest can follow once the locking tab on the drive pinion has been tapped back. This is the drive assembly in its entirety. Make sure you don't damage the (relatively) soft bronze bush during the removal process.

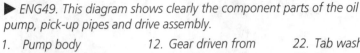

▶ *ENG49. This diagram shows clearly the component parts of the oil pump, pick-up pipes and drive assembly.*

1. Pump body
2. Rotor assembly
3. Cover
4. Setscrew
5. Setscrew
6. Spring washer
7. O-Ring
8. O-ring
9. Distributor driveshaft
10. Bush
11. Washer
12. Gear driven from crankshaft
13. Woodruff key
14. Nut
15. Special washer
16. Coupling sleeve
17. Dowel bolt
18. Dowel bolt
19. Tab washer
20. Oil delivery pipe
21. Gasket
22. Tab washer
23. Strut
24. Clip
25. Oil pick-up pipe
26. Clip
27. Strut
28. Strut
29. Strut
30. Sealing plate
31. Spring

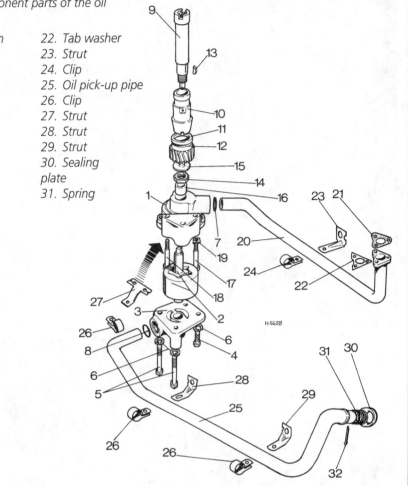

▲ *ENG50. Malcolm tapped off the front damper cone revealing the woodruff key in the end of the crankshaft. This has to be tapped free and stored safely.*

▲ *ENG51. The timing chest cover is held by three ½ in bolts and five ⁹⁄₁₆ in bolts. Malcolm had to tap the casing gently with a rubber mallet to get it to break free of the gasket.*

▶ *ENG52. The timing chain layout is quite complex, so it's important to have a good grasp of what goes where before you start.*

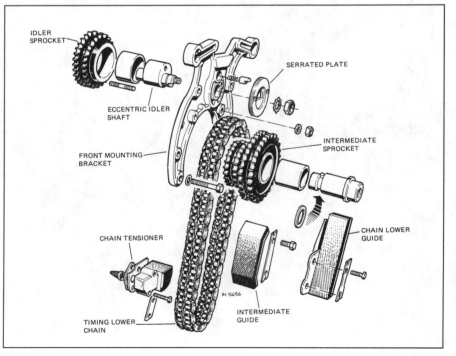

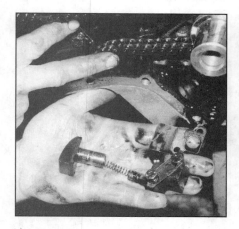

▲ ENG53. There are two chain tensioners – a 'manual' intermediate guide and a hydraulic tensioner, and both feature tabbed washers which have to be tapped back before they can be removed. Here, Malcolm is holding the parts that make up the hydraulic tensioner, and in the hole behind this there should be …

▲ ENG56. Malcolm then loosened – but did not remove – the bolts holding the timing cover top plate. He then removed the complete timing chain assembly. Chains are always replaced at VSE, though it's rare to find a sprocket with any serious wear problems.

▲ ENG58. Malcolm turned the crank so that he could easily access the two nuts on No. 1 con-rod. Note that the nuts have double the number of 'flats', to ensure that a socket is used for removal. He removed the cap and checked out the bearing for signs of wear; usually this is a bronzing effect. It's generally wise to replace all such bearings as the cost is minimal. If you are re-using them, wipe off the oil and stick on a piece of masking tape, marked with their location before storage.

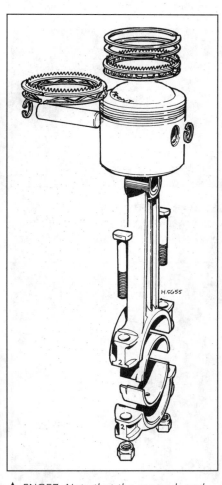

▲ ENG54. … a tiny conical filter.

▲ ENG55. This is the intermediate guide with its mounting bolts and lock washer.

▲ ENG57. Note that the con-rods and caps are numbered, with the highest figure (6) being at the front of the engine. The numbers should always align as shown here. Two types of oil control rings have been fitted over the years.

▲ ENG59. Malcolm pulled the piston out of the bore – fit was quite sloppy, indicating a little too much wear and pointing to an impending rebore. He kept each piston and con-rod assembly together.

▲ ENG60. The main bearing caps are held by 14 nuts, and locking tab washers (don't reuse old washers). There should be a number stamped into the caps or alongside them in the crankcase. If there isn't, use a dot punch to make an identifying mark so that they can be returned to their original positions at rebuild time.

▲ ENG61. The centre cap is the only one to feature a thrust washer at each side.

▲ ENG62. With all the bearing caps removed, Malcolm lifted out the heavy crank ready for examination.

▲ ENG63. A small drift was used to tap out the engine oil dipstick tube, and a large socket was required to undo the rear gallery oil plug. There should also be a copper washer – this has to be discarded, as the sealing properties cannot be guaranteed a second time.

▲ ENG64. Seven bolts hold the rear water chamber plate, and when it's removed there's more thick, sludgy rust.

▲ ENG65. The upper rear oil seal housing is held by three Torx head bolts. Note the hollow locating dowels which fit into the cover at either side.

▲ ENG66. Malcolm then turned the engine upright and removed the water drain bolt from the rear left of the engine.

▲ ENG67. Removing the studs can be a nerve-wracking business, as they often rust badly and shear. Malcolm is using the S-P stud remover – essential for this job.

▲ ENG68. Nasty! The front stud has been ravaged by rust – compare with the unaffected stud above it. The 14 studs are not all the same length; so take careful note of which goes where.

▲ ENG69. Remove the core plugs after the studs, as the plugs could foul on some of the studs. There are five plugs on the RH side and six on the left. Tap them at the edges to make them tip out, rather than in their centres. Uncared for engines can silt almost all the way up, particularly from the back of the engine. You should use only top-quality anti-freeze with anti-corrosion inhibitors, all year round.

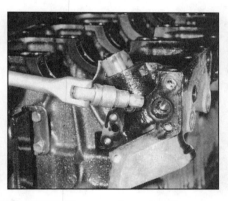

▲ ENG70. There are four oil gallery plugs and copper washers on the RH side of the engine, and an oil gallery plug alongside the distributor drive at the front. This requires a large Allen key.

▲ ENG71. Malcolm then removed the intermediate tensioner.

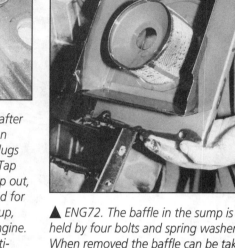

▲ ENG72. The baffle in the sump is held by four bolts and spring washers. When removed the baffle can be taken out, as here.

CLEANING

▲ CE1. Many parts of the engine were automatically binned, notably where their replacements were relatively cheap and/or where excess wear had occurred. Many other items, however, were to be re-used, but not in the condition they came off the car. Here are parts of the timing chain assembly and the con-rods going into the VSE acid bath.

▲ CE2. Smaller items were put into a cage or can for safety – no one was volunteering to grope around in the acid for lost bits of engine!

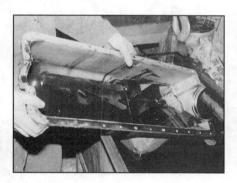

▲ CE3. The sump was in a real state when it went for its dip in a special aluminium cleaner, but ...

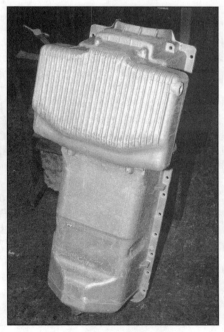

▲ CE4. ... this is how it looked when it came out.

CYLINDER HEAD

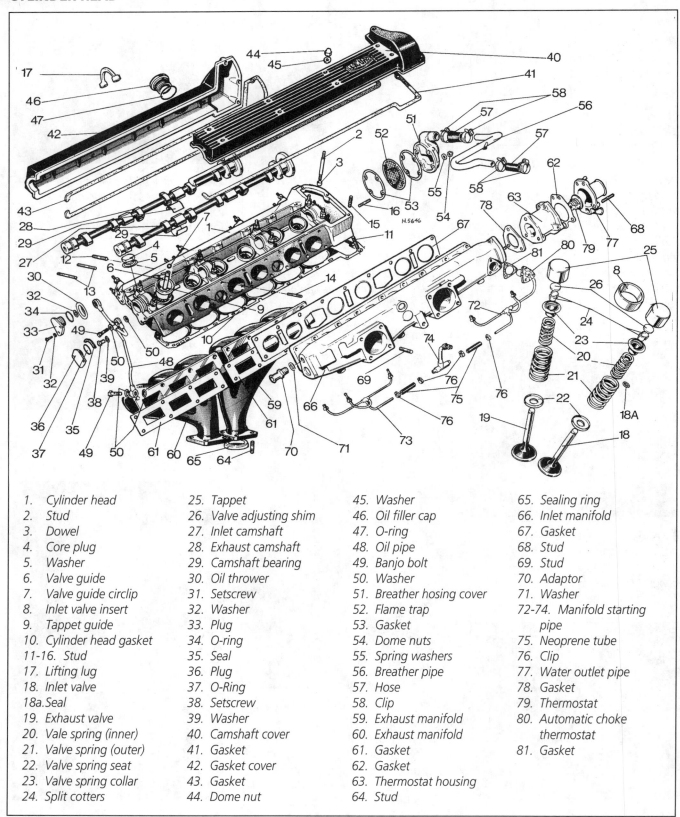

1. Cylinder head	25. Tappet	45. Washer	65. Sealing ring
2. Stud	26. Valve adjusting shim	46. Oil filler cap	66. Inlet manifold
3. Dowel	27. Inlet camshaft	47. O-ring	67. Gasket
4. Core plug	28. Exhaust camshaft	48. Oil pipe	68. Stud
5. Washer	29. Camshaft bearing	49. Banjo bolt	69. Stud
6. Valve guide	30. Oil thrower	50. Washer	70. Adaptor
7. Valve guide circlip	31. Setscrew	51. Breather hosing cover	71. Washer
8. Inlet valve insert	32. Washer	52. Flame trap	72-74. Manifold starting
9. Tappet guide	33. Plug	53. Gasket	pipe
10. Cylinder head gasket	34. O-ring	54. Dome nuts	75. Neoprene tube
11-16. Stud	35. Seal	55. Spring washers	76. Clip
17. Lifting lug	36. Plug	56. Breather pipe	77. Water outlet pipe
18. Inlet valve	37. O-Ring	57. Hose	78. Gasket
18a. Seal	38. Setscrew	58. Clip	79. Thermostat
19. Exhaust valve	39. Washer	59. Exhaust manifold	80. Automatic choke
20. Vale spring (inner)	40. Camshaft cover	60. Exhaust manifold	thermostat
21. Valve spring (outer)	41. Gasket	61. Gasket	81. Gasket
22. Valve spring seat	42. Gasket cover	62. Gasket	
23. Valve spring collar	43. Gasket	63. Thermostat housing	
24. Split cotters	44. Dome nut	64. Stud	

▲ CL1. The cylinder head is a complex assembly, as can be seen here in this exploded view.

UNLEADED FUEL

According to Tim Camp, all XK engines can run on unleaded fuel as long as the heads are equipped with hardened valve seats. The Series 3 cars had these as standard, but VSE can easily fit them to the Series 1 and 2 cars. The ignition timing has to be altered slightly and, in some cases, the carburation, too. In general, Tim finds that better performance results from using the current Super unleaded fuel, although this depends very much on the individual engine.

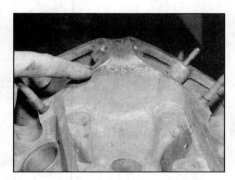

▲ CL2. The XJ6 head has a cast front and there is a reference number stamped into the back of the cam alley.

▲ CL3. Russ removed and discarded the spark plugs. Note the casting numbers in the cams.

▶ CL4. There are four main caps holding each cam, with two nuts and two washers on each. Undo the nuts vertically so that the cam comes up evenly. Each cap is numbered to correspond with a number on the head, from 1 to 8, where 1 is the LH front (exhaust front) and 5 is the inlet side rear.

▲ CL5. Inlet and exhaust cams are different. They're not marked, but when in position correctly, the lobes will both turn outward to form the 'rabbit's ears'. Crossed over, the cam lobes will both point inward. The ends of the cams wear, particularly if the engine has been standing for some time and the cams have been touching the followers. XJ6 cams tend to wear on the side of the cams just before the base circle starts.

▲ CL6. The eight cam bearings can be tapped out using a suitable drift. VSE always replaces them. Russ removed the cam followers with a magnet. If they stick, gently tap the top of the follower with a hammer. If worn, they must be skimmed and re-hardened.

▲ CL7. Unless you are doing a complete head overhaul job, keep the tappets and tappet shims in pairs.

▲ CL8. Russ applied the spring compressor and used a small screwdriver to ease out the two collets per valve. If they're not too badly worn, they can be re-used.

▲ CL9. Left to right, each valve assembly comprises: valve, rubber stem seal (inlet valves only), spring seat, two springs (inner and outer) valve top and collets (at front).

▲ CL10. Early valve tops are deeper, spring seats are deeper and collets are longer. Early engines do not have valve seals and this can lead to smoking. The answer is to use a later spring seat, top collet and valve seal – inlet only. VSE always fit new valves, springs and seals.

▲ CL11. Russ dipped the head into an acid bath to make baked-on oil and carbon easier to remove. The spring seats, collets and valve tops are also put in for a good cleaning.

▲ CL12. The cylinder head specialist is Doug Whittingham. He noticed signs of a gasket blowing between No. 4 and 5 cylinders. The leaking water gets into the combustion chambers up behind the exhaust valve seats and causes damage.

▲ CL13. The felt-tip pen marks the path of a crack in the top of the cylinder head near a core plug. This needs professional repair, of which stitching – drilling a series of small holes and inserting screws into it – is easier and safer than welding.

▲ CL14. Two inlet valve seats (No. 4 and 5 cylinders) needed attention on our head. The area around the seat was cleaned up, and Doug drilled out the two valve guides to ensure that the dummy valve used by VSE would slide easily through it. This is used to knock out the seat in the following procedure. Because

it has to be hammered down the guide, the end of the valve gets burred over and won't come out of a standard diameter guide. Old inlet valves are dropped into the other guides to prevent welding spatter getting in there. Doug then applied a neat layer of weld to the seats.

▲ CL15. As the welds cooled, it shrunk the seats and he was able to tap them out. In cases like this, if the recess has not been too badly damaged, it can be machined to take an oversized seat. If it is, then weld will have to be applied to the head to return enough metal back to facilitate machining to the correct size.

▲ CL16. The edges of the two valve seat recesses were chamfered slightly and then smoothed with emery cloth so that the seat would slot into place more easily. To tap the seats into place, the head has to be heated to around 150°C (302°F) – no problem here, as it had to go into the VSE oven anyway to remove the valve guides (see later). Doug applied a little oil to the edge of the new seat and then tapped it into place using another special VSE tool. A feeler gauge was used to make sure the seats were fully down and equal all the way around. This work has to be done quickly while the head is warm and the seat is cold.

▲ CL17. No. 5 seat is in position, but No. 4 required an oversize seat (shown here) and had to be machined to suit. In cases like this, the outside diameter (OD) of the seat is slightly bigger but the inside diameter (ID) is standard. Exhaust and inlet valve seats are both set at a 45 degree angle.

VALVE SEAT INSERTS SPECIFICATIONS

Valve seat material
  Sintered iron

Inside diameter
  Inlet   1.5 in + 0.003 in/–0.001 in
           (38.1mm + 0.076mm/
           –0.025mm)
  Exhaust 1.379 in – 1.383 in
           (35.03mm – 35.13mm)

Interference (shrink) fit in head
           0.003 in (0.076mm)

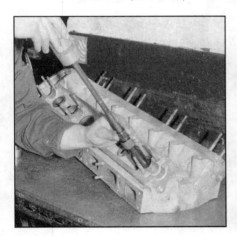

▲ CL18. As seen earlier, the bucket guides can lift up out of their locations as a result of water damage from a leaking cylinder head gasket. Doug removed the damaged bucket guide by using a slide hammer with a special extractor head.

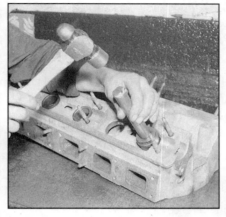

▲ CL19. Another special tool was used to tap home a replacement bucket guide.

▲ CL20. One method used to prevent a recurrence of this problem is to bolt a bracket in between the cylinders. However, this only holds the guide right at its edge, and in extreme circumstances it can move around.

▲ CL21. A better method is to drill a hole through from the inside of the valley into the bucket so that a grub screw can be inserted to secure it firmly.

A taper tap was used first, and when the thread was complete the hole was filled with Loctite 648 to make a good seal and secure the screw. Doug screwed the grub screw into place and filled the hole with plastic metal. VSE's massive experience of developing racing XK engines has shown that this is the best way to keep the bucket guides where they should be.

▲ CL22. Inlet guides (left) have two circlip guides and exhaust guides have one. The circlips are tapped on to the guides and act as locators as the guides go into the head. On the inlet guides, one groove is for the circlip, the other is for the oil seal (no oil seal on the exhaust side, of course). An oversize guide should have markings below the circlip grooves, as on the guide at the far left of this photo.

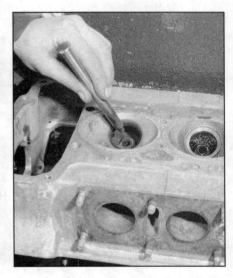

▲ CL23. The head had to be heated to 150°C (302°F) before the guides could be removed. Once more, VSE have designed their own special tool for this.

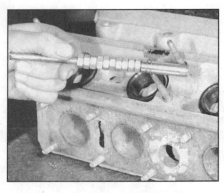

▲ CL24. Once removed, Doug checked the diameters with a micrometer, to make sure they are not oversize already. Although they should be marked, not all are. He used yet another special VSE tool to tap the guides into place.

▲ CL25. No. 5 inlet guide was loose as it was put in, so it was reamed out and an oversize guide inserted. After this, the head was put outside and allowed to cool naturally and evenly. The oversize guide was reamed out to the correct ID and the others were also reamed out very gently to ensure that there were no burrs from the tapping-in process.

▲ CL26. It's important for the angles and the valves to be correct. The two new valve seats had to be cut into the correct

angle, using this Mira machine. New guides had been fitted and so the Mira was used to confirm that the guides, valves and seats were at the right angle and also to clean up the valve faces.

VALVE GUIDE SPECIFICATIONS

Material	Cast iron
Length	
Inlet	1.86 in. (47.24mm)
Exhaust	1.95 in. (49.53mm)
Inside diameter	
Inlet & Exhaust	5⁄16 in. (7.94mm)
Interference (shrink) fit in head	0.0005 in.-0.0022 in. (0.013mm-0.055mm)

▲ CL27. The head was then taken to the machine shop where the combustion chambers were thoroughly cleaned up, and then the head was skimmed. A steel straight edge and feeler gauges were used to ensure that it was absolutely flat.

▲ CL28. Doug fitted the valves into the lapping tool and 'painted' a layer of fine

grinding paste around the very edges before inserting the whole lot into the head in order to match each valve to its seat. Always keep the paste off the valve stems, or they will soon wear away.

▲ CL29. The finished article, the last perfectly matched valve and stem.

▲ CL30. Doug collated the components required to build up the valve assemblies.

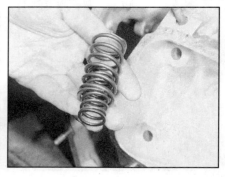

▲ CL31. He oiled the valves before sliding them into their respective holes. There are two springs per valve; the outer one is a standard spring and the inner one is a damper spring. These are heavy-duty because the head is from a fuel-injection engine.

▲ CL32. The valve top was fitted and then the valve spring compressor was applied. To make fitting the small collets easier, Doug put a dab of grease on the end of a small screw driver, and 'stuck' them to it. Simple, but effective, and it also gives a little start-up lubrication. Always ensure that the groove in the collet aligns with the groove in the valve stem.

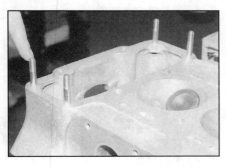

▲ CL33. Once Doug had fitted all the valve assemblies, he upended the head and inserted the four studs at the front of the block. This is so that when the head is tipped the other way up for cam fitment, the rotation of the cams causing the valves to move in and out won't foul them on the bench top.

VALVE ASSEMBLY SPECIFICATIONS

VALVES

Material

Inlet	Silicon chrome steel
Exhaust	21 – 4 – NS

Valve head diameter

(Series 1 & 2)

Inlet	1.75 in +/– 0.002 in (44.45mm +/– 0.05mm)
Exhaust	1.625 in +/– 0.002 in (41.28mm +/– 0.05mm)

(Series 3)

Inlet	1.87 in-1.880 in (47.50mm-47.75mm)
Exhaust	1.620 in-1.630 in (41.15mm-41.40mm)

Valve stem diameter

Series 1 & 2

Inlet & exhaust	0.3125 in (7.94mm)

Series 3

Inlet & exhaust	0.3100 in-0.3125 in (7.87mm-7.94mm)

Valve lift	0.375in. (9.53mm)

Valve clearance (cold – inlet & exhaust)
0.012 in- 0.014 in
(0.30mm-0.35mm)

VALVE SPRINGS

Free length

Series 1	Inner	1 21/32 in (42.0mm)
Series 1	Outer	1 15/16 in (49.2mm)
Series 2	Inner	1.734 in (44.04mm)
Series 2	Outer	2.103 in (53.42mm)
Series 3/3.4	Inner	1.734 in (44.04mm)
Series 3/3.4	Outer	2.103 in (53.42mm)
Series 3/4.2	Inner	1.656 in-1.719 in (42.06mm-43.66mm)
Series 3/4.2	Outer	1.938 in-2.000 in (49.23mm-50.80mm)

FITTING THE CAM ASSEMBLY

▲ CL34. VSE always fit new Glacier cam shells whenever a cylinder head is rebuilt.

▲ CL35. He put the shells into the head 'dry' and then repeated the procedure for the caps, which are numbered 1-8.

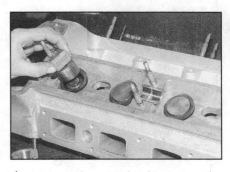

▲ CL36. He then put the shims on to the tops of the valves. The right shim value is important; Doug usually starts with 85/95 thou and adjusts from there. The shims must be clinically clean, as dirt and swarf on the surface could throw the figures way out. The valve assemblies are always filled with engine oil before the new buckets are installed, using the magnet.

◄ CL37. Doug inserted two bolts into the end of the cam for some leverage once it's bolted into place. When setting up one cam, make sure the other is out altogether to prevent the valves colliding. Doug applied a drop of oil to the tops of the buckets and then laid the cam in place with the front lobes pointing outward, like 'rabbit's ears'.

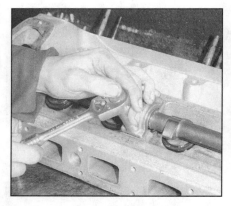

▲ CL38. He oiled the shells in the caps before putting them in position and tightening them up evenly.

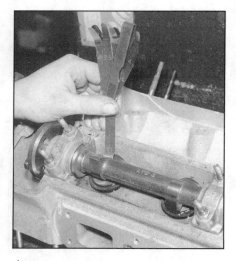

▲ CL39. Doug checked the valve clearances on each valve until they were spot-on (see separate chart) and …

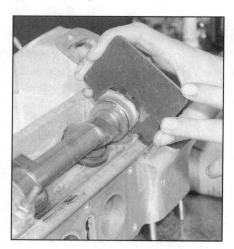

▲ CL40. … set up the cam with this special gauge. It's possible to hire or buy one from the Jaguar clubs.

▲ CL41. Having got the shimming correct, Doug added the special washers under the nuts and tightened the cam down. Take care here, as they are alloy and can easily be damaged – they should only be tightened to 9 lb/ft, which is more or less hand tight.

CAMSHAFT SPECIFICATIONS

Number of bearings	4 per shaft	
Journal diameter		
Series 1 & 2	1.00 in. (25.4mm)	
Series 3	0.9990 in.-0.9995 in. (25.375mm-25.387mm)	
Running clearance	0.0005 in.-0.002 in. (0.013mm-0.05mm)	
Endfloat (max.)	0.004 in.-0.006 in. (0.10mm-0.15mm)	

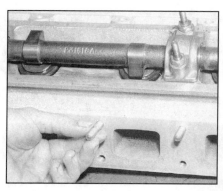

▲ CL42. VSE always fit new manifold studs – 18 on the inlet side and 16 on the exhaust side. Note that the inlet studs (right) are shorter.

CAM COVER CLEANING

▲ CL43. Russ shot-blasted the covers to clean off all the original paint and to make a good key for the heat-resistant, competition black Spectra spray paint. Then he ran a 3M Scotchbrite CSD-S plastic paint stripping wheel across the tops of the covers to remove the paint on the ribs, producing …

▲ CL44. … a final effect that looks straight off the production line at Browns lane.

SKIMMING AND REBORING THE CYLINDER BLOCK

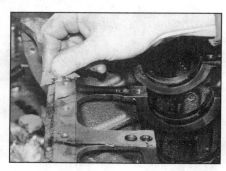

▲ CC1. Having got the block down to its basics, Malcolm used a sharp blade to remove the excess gasket material from the bottom of the block. It was then soaked overnight in a paraffin-based solvent in a large 'bath', then spray-cleaned the block with water heated up to 60°C (140°F).

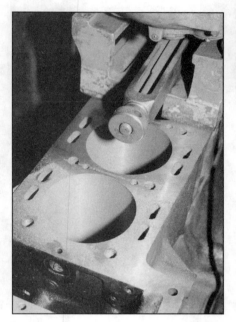

▲ CC2. In the machine shop, VSE boss, Tim Camp, set about surface grinding. It's vital to ensure that the timing case cover is in place at this point, otherwise there'll be a 'step' when the cylinder head is replaced.

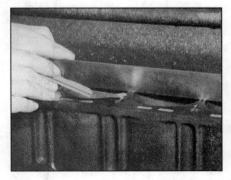

▲ CC3. Even with all this technology, the only foolproof way to ensure that the surface is exactly level is to check it with a steel straight edge and a set of feeler gauges, as Tim did here. In this case, the head required just 4 thou off the top – it's common to find that 8 thou is needed.

▲ CC4. Tim checked the bores carefully for signs of taper, ovality, scoring and scratches. A good idea of what the bores will be like can be gained by knowing how the engine performed when in the car; excessive oil consumption and lots of blue smoke indicates worn bores. He used a micrometer to measure the diameter at the top of the bore and then again at the bottom, where there is no wear. If the difference is more than 0.006 in (0.15 mm) then a rebore with oversize pistons will be required – and this was the case with this engine. Tim set up the cutting head and wound it down into each bore in turn. It was set to 20 thou oversize, because 10 thou oversize pistons are not available. Note that reboring can only be carried out up to 30 thou – if any more is required it means that the liners must be pressed out and new ones fitted in order to start all over again.

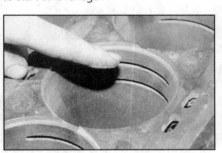

▲ CC5. Important note: More wisdom from Tim tells us that from engine number 8L89109 the maximum rebore is +0.020 in because of a change of waterway position between bores. In early 4.2 litre engines (Series 1 and 2 XJ6 models), the block has waterways between the bores behind the liners. There's a very good chance of small cracks between the bores. If left, the head gasket will blow, with possible cracking of the liner.

▲ CC6. The best solution is to remove liners and machine block for a flanged liner (often referred to as a top-hat liner, for obvious reasons). This allows for the sealing ring of the head gasket to seat on to the top of the liner, ensuring a 100 per cent seal. With the liners removed, it is possible to clean out the waterways completely.

▲ CC7. The bores were finished off by Russ, who used a flex, or bottle brush, honer. After oiling the cylinder bores, the brush was connected to an electric drill and moved up and down the bore. Note that it is important NOT to remove the brush while the drill is rotating. This honing produces a crosshatch finish and a good key for piston rings to work in, and it is essential that newly machined bores are honed before fitting the pistons.

▲ CC8. With honing complete, he chamfered the top edges of the cylinder bores with a small file so that the rings wouldn't foul when the pistons were installed.

▲ CC9. The block was then steam cleaned. Once dried, it was wire-brushed and painted with a heat-resistant synthetic black enamel paint.

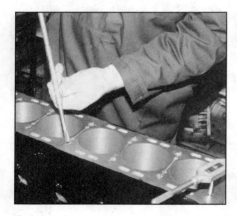

▲ CC10. Malcolm was in charge of engine reassembly and he took the trouble to run a tap through all the threads on the cylinder block. More attention to detail that is typical of the business as a whole and essential when you're building engines that go all over the world.

CRANK STRIP, EXAMINATION, BALANCE AND REBUILD

▲ CC11. The sprockets and worm gear on the end of the crank are usually OK. On earlier models there is sometimes an oil thrower plate which can often be damaged and has to be replaced – check for diagrams. The crank has six Allen-headed recess plugs, but each has a peen mark which has to be drilled out and then the plugs removed.

▲ CC12. There's bound to be plenty of messy silt behind each plug …

▲ CC13. … and VSE always chase out the threads before going on to the next stage.

▲ CC14. VSE has complete facilities for all aspects of engine building including full crankshaft testing facilities. Here, Tim is checking 'our' crank for cracks. The crank is magnetised by inducing a current through it. He then sprays a fluid over it which contains dyed magnetic particles which show up in ultraviolet light (hand-held in this photo). In the darkness of the covered booth, a crack will show up as a bright yellow line. Tim reckons that cracks usually occur where the journal joins the webs of the crank, although this is rare on the 4.2 litre cranks.

▲ CC15. Tim used a micrometer to check the journals for size and ovality. Our crank was within specified limits, so he …

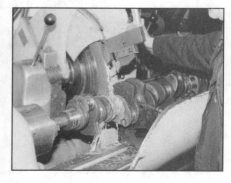

▲ CC16. … ground it as required. He ground the first journal and then the others to match it, repeating the process for both big end and mains surfaces. Tim found that the only real way to ensure total quality was to install the necessary machinery and carry out the work on the premises.

Technical note: According to Tim, Series 3 XJ6s have a crank that is surface-hardened by the 'Sursurf' process (from engine no 8L147650 4.2 litre and 7M4796 3.4 litre). In theory these cranks can't be reground as it removes the hard surface. However, it is possible to regrind and retreat the crank to restore its hard surface – a job for the professionals. He checked and rechecked the journals at regular intervals, and when they were correct ...

▲ CC17. ... he transferred the crank to yet another complex machine for balancing. Here, the crank was mounted on a pair of rollers with vibration sensors underneath that transmit the imbalance to the in-built computer. Imbalances show up as a digital display so Tim knows exactly where to remove metal from. Once balanced, Tim added the flywheel drive plate and front damper so that everything was balanced to itself.

▲ CC18. With the crank perfectly balanced and cleaned-up, new plugs were fitted and new peens made using a suitable punch. Standard plugs only have one peen, but Malcolm, ever the perfectionist, prefers to make two – just in case.

TIMING GEAR DISMANTLING, PREPARATION AND REASSEMBLY

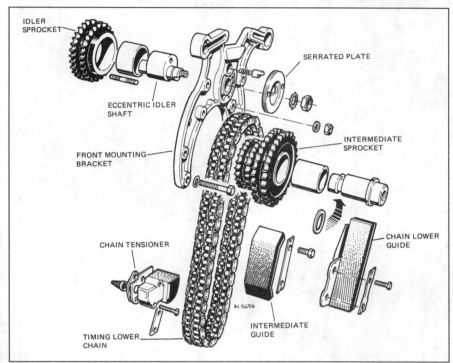

▲ TG1. This diagram shows the lower timing chain and gears and ...

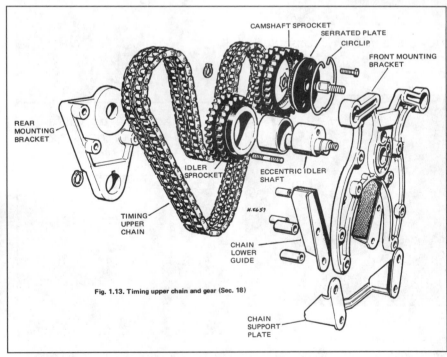

▲ TG2. ... this one shows the upper timing chain and gear. After removing the assembly from the engine, Malcolm removed the elastic band that held them together and started the dismantling procedure. In every case VSE discard the timing chains – always fitting new chains is a pre-requirement for a good new engine.

▲ TG3. With the circlips removed, he was able to tap the two timing chain brackets apart.

▲ TG4. These are the two camshaft sprockets with the serrated plates and securing circlips.

▲ TG5. Sprockets rarely need replacement and they were cleaned up by Russ along with other timing gear hardware in the Clarke washer with Safety Kleen before being buffed up on the wheel – note the safety goggles and gloves.

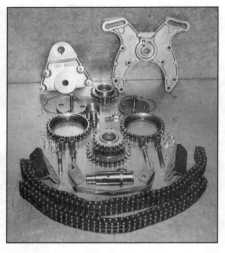

▲ TG6. The timing chain components ready for reassembly, with new chains, nuts, bolts, washers and circlips, but the original mounting brackets, sprockets and guides.

▲ TG7. The camshaft sprockets have serrated plates in their centres that are held in place by large circlips.

▲ TG8. The pin was lightly oiled before being inserted into the intermediate sprocket. The bush in the centre of this sprocket and the idler sprocket can wear. Malcolm fitted new bearings into the two sprockets. Test by inserting the shaft

and rocking side to side – if you can feel any play, then the bush(es) will have to be replaced.

▲ TG9. The assembly was pushed into position on the front mounting bracket and held by a circlip. The eccentric idler shaft was given a coating of engine oil before being put into position.

▲ TG10. The longer of the two new Rolon chains, was looped around the sprockets, then the shorter one was added.

▲ TG11. Malcolm put the front mounting bracket in place and, before tightening the nuts (which fit on to studs in the bracket), used an elastic band across the camshaft sprockets to prevent them going for an unauthorised 'walkabout'. The lubricating spring and plunger were placed in position and ...

▲ TG12. ... the eccentric idler shaft fitted and secured by a washer and nut. The lower chain tensioners were put in place. The 4.2 litre engine also has a bridging plate.

▲ TG13. Two completed timing chain assemblies; the one on the left is for 'our' 4.2 litre engine and the one on the right is from a 3.8 litre XK unit.

THE PISTON AND CONNECTING ROD ASSEMBLIES

▲ PS1. Malcolm started by removing the circlips from the piston gudgeon pin (little end). Note that the caps have been replaced on the con rods as the pistons were removed from the engine so that

they can be put back together as matched sets. He threw away the little ends and then checked the rods for condition. If the stamping inside the big end, showing the rod designation, is still clearly visible, then the bearing shell hasn't been loose and wriggling about. If the little end bronze bearing can be pushed out by hand, it's very bad news, but also extremely rare.

▲ PS2. The con rods went to Russ for cleaning and came back looking like new. Here, they are lined up ready to be assembled with new little ends, circlips, pistons rings and Hepolite pistons.

▲ PS3. The bronze bush in the little end should have a diameter of 0.875 in + 0.002 in (22.22mm + 0.005mm). Anything more than that means it will have to be replaced, although Malcolm usually replaces them as a matter of course. Getting the bush out of the con rod is virtually impossible without the use of a hydraulic press. Here, Malcolm is using a suitably-sized drift and taking care to ensure that it is being pushed out 'square'.

▲ PS4. The bronze bushes have an oil hole half way along their length, and it's vital that these holes line up exactly with the corresponding holes in the con rods during assembly.

▲ PS5. The bush has to be reamed out for an exact fit with the new little end. For DIY purposes, this would probably be done in a vice, but great care must be taken to ream absolutely straight. Malcolm devised this impressive device, comprising a piece of round bar with the same diameter as the crank and two old con rods. Having pressed the new bush into the con rod, it goes in the middle of the device and the reamer is pushed through from one side to the other.

▲ PS6. Malcolm reamed a little and checked, then reamed some more until the fit was almost right. He then used a little emery paper and a lot of skill to bring the size just right.

▲ PS8. For the 4.2 litre engine there are three rings; the lower is the oil control ring, which comes in two parts (seen at left) and when assembled must not overlap – it should abut perfectly. The other two rings are scraper/compression rings and are tapered, so it's important that they are fitted with the word 'top' uppermost. Malcolm weighed the piston assemblies and balanced them by removing small amounts of metal from inside the lower skirt area. Naturally, they have to be balanced to the lightest piston and the same principle applies to the con rods.

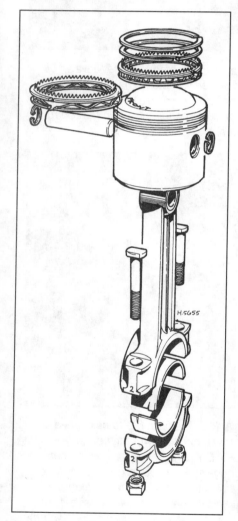

▲ PS7. This exploded diagram shows clearly the piston and con rod assembly.

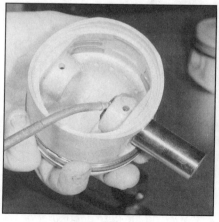

▲ PS9. He then fitted one of the little end circlips and oiled the little end ready for it to be pushed into the piston. Once it was in this position, he applied more oil into the oil hole to help lubricate it and …

▲ PS10. … the con rod bronze bush as the little end was pushed fully home, at which point the second circlip was fitted. Missing off a little end circlip is a very common DIY affliction and a very simple way to wreck your new engine.

▲ PS11. Malcolm also had other rebuilds in progress – these are the piston assemblies for a 3.4 litre XK unit. Spot the difference? There's an extra piston ring.

▲ PS12. Early XJ6s used a pressure-fed con rod, which had a hole running up its centre (i.e. the rod was hollow), as seen here at centre. Later cars kept the hole up the middle of the forging but not at the bottom, and latterly there were no holes or galleries.

FUEL – CARBURATION AND FUEL INJECTION

SAFETY WARNING: Before carrying out *any* operation on the fuel system, refer to the precautions in Chapter 2 and follow them implicitly. Petrol (gasoline) is a highly dangerous and volatile liquid and the precautions necessary when handling it cannot be over-stressed. Ban smoking and do not use naked flames. Always remove the battery earth terminal when dealing with your fuel system, to prevent the possibility of accidental sparks from short circuits. For tests where it needs to be connected and/or where the engine needs to be cranking or running, your safety efforts should be redoubled. Ensure that there is a suitable fire extinguisher (not a water-based model) to hand.

CARBURATION

All XJ6s were fitted with twin carburettors with the exception of later model 4.2 litre cars, which had Lucas-Bosch L-Jetronic airflow fuel injection. All markets utilised SU carburettors with the exception of North America, where Stromberg 175 CD2SE carburettors were fitted. Early cars used HD8 carbs, with an auxiliary carb to aid cold starting. An AED (Automatic Enrichment Device) was used for the same reason on the HS8 carbs which followed on, and also on the HIF7 (horizontal integral float) carbs used latterly. Carburettor-equipped models were fitted with dual electronic fuel pumps to bring the fuel from the twin rear-mounted tanks to the carburettors. Early models had them fitted inside the under floor area to the rear of the spare wheel well, but in later models, they were installed in the fuel tanks. Shown here are basic details of XJ6 carburation and details of removal. Haynes Manual 299 gives full details on how to dismantle, rebuild and set up all types of SU carburettor. Don't forget that the most important thing to remember when

dismantling/repairing carburettors is the need for total cleanliness; even the smallest piece of debris can cause havoc once the carbs are back in place. If you have a compressor and air gun, it can be used to great effect in cleaning out those intricate internal carburettor passageways. Use a proprietary carburettor cleaner to remove the gunge that builds up inside them over the years.

CARBURATION SPECIFICATIONS UP TO 1975

Size	Year	Spec	Pos	Type	Needle	Piston spring
2.8	1968-71	AUD 321F	F	HD8th	UVV	Blue/black
		AUD 321R	R	HD8		Blue/black
2.8	1971-72	AUD 415F	F	HS8 AED	BAU	Blue/black
		AUD 415R	R	HS8 AED	BAU	Blue/black
2.8 (lhd)	1972-73	AUD 536F	F	HS8 AED	BBL	Red/green
		AUD537R	R	HS8	BBL	Red/green
4.2	1968-71	AUD 357F	R	HD8th	UM	Red/green
		AUD 357R	R	HD8	UM	Red/green
4.2 (lhd)	1972-73	AUD 538F	F	HS8 AED	BBK	Red/green
		AUD 538R	R	HS8 AED	BBK	Red/green
4.2	1971-73	AUD 397F	F	HS8 AED	BAW	Red/green
		397R	R	HS8 AED	BAW	Red/green
4.2	1973	AUD 647F	F	HS8 AED	BAW	Red/green
		AUD 647R	R	HS8 AED	BAW	Red/green
4.2	1973	AUD 653F	F	HS8 AED	BCC	Red/green
		AUD 653R	R	HS8 AED	BCC	Red/green

CARBURATION SPECIFICATIONS FROM 1975 ONWARD

Size	Year	Spec	Pos	Type	Needle	Piston spring	Jet
3.4	1975-76	AUD 710F	F	HS8 AED	CUD 1169	AUC 4826	CUD 2753
		AUD 710R	R	HS8	CUD 1169	AUC 4826	CUD 2752
3.4	1975-76	FZX 1001R	R	HIF7 AED	CUD 8013	AUD 4355	LZX 1068
		FZX 1049R	R	HIF7	CUD 8013	AUD 4355	LZX 1068
3.4	1976-79	FZX 1053F	F	HIF7 AED	CUD 8021	AUD 4355	LZX 1068
		FZX 1053R	R	HIF7	CUD 8021	AUD 4355	LZX 1068
3.4	1979	FZX 1330F	–	HIF7	CUD 8021	AUD 4355	LZX 1068
		FZX 1330R	R	HIF7	CUD8021	AUD 4355	LZX 1068
4.2	1975	AUD 667F	F	HS8 AED	CUD 1150	AUD 4826	CUD 2753
		AUD 667R	F	HS8	CUD 1150	AUD 4826	CUD 2752
4.2	1975-76	FZX 1049F	FZ	HIF7 AED	CUD 8013	AUD 4355	LZX 1068
		FZX 1049R	R	HIF7	CUD 8013	AUD 4355	LZX 1068
4.2	1976	FZX 1252F	F	HIF7 AED	CUD 8023	AUD 4355	LZX 1068
		FZX 1252R	R	HIF7	CUD 8023	AUD 4355	LZX 1068

AED = Automatic Enrichment Device

CARBURETTOR	IDLING SPEED RPM
HD8 manual/auto	600/70
HS8 manual/auto	650/700
HIF7 manual and auto	750

JET NEEDLES

2.8 litre

HD8	UVV
Auxiliary carb needle	425/8

4.2 litre

HD8	UM
Auxiliary carb needle	425/8

3.4 litre

(HS8)	BCX
HIF7	BDW

4.2 litre

HS8 (no intake air control – ITC)	BAW
With ITC up to engine number 7L80999	BBK
With ITC from engine number 7L81000	BCC
HIF7 – external vent	BDY
Internal vent	BDN

▲ FUL1. It's more than handy to have the right tools for the job and this S-P fuel-kit includes adjustment and tune-up tools for most kinds of popular fuelling systems. One included is …

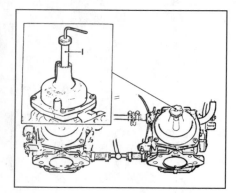

▲ FUL2. … this one required to set-up the Stromberg carburettors.

1. Screw
2. Body
3. Throttle spindle
4. Bush
5. Retaining ring
6. Retaining ring
7. Throttle disc
8. Adaptor
9. Gasket
10. Ignition union
11. Suction chamber
12. Damper assembly
13. Washer
14. Spring
15. Jet needle
16. Jet assembly
17. Jet bearing
18. Nut
19. Spring
20. Jet housing
21. Float chamber
22. Lid
23. Float
24. Needle and seat
25. Lever
26. Knurled pin
27. Gasket
28. Cap nut
29. Serrated washer
30. Aluminium washer

31. Filter
32. Banjo bolt
33. Fibre washer
34. Starter carburettor body
35. Acceleration needle assembly
36. Spring
37. Jet
38. Spring plate
39. Dust shield
40. Screw
41. Shakeproof washer

42. Solenoid
43. Bracket
44. Connecting arm
45. Banjo bolt
46. Washer
47. Washer
48. Banjo bolt
49. Fibre washer
50. Aluminium washer
51. Valve
52. Spring
53. Gland washer
54. Dished washer

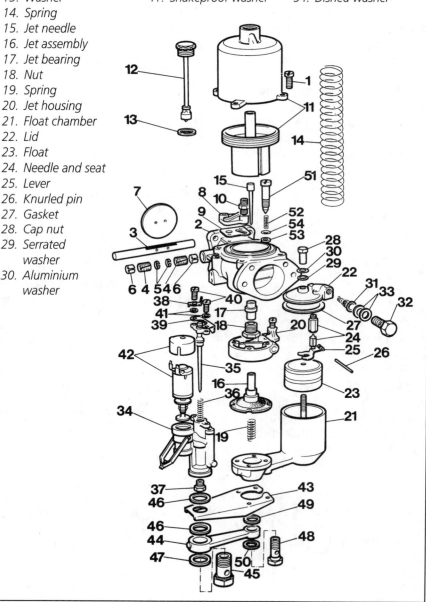

▲ FUL3. This diagram shows an exploded view of the SU HD8 carburettor as used on early models.

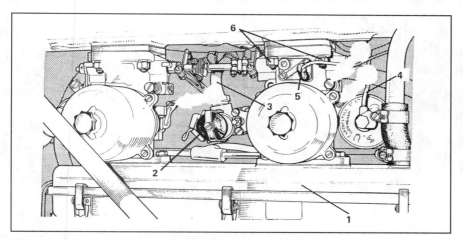

▲ FUL4. This diagram shows the layout and the positioning of the small auxiliary carburettor which took information from a thermostatic engine switch. The latter was dependent on engine coolant temperature.
1. Air cleaner assembly
2. Auxiliary carburettor
3. Mixture delivery pipe (auxiliary carb)
4. Carburettor fuel pipe
5. Vacuum ignition advance pipe
6. Flange nuts

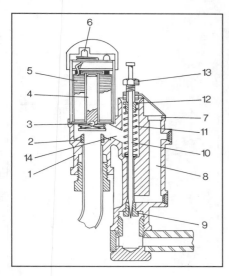

▲ FUL5. The auxiliary carburettor is a relatively simple device, as can be seen in this cutaway diagram.
1. Main body
2. Valve seating
3. Solenoid valve
4. Solenoid core
5. Solenoid winding
6. Solenoid terminals
7. Air intake
8. Air intake passage
9. Jet
10. Metering needle
11. Spring
12. Disc
13. Adjustable needle stop
14. Interconnecting passage.

▲ FUL6. This photo shows a pair of HS8 carburettors. Note that with these (and the later HIF7 carbs), the auxiliary carburettor had been replaced by an AED (automatic enrichment device), sitting between the carbs. The sequence here shows the removal of these carburettors from an engine that has already been removed from the car, with basic instructions assuming it is in the vehicle – adapt where required. Remove the air cleaner including back plate and filter element, close the tap on the fuel filter and disconnect the fuel line banjo unions for the carburettor float chambers.

▲ FUL7. Remove the crankcase breather pipes and …

▲ FUL8. … the distributor vacuum advance pipe.

▲ FUL9. Disconnect the throttle cables and the leads from the choke solenoid. On cars with auto transmission, remove the spring clip which secures the kick-down link at the rear of the rear carburettor. Disconnect the throttle return springs. Shown here is the removal of the hot air delivery pipe.

▶ FUL10. Remove the four nuts which secure each carburettor to the inlet manifold – the top inner nuts are a little tricky to get at. Note that there isn't room to get the ring of this combination spanner on the nuts at all four corners.

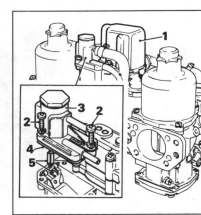

▲ FUL14. The HS8 and HIF7 SU carburettors were fitted with an AED (Automatic Enrichment Device) which increases the fuel/air mixture ratio when the engine is running below normal operating temperature. This diagram shows its component parts.
KEY
1. AED
2. Screws
3. Cover
4. Gasket
5. Needle valve

▲ FUL11. The carbs will almost slide straight off the manifold mounting studs, but it may be necessary to ease the carburettors away from the manifold before the last two nuts can be reached in order to release them from the last few threads. If the carbs stick on the manifold gasket, a sharp tap with the flat of the hand on the smooth dashpots should do the trick.

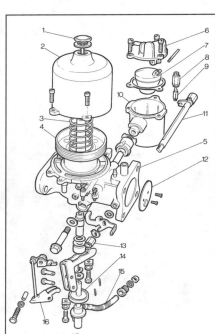

▲ FUL13. This is an exploded view of a HS8 carburettor.
KEY
1. Piston damper
2. Suction chamber
3. Piston spring
4. Piston/needle
5. Body
6. Float chamber lid
7. Float
8. Fuel inlet valve seat
9. Fuel inlet needle valve
10. Float chamber
11. Throttle valve spindle
12. Throttle butterfly valve plate
13. Hollow nut
14. Jet assembly
15. Flexible pipe
16. Jet fork.

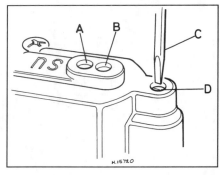

▲ FUL15. Where required, the AED can be adjusted. At routine service intervals, remove the plug and aluminium washer from the float chamber and withdraw the filter gauze. Clean with fuel and allow to air dry – use an air gun with your compressor if you have one. Refit carefully.
KEY
1. Main valve probe hole
2. Main valve adjustment screw
3. Screwdriver
4. Jet needle lift adjustment screw

▲ FUL12. The two carbs and the AED complete with linkages can be lifted clear all-of-a-piece and taken to the bench for examination and strip-down if required. Always renew the gaskets or O-rings located on the flanges, whichever type of sealing device is used.

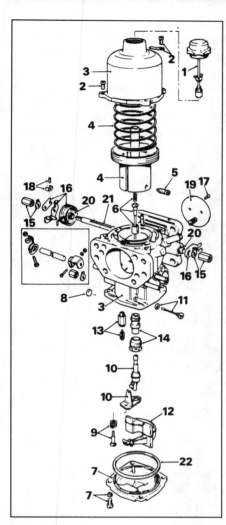

18. *Idle speed adjustment screw/clip*
19. *Throttle disc*
20. *Throttle spindle seals*
21. *Throttle spindle*
22. *Sealing ring*

FUEL INJECTION

Lucas-Bosch L-Jetronic airflow fuel injection was only fitted as standard in the UK to the latter 4.2 litre models, although it was introduced earlier on North American cars.

SAFETY NOTE: All the usual safety precautions relating to carburettor cars apply here, but even more so, because the nature of the system is that the fuel is under pressure. As such, extra care must be taken when dealing with the injected Series 3 models. Do not attempt to work on any part of your car's fuel injection system unless you are qualified to do so.

Fuel is drawn from the tanks by electric pumps from where it goes to the fuel injector rail after passing through a changeover valve, filter and pressure regulator. On air-conditioned cars, the fuel passes through a fuel cooler before being returned to the tank.

An electronic control unit (ECU) monitors information it receives from various sensors relating to engine load, speed, coolant and induction air temperatures and throttle opening, and from this it allows more or less fuel to be supplied to the cylinders, as required. There are six electro-mechanical fuel injectors (one per cylinder) which form part of a fuel 'rail' and a cold-start injector, acting as a choke would on a carburettor.

TECH SPEC

Idle speed	750 rpm
CO level	1.25-1.75%
Fuel pressure	2.55 bar (+/– 0.05 bar)

▲ *FUL16. Exploded view of an SU HIF7 carburettor*
KEY
1. *Piston damper*
2. *Suction chamber screws*
3. *Suction chamber*
4. *Piston and spring*
5. *Needle retaining grub screw*
6. *Needle, spring and guide*
7. *Bottom cover and screw*
8. *Sealing plug (jet adjusting screw)*
9. *Jet adjusting lever screw and spring*
10. *Jet and adjusting lever*
11. *Float pivot pin*
12. *Float*
13. *Needle valve and seat*
14. *Jet bearing and locknut*
15. *Throttle spindle nuts and lock washers*
16. *Throttle levers and spring*
17. *Throttle disc screw*

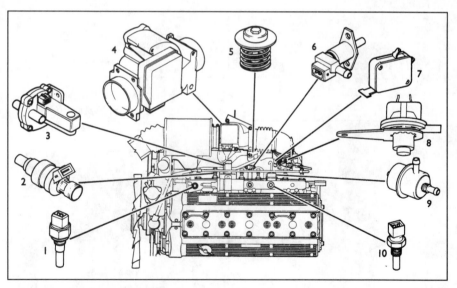

▲ *INJ1. Though fuel injection systems are inherently more complex than a comparable carburettor set-up, it has several advantages in that it offers better, smoother performance, better mpg and low emissions levels. The Lucas system as fitted to the XJ6 is far from being the most complex system. In most cases, faults can be traced to faulty sensors rather than a faulty electronic control unit (ECU) – which is what many owners worry about most. This diagram shows the sensors used on the XJ6.*
KEY
1. *Thermo time switch*
2. *Fuel injectors (6)*
3. *Auxiliary air valve*
4. *Airflow meters*
5. *Overrun valve*
6. *Cold start injector*
7. *Throttle switch*
8. *Full load vacuum switch*
9. *Fuel pressure regulator*
10. *Water temperature sender*

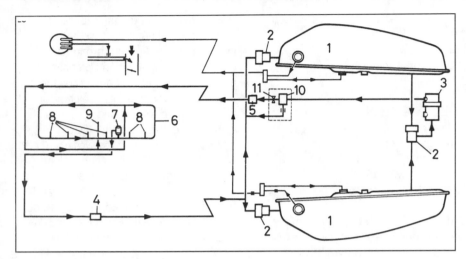

▲ INJ2. Schematic view of the fuel injection components and how they operate.

KEY
1. Fuel tanks
2. Tank changeover valves
3. Fuel pump
4. Fuel cooler (aircon cars only)
5. Fuel filter
6. Fuel rail
7. Fuel pressure regulator
8. Fuel injectors
9. Cold start injector
10. Air bleed valve
11. Non-return valve

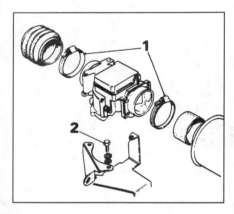

▲ INJ3. This diagram shows the component parts of the air flow meter (as removed earlier in this chapter). Undoing one bolt and loosening the Jubilee clips on the flexible air connections is all that is required.

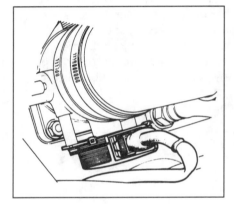

▲ INJ4. Two types of throttle switch were fitted. This is the type which is operated directly by a spindle and …

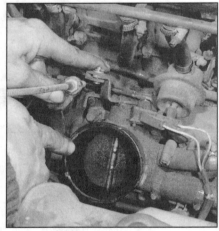

▲ INJ5. … this type is operated by a lever, seen at top, which moves the flap as in a carburettor.

DEPRESSURISING THE INJECTION SYSTEM

Early models did not feature a separate fuel pump relay, so the best way to disable the pump is to access it in the spare wheel well and remove the earth lead. On later models, remove the fuel pump relay from the bulkhead in the engine bay. In both cases, with the fuel pump disabled, crank the engine for 5/10 seconds. Replace the earth lead/relay and at this point, the system should be depressurised and will remain so until the next time the engine is cranked. Though the full pressure will not be present, there will inevitably be some spillage from various components if they are disconnected/removed. As such, it is vital to take all the usual safety precautions.

FUEL INJECTION BASIC COMPONENTS ELECTRONIC CONTROL UNIT (ECU)

The ECU is a very complex box of electronic components and is non-serviceable by the DIYer. However, most fuel injection problems tend to relate more to the sensors which supply information to the ECU than that device itself. As such, it's usually wise to assume that a fuel injection fault is being caused by a (relatively) cheap sensor rather than the expensive ECU.

FUEL RETURN VALVES

There are two fuel return valves, one situated under each rear wheel arch. It is important to note that they are 'handed' and, as such, are not interchangeable. This should also be mentioned when ordering replacement valves.

THROTTLE SWITCH

The basic aim of a throttle switch is to inform the ECU when the throttle is fully open so that maximum fuel enrichment is provided. European specification cars actually featured two throttle switches, the extra one of which was linked to the manifold vacuum. Subject to an adequate engine speed being maintained, the fuel is shut-off totally on the overrun.

INERTIA SWITCH
As a safety measure in case of an accident, the fuel injected XJ6 also features an inertia switch. This is fitted in the passenger side of the vehicle near the door pillar. Its object is to cut the power to the fuel pump in an emergency. Access for resetting can be gained simply by removing its cover.

AUXILIARY AIR VALVE
This is an idle air valve which allows extra air past the throttle butterfly to compensate for the additional fuel injected at very low temperatures. It is solenoid operated and controlled by the ECU. The air allowed to enter the engine via this valve is measured by the ECU via the airflow meter.

FLOODING PROTECTION
To prevent the engine being 'flooded' with fuel, a special circuit prevents the fuel pump from operating when the ignition is on except when the engine is being cranked or it is actually running.

OXYGEN SENSOR
North American models were fitted with a catalytic exhaust system which required an oxygen (or Lambda) sensor to be fitted in the manifold downpipe. Its function is to measure the oxygen/fuel ratio many times per second and pass the information to the ECU. When the mixture is too weak, the ECU puts more fuel to the injectors; when it is too rich, it reduces the amount of fuel, thus increasing the oxygen level. The ultimate aim is to achieve a fuel/air mixture of 14.75:1, a figure known as the Stoichiometric level. This is also denoted in scientific terms as the Greek letter Lambda – hence its adopted name.

BASIC CHECKS
If you have a multimeter, you can make several checks on your fuel injection system. WARNING – *never* connect a multimeter set to a resistance setting (Ohms) into a circuit which has power in it, as it could seriously damage the meter. Before making resistance checks it is wise to turn off the ignition. If you are making a check where the engine needs to be cranking, prevent it from starting by removing the negative (–) cable from the ignition coil.

COOLANT TEMPERATURE SENSOR (RESISTANCE – OHMS)
If the coolant temperature is reading incorrectly, this can affect the fuelling to the engine. Pull off the multi-plug and remove the switch itself. Connect the meter leads to the two terminals in the sensor. The resistance reading is related to the coolant temperature, getting lower as the temperature gets higher, as follows:

Resistance (Ohms)	Temperature (°C)
9.2K	–10
5.9K	0
2.5K	20
1.18K	40
600	60

The switch cannot be repaired and, if faulty, must be replaced.

THERMO-TIME SWITCH (Resistance – Ohms)
Poor starting and idling is often a faulty thermo-time switch which is failing to activate the cold start valve – hence it is similar to starting a cold carburettor'd engine without the choke. Pull off the multi-plug and then remove the switch itself. This should be immersed in coolant (many owners repeat the old method of thermostat checking – that of heating a pan of water on the kitchen stove!) whilst the meter is connected between the body of the switch and terminal G. The time readings should match those given here.

Delay (secs)	Temperature (°C)
8	–10
4.5	0
3.5	10
0	36

When the meter is connected between the body of the switch and terminal W, the resistance figure should be extremely low. The switch cannot be repaired and, if faulty, must be replaced.

COLD START VALVE (Voltage – approx. 12v)
Set your meter to VOLTS and connect to the wiring in the back of the cold start valve plug. When the cold engine is cranked, there should be battery voltage recorded. To further check, remove the injector and place in a suitable container so that no fuel can escape, and crank the engine. Fuel should spray into the container. The battery voltage and spraying fuel should both only last a few seconds. With a warm engine there should be no voltage recorded. The valve cannot be repaired and, if faulty, must be replaced.

INJECTORS (Resistance – Ohms/Voltage – 12v)
Before starting work, make sure the whole area is absolutely clean and that no dirt can get into the manifold or the injector itself. Do not remove the injectors unless the engine is stone cold. Remove each injector multi-plug and connect the meter across the two terminals on the injector. At an ambient temperature of around 20°C (68°F), you should get a reading of around 2.4 Ohms. With the multi-plug still removed, switch the meter to volts and, with ignition on, put the meter across the two contacts in the plug. There should be a battery voltage reading (around 12v). If not, it points to a break in the circuit somewhere, or possibly a blown fuse.

With a COLD engine and a depressurised system (see earlier) remove the injectors. Though the spray pattern can be tested on a DIY basis, it is better and safer to have the injectors checked for performance by a professional, preferably one of the Lucas/Bosch service centres. It is important that the injector pattern should be smooth and even in order to get the best performance. According to David Abbott of injection specialists, Performance Car Services, unless the injector is very old and/or damaged, he will usually be able to clean it electronically to bring its performance back to standard. Better still, the checking, cleaning and re-checking process usually works out to be less than half of the cost of new injectors.

AIR TEMPERATURE SENSOR
(Resistance – Ohms)
Remove the battery earth cable and the multi-plug at the air flow sensor. By definition, the resistance across terminals 6 and 27 of the sensor will vary depending on the temperature. Compare with the following table:

Resistance (Ohms)	Temperature (°C)
9.2K	–10
5.9K	0
2.5K	20
1.18K	40
600	60

OVERRUN VALVE
For this check the engine must be running, and so great care must be taken to avoid hot and moving parts.

Remove the valve (it's under the air distribution block) and the rubber hose between it and the throttle body. Start the engine and check the idle speed. If it is correct, then the idle valve is OK. If it decreases, the idle valve is faulty – it cannot be repaired and so should be replaced.

AUXILIARY AIR VALVE
The auxiliary air valve should only be operational when the engine is cold. Start the engine (cold) and, taking the usual care, gently squeeze the rubber hose linking the valve to the inlet manifold. The idle speed should drop – if it does, it shows the valve to be working properly. With a hot engine, repeat the test, at which point it should have no effect at all. If the valve fails either of these test, it should be replaced.

THE COOLING SYSTEM

The cooling system features a crossflow radiator and a pressurised header tank which is thermostatically flow-controlled. On smaller-engined models, the header tank is mounted above the radiator matrix. On those cars with larger engines it is attached to the inlet manifold, and an expansion tank is mounted on the left-hand wing valance. Coolant circulation is assisted by an impeller type pump driven by a belt from the crankshaft pulley.

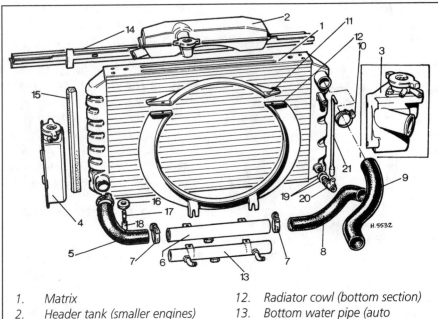

1. Matrix
2. Header tank (smaller engines)
3. Header tank (larger engines)
4. Expansion tank (larger engines)
5. Radiator hose
6. Bottom water pipe (manual 'box)
7. Hose clip
8. Radiator
9. Radiator top hose
10. Hose clip
11. Radiator cowl (top section)
12. Radiator cowl (bottom section)
13. Bottom water pipe (auto transmission)
14. Upper cross panel
15. Sealing strip
16. Mounting rubber
17. Stud
18. Distance piece
19. Fibre washer
20. Drain tap
21. Tap remote control

▲ RAD1. This diagram shows the basic radiator component layout.

▶ RAD2. The cooling system was changed slightly for Series 2 and Series 3 cars, although principles and basic layout were the same. Some air-conditioned cars were fitted with one or two cooling fans in front of the condenser and radiator. These were triggered by a thermo-switch which brought them into play when the coolant temperature reached 96°C (205°F). As ever with electric fans, they can operate after the ignition has been switched off. Later models had a generally improved cooling system which didn't require these fans (unless the cars were for export to very hot climates). Auto transmission cars featured a fluid cooler in the centre section of the radiator bottom hose. From 1982

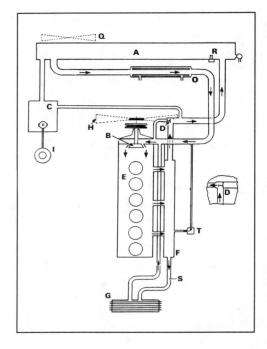

model year cars, the header tank was deleted and, instead, a combined header and expansion tank was fitted to the LH inner wing. The expansion tank vents into an atmospheric recovery tank, unless headlamp wash/wipe components are fitted. Later models were fitted with a low-coolant sensor, linked to a warning light on the dash. In pre-1982 cars it was in the radiator, in later models it was in the expansion tank.

KEY

A. *Radiator*
B. *Water pump*
C. *Expansion tank*
D. *Thermostat*
E. *Engine*
F. *Inlet manifold rail*
G. *Heater*
H. *Fan (engine driven)*
I. *Atmospheric recovery tank*
J. *Transmission fluid cooler*
K. *Fan (electric)*
L. *Fan thermo-switch*
M. *Heater water valve location*
N. *Throttle housing.*

VISCOUS FAN

The cooling fan is of a viscous type where a fluid driven coupling slips at between 1500/1900 rpm. The centre finned assembly to which the fan is bolted is called a Torquatrol drive unit and it is this which 'slips' as the engine speed rises, thus effectively removing the drive to the fan. It is fitted to early water pump pulleys by four bolts and to later pulleys by a single, centrally-positioned bolt.

▲ *RAD3. This photo shows the general layout of the fan and associated pulleys. This is the later-style unit.*

▲ *RAD4. This diagram shows the fan and fluid couplings for (a) early cars and (b) later cars.*

WATER PUMP

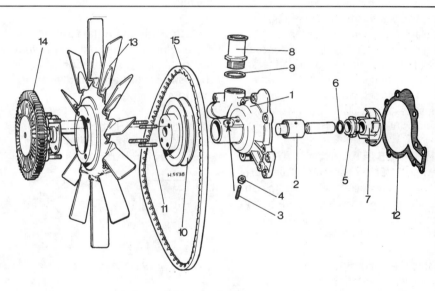

1.	Pump body	5.	Thrower	9. Copper washer	13.	Fan
2.	Spindle	6.	Seal	10. Fan pulley	14.	Fluid coupling
3.	Lock screw	7.	Impeller	11. Stud	15.	Belt
4.	Lock nut	8.	Adaptor	12. Gasket		

▲ *RAD5. Water pump removal is shown elsewhere in this chapter. This diagram shows the layout and component parts of the water pump and fan.*
It is possible to overhaul the water pump, but in reality, it is far more time and cost-efficient to obtain a new or exchange unit from a specialist, such as SNG Barratt.

CAPACITIES

ENGINE	UP TO 1977 Imp pints/litres/US pints	1977 ONWARD Imp pints/litres/US pints
2.8 litre	30/17/36	N/A
3.4 litre	30/17/36	32/18/38.5
4.2 litre	32/18/38.5	32/18/38.5

Torque wrench settings	lb/ft	Nm
Radiator mounting bolts	26	35
Retainer to radiator crossmember	18	25
Expansion tank to wing valance	18	25
Fan cowl upper bracket to body	7	10

ANTI-FREEZE

Your XJ6 always requires at least a 50/50 mix of water and anti-freeze; the latter prevents freezing up in the cold and it also raises the boiling point in summer. Drain the coolant and refill every two years.

PRESSURE CAP

The pressure cap puts the coolant under pressure which raises its boiling point – for every psi increase in pressure, the boiling point rises by around 1.7°C. A faulty cap allows the engine to boil its coolant early. Remove the cap (cold engine) and check the large outer rubber seal. If it's deteriorated, replace the cap. Check the inner vacuum seal by easing it open with a screwdriver. Replacement caps are now available from Halfords, and cost very little.

THERMOSTAT SPECIFICATIONS

Setting	Start operating temperature	Fully open temperature
Standard	159°F (70.5°C)	165°F (74°C)
High (extreme winter conditions)	174°F (78.8°C)	179°F (82°C)

Places like Halfords have thermostats available for all XJ6 models, so there's no excuse for running with an old one.

FLUSHING THE COOLING SYSTEM

Remove the radiator cap (cold engine) and look inside. Run your finger around the inner lip of the radiator and if it comes out covered in slimy brown sludge, flushing is overdue.

FLUSHING THE RADIATOR

Remove the radiator from the car and turn it upside down. Insert a *standard* hose pipe into the bottom hose hole. Make sure that water only comes from the top hose hole and is not leaking from elsewhere. You'll probably see brown sludge coming out at first, but then you should get clear water.

FLUSHING THE ENGINE

Open or remove the drain tap from the engine block and also the thermostat. Insert the hose into the thermostat hole and flush through until clear water runs from the drain tap.

DRAINING THE COOLING SYSTEM

IMPORTANT NOTE: With Series 2 cars fitted with air conditioning, the system MUST be discharged before removing the radiator. On Series 3 cars it is not necessary as long as the condenser and receiver/drier can be moved out of the way without placing undue strain on the hoses.

SAFETY: Only drain the coolant when the engine is stone cold, to prevent personal injury. In addition, there is the risk of cylinder head distortion and lots of expense!

For practical work in this section, reference should be made to the explanatory diagram in RAD1.

▲ *RAD6. Set the heater controls at 'hot' and ensure that you have a large enough receptacle to catch the coolant. There are two drain taps, one on the rear LH side of the cylinder block and one at the base of the radiator. This is operated from the top of the radiator by a remote rod. It will probably have seized, and you may be able to release it by using a strong piece of wire, but don't force it. Soaking in releasing agent can help.*

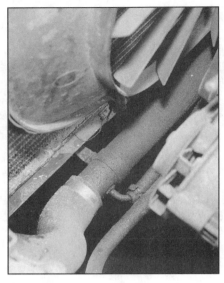

▲ *RAD7. Unscrew and remove the header tank/expansion chamber filler caps. The system is pressurised, so this is another reason for NOT working on the cooling system when it is anything other than cold. The expansion/header tanks can only be emptied by removing them from the car. Being an automatic transmission car, this particular model had a fluid cooler in the centre section of the radiator bottom hose, as seen here.*

▲ *RAD8. We opened the rear tap and, with the radiator tap seized, Phil removed the plug from the bottom water pipe, and drained the coolant from there also. Never re-use anti-freeze, but make sure you dispose of it responsibly, in the same way as used oil (see Chapter 2).*

REMOVING THE RADIATOR

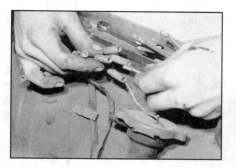

▲ RAD9. With the bonnet off, remove the radiator upper cross panel which comes off as a complete assembly with its own mini-wiring loom. Ensure that all wiring and other connections are removed beforehand.

▲ RAD10. For practicality, Phil bent the wires back and put them into the nose of the air inlet, taping them together with electrician's tape for extra safety.

▲ RAD11. He loosened the clip holding the air inlet pipe, so that the section fixed to the top of the upper cross panel could be removed with it. As well as the wiring attached to the upper cross panel, Phil had to remove all the hoses, too, including the two on the header tank. One of the hoses pulled off easily, but the other was more reluctant to leave

home, which shows that the hose was old and perished. A squirt of WD40 will usually free any sticking hose. Most jubilee clips are likely to be well-rusted and it's as well to bin them and replace when the radiator is refitted.

▲ RAD12. The plastic fan cowl is in two parts. The top part is secured to the radiator by two set screws and a further two secure it to the low fan cowl. Don't forget to remove the clip which secures the horn wire to the upright.

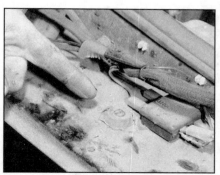

▲ RAD13. The radiator locates in rubber bushes in the upper cross panel at two points, one either side (this being at the RH side).

▲ RAD14. Phil removed the three captive bolts per side and then he was able to ...

▲ RAD15. ... remove it complete with various sections of wiring, part of the air inlet, relay, etc. Dismantling as a sub-assembly off the car is far easier!

▲ RAD16. Phil then removed the radiator top hose and bottom hose ...

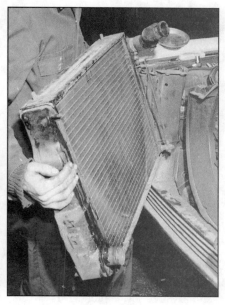

▲ RAD17. ... and lifted the radiator free. It fits by means of pegs which locate in rubber bushes.

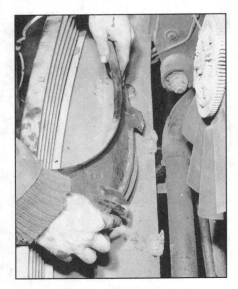

▲ *RAD18. The fan cowl lower section should be secured by two screws. However, it's common to find that at least one has been removed on a previous occasion and not been replaced by a less than fastidious owner. They are also prone to rusting solid.*

▲ *RAD19. The fluid cooler/lower hose section is held by two brackets mounted under the front crossmember in the position shown here.*

HOSES AND REPLACEMENT

Hoses should always be regarded as suspect unless you can be absolutely sure that they are fairly new. Even so, inspect all the hoses carefully – bend them back harshly and look for even the slightest sign of a hairline crack or perishing. If you find any, throw it away and replace it. A small crack may not look bad, but eventually it will give up under the pressure and heat to become a 3 in split, out of which will come litres of coolant. If you're on the motorway when it

happens, you could have wrecked your engine by the time you can stop! Check the jubilee or spring wire clips securing the hoses at either end for tightness.

RADIATOR RUDIMENTS

The radiator is a core of thin-walled, metal tubes with fins attached. The tubes used to be brass with copper fins, whilst the tanks were brass. In common with most manufacturers, modern Jaguar radiators tend to be aluminium cores (tubes and fins) with plastic tanks, although some brass/copper cores can have plastic tanks.

As the car moves along, the cool air flow passes over the tubes and cools the water inside them. The fins also help dissipate the heat. The hot water from the engine goes into the radiator at the top and by the time it reaches the bottom it is much cooler and ready to re-enter the system and start its journey once more.

INSPECTION

Take some time to inspect the radiator thoroughly, paying particular attention to the condition of the cooling fins and checking for obvious signs of leaks (if you have been using plenty of anti-freeze, there will be a tell-tale trail of dried blue/green coolant showing where it has been escaping).

The radiator is almost universally overlooked until it is seriously clogged up or rotten (or both). The trouble is that, it may have been under-cooling for some time before it is evident to the driver, which means that the engine could have been running too hot for many thousands of miles. The relatively small expense of replacing or repairing the radiator can often offset the relatively large expense of a major engine rebuild. And, of course, a failing radiator places extra strain on other cooling system components, notably the hoses.

RADIATOR RENOVATION

Northampton Autorads have a wealth of experience in repairing and making radiators and associated parts, stretching back over 30 years to when Don Goodwin first started the business. It has

grown since then, and now his son Bob is involved along with an enthusiastic staff headed up by workshop manager David Chater.

Autorads is heavily involved with the Jaguar scene, dealing with over 1,000 rebuilds/repairs every year for just about any breed of 'cat' you can name, going all the way back to the SS series! As a further measure of quality, since 1975, Aston Martin have fitted Autorads radiators to every Aston Martin that has left Newport Pagnell! Perhaps it's no surprise that there's now a family link with Jaguar and Aston?

Their knowledge and expertise extends across all areas of Jaguar cooling, including air conditioning, heater matrixes and metal water pipes. They recommend that, when the engine is out, the radiator should be checked/replaced unless known to be excellent. You can ruin a lot of hard work by not doing so. And, of course, you should check all hoses and metal water pipes – something else that can be supplied by Autorads.

XJ6 RADIATORS

All Series XJ6 models featured brass tanks. However, the Series 1 and 2 cars had pipes and nozzles which were SOFT-soldered into place. As a result, during the dismantling process, these have to be removed (in truth, they simply fall off with the effects of the blow torch) and, at a later date, replaced. This isn't a difficult job for the Autorads staff, but it does add a fair amount of time to the job. Our Series 3 radiator (as seen in this section) had the various tank attachments SILVER-soldered into place, and so remain in place during the core checking/replacement operation. All are called 'crossflow' radiators because the tanks are on either end of the core, rather than the more usual top and bottom. Andrew Hurlock at Autorads was responsible for turning our rusty, inefficient old radiator into a beautiful and perfectly functioning unit. My thanks to him for his skill and patience.

▲ RAD20. His first task was to check the core for physical damage and rotted fins. XJ6 radiators tend to be at their worst at the bottom front corners, as here, where they are vulnerable to collecting stone damage and rock salt from winter roads. Where the fins are not solid around the tubes, it allows them to overheat, which can cause splitting, as seen here. In this case, the fins had rotted quite badly, meaning that the core would have to be replaced. Even if the fins are OK, a core that is more than a few years old needs checking from the end to ensure that the tubes are not blocked (see later).

▲ RAD21. Andrew wire brushed the tank while applying heat from the blow torch in order to remove most of the paint. With the paint gone, a little more heat is applied until the original solder runs out.

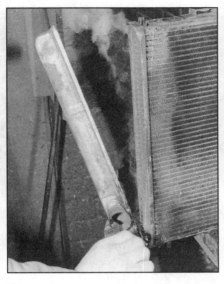

▲ RAD22. Then Andrew took a pair of pliers to remove the tanks from the core. This is quite simple, as any few remaining globules of solder will still be quite soft. Getting the tank clean is all-important, and the job is not finished yet.

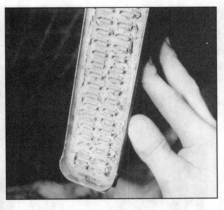

▲ RAD23. While the tanks cooled, Andrew checked the ends of the core for signs of blockage. At one end, it wasn't bad, with just two tubes being partially blocked. But at the other end, far more of the tubes were blocked and would have been contributing to any cooling problems. Any more than 10 blocked tubes will cause a noticeable difference in cooling performance. Where the fins are not damaged, Autorads would usually be able to clear blocked tubes, using special rods and water under pressure, removing the necessity for core replacement. It's no use ignoring either fin damage/corrosion or blocked tubes, because it can only get worse.

▲ RAD24. The now cooled tanks were given yet another wire-brushing before being heated up again and dipped briefly into a vat of hydrochloric acid for a final clean. This effectively takes a very thin layer off the top of the brass tanks. Once it has been cooled and rinsed in the water tank, a wire brush is used to brighten the tanks and ensure that there are absolutely no traces of dirt, grime or grease.

▲ RAD25. Each tank was given yet another going over with the wire brush. The difference between the 'before' and 'after' is obvious.

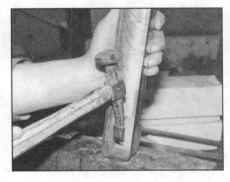

▲ RAD26. Andrew checked each tank for dents, and where they were found they were tapped out gently. It's important that the 'lips' of the tanks are perfectly flat in order to make a perfect join with the new core.

▲ RAD27. A new core was fitted. In case you can't see the difference, the old one is on the right!

▲ RAD28. Andrew checked the tube end plates for damage which could have occurred during storage or in transit. The edges have to be perfectly straight, and if they're not, Andrew has to tap them gently out with a hammer and flat edge as shown.

▲ RAD29. He wire-brushed the edges of the tanks to make sure that there were no foreign bodies to impede the soldering process, and then tapped the tank gently into place. It is not unknown for the tube plates to bow a little during manufacture, so he was very careful to ensure that the fit was tight all along the edge of the core.

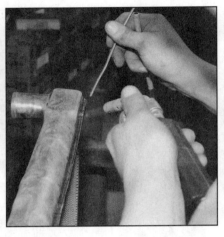

▲ RAD30. Flux was brushed on all around the tank join, and then the first of two soldered joins was made. This one actually sealed the tank, so the flame was set high and aimed deep down into the 'valley' of the tank. Andrew tinned the join as he went along, expertly using the solder and flux brush in the same hand.

▲ RAD31. When this join had been completed, Andrew fluxed around the join again ready for the second soldered join to be made. Because this was as much for appearance as anything else, it was important not to apply too much heat and disturb the original join. As such, the flame was set low and angled high. When finished there was a nice neat layer of solder filling the valley around the lip of the tank. Note how the top of the second join is exactly flush with the rim of the tank. It looks easy, but that's only because Andrew has had years of experience!

▲ RAD32. Once the tank had cooled, Andrew lightly used a dual-action pneumatic sander to remove any slight imperfections and blobs of solder from the tank, to provide a smooth surface for the paint.

▲ RAD33. Andrew then checked the front of the radiator for any fins which may have been damaged in transit or during the fitting process. It may seem like nit-picking, but bent-over fins can soon lead to cooling problems. With the other tank soldered into place in the same professional manner, it was time to head for the acid – or, rather, water – test. All orifices were plugged, and a compressed air line connected to feed air into the radiator at around 20 psi – in the car it usually only runs at around 10 psi. The radiator was then completely immersed in water and Andrew checked carefully for signs of those tell-tale bubbles which would mean a leak. Both sides were checked and, as the glassy smooth water surface proves, there were no leaks.

▲ RAD34. The finished article? Not quite – it requires a coat of paint and so it first had to spend 30 minutes in the drier to get rid of every last trace of moisture.

▲ RAD36. All Autorads radiators carry a brass plate which shows their name, telephone number and a serial number which they keep on file. This allows them to cross-reference the vehicle, date of manufacture and even the name of the employee who built the radiator, in this case …

REASSEMBLING THE BLOCK

▲ RB1. The rear circular oil seal cover is in two halves which locate by a hole/dowel at each side. Tim fitted the seal into one half, 'rolling' it firmly into the groove by using a steel shaft, and then cutting off any excess with a sharp blade. To prevent the seal moving around in the cover, a small amount of PU adhesive is used. The seal was sized using a special VSE tool (but the same as Jaguar used on the production line) in an old XK block.

▲ RAD35. Once totally dry, Andrew sprayed it matt black, making four passes per side in an effort to get paint right down into all the fins. Most owners opt for this finish, although gloss black is an option.

▲ RAD37. … Andrew, who presents the finished package here.

▲ RB2. The seals and covers were soaked overnight in engine oil.

COOLING TROUBLE-SHOOTING GUIDE

Symptom	Most likely cause	Answer
Overheating	Thermostat broken	Replace the thermostat
	Radiator blocked	Physically clear the radiator
	Water pump broken	Replace the water pump
	Incorrect anti-freeze mix	Drain and top up with 50/50 solution
	Engine out of tune	Adjust plugs/points/timing, etc.
	Dirty engine oil	Drain and refill with new filter
	Fan belt loose	Tighten to correct tension
	Viscous fan not working	Replace fan
Overcooling	Thermostat broken	Replace the thermostat
Loss of coolant	Damaged radiator	Repair or replace radiator
	Leaking/damaged hoses	Check and replace
	Cylinder head leak	Remove cylinder head to check
	Loose head bolts	Tighten bolts in correct sequence

▲ RB3. Meanwhile, Malcolm was preparing the block. He replaced the front oil gallery plug/washer, the four side plugs/copper washers, the large rear hexagon plug and the water drain plug (some models have a tap here).

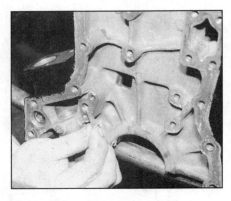

▲ RB4. He put the tiny cone filter in place – this will ultimately be behind the hydraulic tensioner.

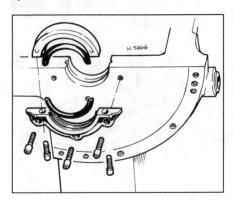

▲ RB5. This shows how the crankshaft oil seal assembly fits.

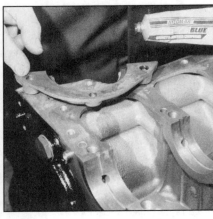

▲ RB6. Malcolm then turned the engine upside down and fitted the lower part of the crankshaft oil seal, using Hylomar universal blue gasket compound.

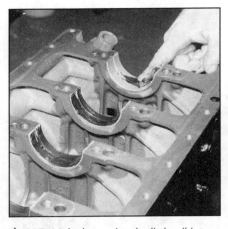

▲ RB7. Malcolm squirted a little oil into the galleries, before putting the main bearing shells in place and smearing some Graphogen colloidal graphite grease on the inner surfaces to provide some start-up protection for the bearings.

▲ RB8. He carefully placed the freshly balanced and cleaned crankshaft into position.

▲ RB9. The crank shells were put into the main bearing caps 'dry', but again Graphogen grease was used on the inner surfaces, and on the sides of the centre bearing cap thrust washers. Thrust washers are available in two sizes; standard and oversize +0.004 in (0.10 mm). They should be fitted according to the amount of endfloat in the crank (see later) and, if required, it is permissible to use standard and oversize at either side of the centre bearing cap.

▲ RB10. Malcolm fitted the main bearing caps, ensuring that the numbers aligned correctly – the block is stamped 1-6 and so are the caps.

▲ RB11. He used a Sykes-Pickavant torque wrench to ensure that the main bearing bolts were accurately torqued to 72 lb/ft (98 Nm).

▲ RB12. The top half of the crankshaft oil seal was fitted, again using Hylomar universal blue gasket compound and a test dial indicator used to check the crankshaft endfloat. This should be between 0.004 in and 0.006 in (0.10mm-0.15mm). He also checked that the crank rotated freely and that there were no 'tight' spots. Each main bearing bolt has a tab washer to be bent back. Those for the rear main bearing bolts being longer than the others – the plain ends should be tapped down round the bolt hole bosses.

▲ RB14. There's an arrow stamped into the top of each piston and this MUST face toward the front of the engine. The con rods are numbered and must go in the right order. An S-P ring compressor was used to get the pistons into the bores. It's virtually impossible to do this without a compressor, with the very real risk of snapping the rings and/or damaging the bore. Once the piston is squarely in the bore, use a wooden hammer handle to tap it gently down, making sure the crank is turned to a suitable position.

▲ RB16. … fitted the lower timing chain guide, followed by the intermediate guide – it's important not to tighten the securing bolts at this stage.

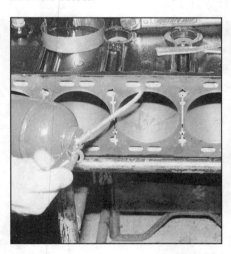

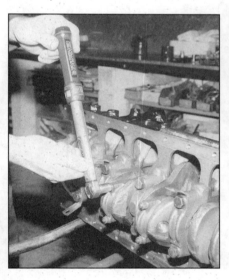

▲ RB13. Each con-rod bearing shell was fitted dry and Graphogen grease applied to the inside of the shell. The bores were all liberally oiled, as were the piston rings.

▲ RB15. The con rod caps were fitted and Malcolm applied a dab of Loctite 243 thread locker as a belt and braces measure to ensure the bolts didn't work loose. Once more, it is important that the bolts are torqued up correctly. Note that the figure of 37 lb/ft (50 Nm) is around half that required for the main bearing cap bolts. Malcolm put Nos. 1 and 6 pistons at TDC and went to the front of the engine, and …

▲ RB17. The complete timing chain assembly was fitted, and the bolts tightened.

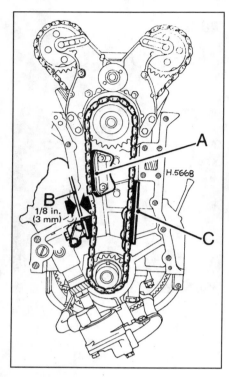

▲ *RB20. The two timing cover gaskets were put into place, using a smear of PU adhesive to keep them in place until Malcolm fitted the timing cover itself. He also fitted the front oil seal, using Hylomar compound, and smeared grease around the front of the crank.*

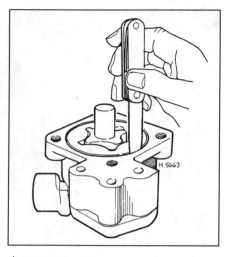

▲ *RB22. The oil pump outer rotor to body clearance should be no more than 0.010 in (0.25mm).*

▲ *RB18. Then the intermediate tensioner was tightened and the tabs on the locking plate prised over. The hydraulic tensioner was fitted and adjusted to have around ⅛ in (3mm) play, as detailed in this diagram – remember that the engine shown in the sequence here is upside down on the workbench. Again, all the locking tabs were prised over.*
KEY
A   Intermediate guide
B   Slipper-to-body clearance
C   Lower guide

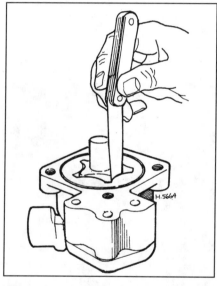

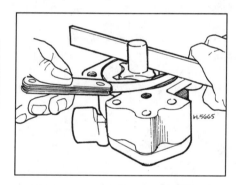

▲ *RB23. Use a straight edge placed across the rotor body to check the gap between the rotor end faces. This should not exceed 0.0025 in (0.06mm). See the strip-down section for an exploded view of the oil pump and distributor driveshaft assembly.*

▲ *RB19. The distributor pinion, crankshaft gear and thrust washer for the oil pump/distributor driveshaft were installed. The gear locates in a Woodruff key on the driveshaft. Here, Malcolm is tapping over the locking tab.*

▲ *RB21. Having removed the oil pump, as described earlier, open it up by removing the four bolts from the pump body. Take out the rotors but do not remove the inner rotor from the driveshaft. If either the rotors or pump body show signs of scoring or heavy wear, the most practical answer is to replace the oil pump complete. If everything looks OK, you will still need to check to ensure that the rotor clearances are within the tolerances specified. Use a feeler gauge to check that the clearance between the inner and outer rotors is no more than 0.006 in (0.15mm).*

▲ *RB24. This photo shows the cleaned-up and checked pump body with the spring and plunger mechanism. A tip from VSE is to always ensure that there is a washer at the end of the spring opposite the plunger; many DIY builders forget this small item – with big (expensive) results! The end cap gasket*

was smeared with Hylomar compound. Malcolm fitted the bush on to the distributor driveshaft, and added the oil pump. Assuming the clearances are OK, VSE always fit new O-rings. It was primed by filling it with oil. The three securing bolts all have locking tabs which have to be bent back.

▲ RB25. Malcolm then fitted the two oil pipes into position, greasing the ends of the pipes where they went into the oil pump to make them an easier fit. Don't forget the triangular gasket where the oil pipe goes into the crankcase – again Hylomar compound was used to make a really good seal. Note that all three pipe brackets are different. The sump gasket was laid carefully in place. It's a large gasket and, because there are 26 holes, it is distinctly flimsy. To aid location, Malcolm put the studs back into their holes.

▲ RB26. He fitted a new sump plug and copper washer, the baffle and the oil seal, before putting the sump carefully into place over the gasket. It's important to tighten the sump bolts in a cross-hatch sequence a little at a time to avoid distorting the sump.

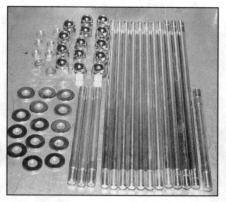

▲ RB27. After replacing the cone and damper on the crank, Malcolm started work on fitting the cylinder head, prepared elsewhere by Doug Whittingham. VSE always use new studs, bolts, washers and nuts. As you can see, the studs are of different lengths, and it's important to get the right stud in the right hole. The studs here are plated and made specifically for VSE, the object being to make them much more corrosion resistant. Because the company buys in such large numbers, the cost to the customer makes these uprated studs cheaper than standard studs from Jaguar.

▲ RB28. Malcolm applied copper grease to the threads going into the block before threading them in by hand and then tightening by using the S-P stud remover.

▲ RB29. The gasket used here is composite, so doesn't require any sealant, but steel-shimmed gaskets do. Make sure the word 'top' on the gasket faces upwards. Malcolm turned the crank so that No. 6 piston (the one nearest the crankshaft pulley) was at TDC. This can be confirmed by checking that the 'O' mark on the crankshaft damper is opposite the pointer on the crankcase. When fitting the new head, patience is required to ensure that neither head, block nor studs are damaged. It is vital at this stage that the mating surfaces are clinically clean.

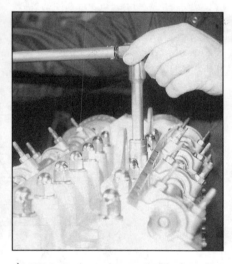

▲ RB30. Each stud was oiled before the washers and new chrome nuts were fitted. Don't forget to refit the engine lifting lugs.

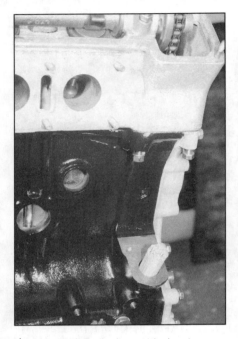

VALVE TIMING

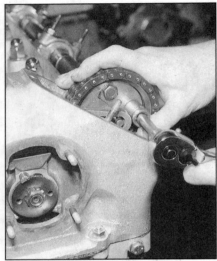

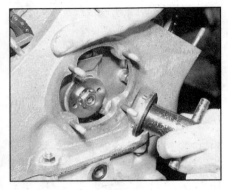

▲ *RB31. When dealing with the six nuts securing the front of the head, note that the harder spring washers go on the back two studs where they tighten up to the cast iron block. The front four tighten up to the alloy head and so have softer copper washers fitted. The cardboard insert in the distributor drive hole prevents dirt getting into the engine.*

▼ *RB32. The cylinder head bolts should be tightened a little at a time in the sequence shown here. It is important to take your time here, as applying too much torque could easily warp the alloy head. Make sure that the head is tightened down 'square'.*

▲ *RB33. With No. 6 piston at TDC (as described earlier) make sure the notches in the camshaft sprocket are at 90 degrees to a line touching the two rocker cover mating surfaces of the cylinder head. The adjusting plates should be pulled forward until the serrations disengage (removing circlips if already fitted). Fit the sprockets to the camshaft flanges and align the bolt holes – if they don't align, then turn the plate through 180 degrees. Fit the circlips to the sprockets, fit the two bolts and turn the sprocket until the remaining two holes are showing, and fit the bolts in them. Remember that each pair of bolts must have the locking tab plate fitted which has to be knocked over the bolts once they're tight.*

▲ *RB34. Tension the chain by inserting the stop peg (plunger) inward and rotating the serrated plate anti-clockwise. You'll need the special tool, as shown here. You can buy this, hire it from one of the clubs. Don't forget to fit the circlips on to the sprockets.*

▲ *RB35. The cylinder head studs are visible through the core plug holes. Malcolm squirted Loctite 648 on to the core plug holes in the block, before tapping the core plugs home using an impact socket just a little smaller than the plug itself to ensure that it went in exactly square.*

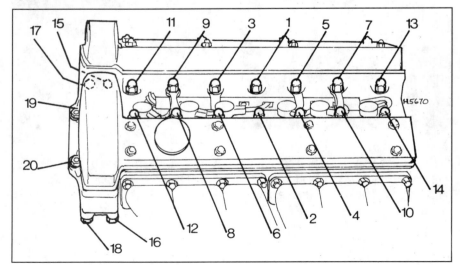

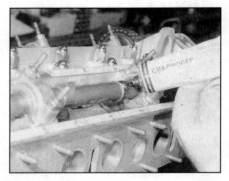

▲ *RB36. The rear water plate cover was refitted, and then the cam lobes were all given a smear of Graphogen grease to prevent them starting 'dry'.*

▲ RB37. A new set of plugs was fitted. Spark plugs are a greatly neglected part of most engines, and yet they have to work in atrocious conditions, dealing with tens of thousands of volts in temperatures upwards of 700° for hours on end. On the one hand they have to be 'hot' enough to allow easy starting and low-speed operation, and on the other they have to stay 'cool' during sustained periods of high engine speeds. If ever there's an unsung hero, it's the spark plug!

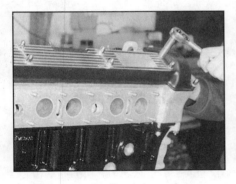

▲ RB38. Malcolm fitted the rocker cover gasket, using Hylomar on the metal surfaces of the head and the rocker cover. It's important not to over-torque the rocker cover nuts. Remember, it's a fairly light aluminium casting and very easily damaged. The oil-sealing capability must come from the gasket and Hylomar.

▲ RB39. A nice final touch is a new Jaguar badge.

SPARK PLUGS

Model		Type	Electrode gap
2.8 litre		Champion N7YCC or	0.032 in (0.8mm)
		Champion N7YC	0.025 in (0.6mm)
3.4 litre		Champion N12YCC or	0.032 in (0.8mm)
		Champion N12YC	0.025 in (0.6mm)
4.2 litre (carb)	UK models	Champion N11YCC or	0.032 in (0.8mm)
		Champion N11YC	0.025 in (0.6mm)
	US models	Champion 2404 or	0.025 in (0.6mm)
		Champion N12YC	0.025 in (0.6mm)

All spark plugs should be tightened to slightly more than hand tight, around 18 lb/ft (25 Nm).

▶ RB40. Every engine VSE produces is thoroughly bench-tested on this purpose-built rig. All aspects of engine running are checked, including timing, oil and water leaks and water temperature. VSE export engines all over the world, so they simply HAVE to be right when they get there. Note that, although this is a fuel-injection engine, it was the work of minutes to bolt two SU carburettors on to the side for testing purposes.

IGNITION TIMING
STATIC

Comp ratio	2.8 litre	3.4 litre	4.2 litre
7.8:1	–	8 BTDC	–
8:1	12 BTDC	–	8 BTDC
8.4:1	–	8 BTDC	8 BTDC
9:1	12 BTDC	–	8 BTDC
9:1	–	–	10 BTDC

DYNAMIC TIMING (using a strobe light)

Comp ratio	2.8 litre	3.4 litre	4.2 litre
7.8:1	–	18 BTDC at 1500 rpm	–
8:1	22 BTDC at 1000 rpm	–	20 BTDC at 1700 rpm
8.4:1	–	18 BTDC at 1500 rpm	10 BTDC at 1700 rpm
9:1	22 BTDC at 1000 rpm	–	10 BTDC at 1700 rpm
9:1	–	–	TDC at 650 rpm

Contact breaker points gap	0.014-0.016 in. (0.36- 0.41 mm)
Dwell angle	35 degrees (+/– 3 degrees)
Firing order	1 – 5 – 3 – 6 – 2 – 4

RUNNING IN YOUR NEW ENGINE

Having spent all that time and money building up your perfect engine, it would be a shame (to say the least!) to blow it up within the month. Tim Camp recommends the following regime as the prelude for a long and happy life with your rejuvenated XK:

SCHEDULE

Make sure that the correct amount of quality oil is in the engine and that the cooling system is sound, operating correctly and has the correct level of anti-freeze (it should contain corrosion inhibitor).

For the first 500 miles, do not exceed 3000 rpm. Do not labour the engine, and avoid constant speed driving situations (i.e. motorways). Vary engine speeds as much as possible up to the rev limit.

500 MILES

Drain the engine oil, fit a new filter and refill with a quality oil. With engine COLD, re-torque the cylinder head nuts to 60 ft/lb (82 Nm – check!). Check all hose clips, security bolts, etc., look around the engine and the engine bay for water/oil leaks. Check the ignition timing and the fuel mixture – this has to be carried out using an exhaust gas analyser, either at your local garage or using the Gunson's Gastester.

500-1000 MILES

Gradually increase the maximum rev limit from 3000 rpm to 4500 rpm for short bursts.

1000-1500 MILES

Build up to maximum revs for your particular model. Do not use sustained high revs for long periods.

1500 MILES

Repeat service instructions as per 500 miles.

The running in period is now complete, and the service intervals are now the same as the factory recommendations for your model.

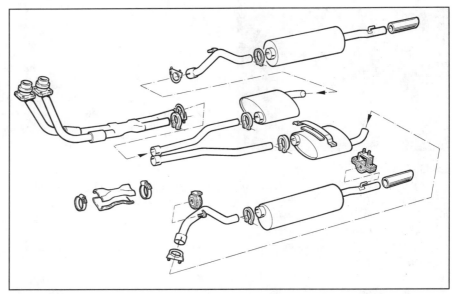

Tim is keen to stress that Jaguar engines suffer most wear and tear on short journeys – those less than 10 miles in total being particularly harmful. Make regular checks on the cooling system, anti-freeze content, ignition timing and carburation. If you do make mostly shorter journeys, make more frequent oil changes than recommended by the factory.

THE EXHAUST SYSTEM

SAFETY:
– **Only ever work on your exhaust system when it is stone cold.**
– **Obey the safety rules outlined in Chapter 2.**
– **If you're working on it whilst it is still on the car, always make sure that the ignition keys are in your pocket, to prevent unpleasant accidents.**
– **When working under your car, always wear goggles to prevent dirt and rust debris falling in your eyes.**
– **Wear gloves to prevent the rusty exhaust pipes/silencers damaging your hands.**
– **If using heat to remove rusted fasteners, keep well away from those petrol tanks!**

▲ *EX1. The XJ6 exhaust system, regardless of model, has always been a serious collection of pipery. There are two manifolds which bolt to a two-into-one down pipe at roughly the height of the engine mounting. They Siamese alongside the gearbox and join a V-shaped exhaust pipe section which runs under the centre section of the car. Each pipe has a large silencer just before the rear suspension subframe. There is then a complex section of exhaust pipe at either side before two more silencers are encountered – these are rubber mounted in recesses cut into either side of the boot floor. The twin pipes exit at either side of the boot. Though the exhaust systems differ in detail over the years, they all follow the same basic lines shown in this diagram.*

EXHAUST EMISSIONS

Exhaust emissions have become an increasingly important part of engine tuning over the years. The emissions total is a good indicator of whether your engine is working at its best, and all the top tuners will relate timing, plus, points and carburation directly to a CO meter, to ensure that all is well.

Moreover, emissions measurement has become part and parcel of the MoT test (see table below). Your Jaguar's exhaust will be linked into special equipment which measures the CO (carbon monoxide) content and also the hydrocarbon content in parts per million (ppm). SU carburettors are easy to tune in order to get the best possible reading. Fuel-injected cars are trickier to fine tune on a DIY basis, though it should be a far more efficient system and require much less attention.

▲ *EEM1. Whilst MoT testing stations use extremely accurate equipment for emissions testing, costing thousands of pounds, it is possible for DIY enthusiasts to check their emissions for rather less of an outlay. The Gunson's Gastester, and its digital 'Professional' sibling shown here, cost a fraction of that but enable surprisingly accurate readings to be made. Checking your emissions like this will help you tune your engine and possibly save the cost of a re-test when it comes to MoT time.*

EMISSIONS REQUIREMENTS RELATING TO NON-CATALYST PETROL-ENGINED VEHICLES

AGE	Hydrocarbons	Carbon monoxide CO
First used between 10th November 1973 and 1st October 1986	1200	4.5%
First used on or after 1st October 1986	1200	3.5%

These figures represent a decrease in the previous limit for older cars from 6% CO to 4.5% – it doesn't sound much, but it will be difficult, if not impossible, to make a worn engine of any age achieve that figure. Later models, i.e. those first used after 1st October 1986, have to achieve 3.5% in order to pass the test.

Most important, the testing procedure now reaches back to vehicles first used

on or after 10 November 1973 – previously, the oldest cars tested were those used on or after 1 August 1975, a difference of almost two years. Jaguars registered before 10 November 1973, at present, will be subject only to a visual smoke test.

CATALYST TESTING

All new cars registered on or after January 1992 were fitted with a catalyst exhaust system as part of EC law, and this forms a separate part of the MoT test. If you have an XJ6 fitted with a 'cat' (if it has been imported from the USA, for example), then in the UK it will only be subject to the normal emissions test, NOT a catalyst-specific test.

CATALYTIC CONVERTERS

No UK spec Series XJ6 cars were fitted with catalyst exhaust systems – only those bound for North America. The catalytic converter is found upstream of the main silencers and it looks like an ordinary silencer. However, its internal catalyst promotes the conversion of unburned hydrocarbons and carbon monoxide to water and carbon dioxide.

The following rules should be obeyed when dealing with a catalyst exhaust system:

1. Do not continue to operate the car if the engine is misfiring or runs-on after switching off the ignition.
2. Do not park on areas of long grass or other combustible materials – the converter gets extremely hot and it could start a fire.
3. Do not overload the car or pull excessively heavy trailer loads.
4. Do not operate the car downhill with the engine switched off.
5. Do not run the engine with a spark plug removed or HT leads disconnected.
6. Do not use the type of tyre pump which can be screwed into the spark plug hole.
7. Do not push or tow-start the car – in emergencies, use battery jumper leads.
8. Do not subject the converter casing to mechanical impact.

9. NEVER use leaded fuel – only unleaded must be used.
10. A damaged converter must be replaced – repair is not possible.

CORROSION

With any exhaust system, rot tends to occur away from the main source of heat – the engine. As such, the down pipes and front part of the system fares quite well. However, by the time we get to the first silencers, things are not so good, especially if the car is used mainly for short trips – the heating up and cooling down of the system causes internal condensation and, of course, rust. At the two rear silencers, the problem becomes worse. It's common to find that if one silencer or part of the exhaust system has failed, the rest won't be far behind. In general, it's better and cheaper to replace the whole lot at once rather than replacing odd components in the hope that the others will last a little while longer. And, of course, it's usual to find it impossible to remove one piece without damaging another.

REMOVING THE OLD EXHAUST SYSTEM

Fitting a new exhaust system – or even part of one – is never an easy task, especially when on a DIY basis without access to a ramp or, as in our case, an NBN Chassis Tilter. By definition, the fixings and clamps are likely to be as rusted as the holed silencers. The application of heat is one way to encourage them free, but this should be used with great caution – remember, there are two fuel tanks above the silencers! For the most part, cutting the offending items free may be the only option.

▲ EX2. The original (mild steel) silencers looked OK, but a little prodding in an area that looked like surface rust soon proved that it was serious rot.

▲ EX3. Where pipes and boxes join is a common rot area, as can be seen here.

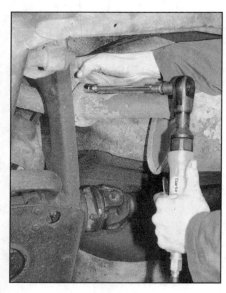

▲ EX4. Here, Phil is removing the bolts from the flange connecting the first silencer to the over-the-axle pipe. It was pointless trying to remove the silencer from the first V-section pipe, because the whole lot was going in the bin anyway.

▲ EX5. After removing the three bolts on each of the two flanges, he was able to lift the entire section away.

▲ EX6. The rear silencers and remaining pipe work will often be corroded together. Phil used an air chisel to get them apart. The more usual option is a hacksaw.

FITTING A STAINLESS STEEL EXHAUST SYSTEM

The golden rule when fitting any exhaust system is that you should never tighten any fitting fully until all the pipes/silencers are in position. That way, it can still be moved around slightly in order to ensure that it doesn't foul anywhere. In most of the photos here, the system was being *positioned*, rather than *fitted*.

▲ EX7. This is a Falcon stainless steel system from SC Parts Group. The cost of the system is little more than a mild steel system and it comes with a lifetime warranty against corrosion. In its component parts, even the full system takes up little space, which enables SC Parts to offer a mail order service.

▲ EX8. These are the silencer boxes. Note the polished tail pipes.

▲ EX9. It's likely that most fittings will be badly rusted, so we used an SC Parts full fitting kit to make life easier.

▲ EX10. Phil started at the back with the rear boxes. We used new mounts because the old ones were well worn. With the new mount in place …

▲ EX13. Phil threaded the rear pipe section over the driveshaft and into the second box. Again, the nuts and bolts on the flanges were only tightened loosely to allow for some movement.

▲ EX15. … final section of pipe to be on the LH side to match up with the manifold.

▲ EX11. … it was simple to insert the silencer into place.

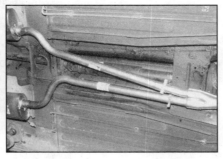

▲ EX14. The centre V-section of pipe is a single piece but it must go the right way round to allow for the unequal distances to the second boxes caused by the requirement for the …

▼ EX16. The final layout. It's at this point, you'll appreciate an extra pair of hands (or two) to help align all the pipes and boxes so that none is fouling the bodywork, propshaft, driveshafts, etc. Once you're happy with the positioning, make sure that none of the parts can move while you tighten up the clamps. It's really a shame to hang such a beautiful piece of engineering under the car where it can't be seen and will get covered in road dirt!

▲ EX12. If you've got a stainless exhaust, why not let the world know? There'll be no doubt, with this sparkling chrome tail pipe.

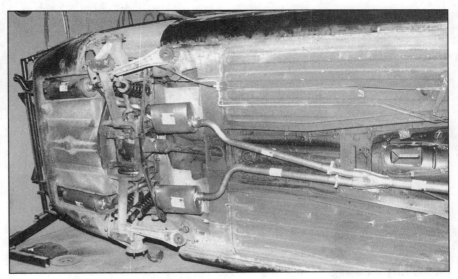

Chapter 7

Transmission

AUTOMATIC TRANSMISSION SPECIFICATIONS

TYPE 8 (Early Series 1 4.2 and 3.4 litre)

1.	2.40:1
2.	1.46:1
3.	1.00:1
Reverse	2.00:1
Torque converter	Infinitely variable

Oil capacity including torque converter:	Imp pints	Litres	US pints
ATF fluid to M2C 33G (Duckhams Q-Matic)	16.5	9.4	19.8

TYPE 12 (Later Series 1 3.4 and 4.2 litre and early Series 2, 3.4 & 4.2 litre)

1.	2.40:1
2.	1.46:1
3.	1.00:1
Reverse	2.00:1
Torque converter	Infinitely variable

Oil capacity including torque converter:	Imp pints	Litres	US pints
ATF fluid to M2C 33G (Duckhams Q-Matic)	16.5	9.4	19.8

TYPE 35F (Series 1 2.8 litre)

Gear	Ratios
1.	2.40:1
2.	1.46:1
3.	1.00:1
Reverse	2.09:1
Torque converter	Infinitely variable

Oil capacity including torque converter:	Imp pints	Litres	US pints
ATF fluid to M2C 33G (Duckhams Q-Matic)	16.5	9.4	19.8

TORQUE FIGURES

Model 8, 12, 35F	lb/ft	Nm
Torque converter to driveplate bolts	30	41
Torque converter housing to engine bolts	35	48
Oil pan securing bolts	13	188
Output coupling flange nut	50	68
Oil cooler pipe unions	21	29
Filler tube union nut	25	34
Transmission case to torque converter housing	60	83
Selector lever to transmission casing nut	35	48

TYPE 65 (Later Series 2, 3.4 and 4.2 litre)

1.	2.39:1
2.	1.45:1
3.	1.00:1
Reverse	2.00:1
Torque converter	Infinitely variable

Oil capacity including torque converter:	Imp pints	Litres	US pints
ATF fluid to M2C 33G (Duckhams Q-Matic)	14.5	8.2	17.4

TYPE 66 (Series 3.4 and 4.2 litre)

1.	2.39:1
2.	1.45:1
3.	1.00:1
Reverse	2.00:1
Torque converter	Infinitely variable

Oil capacity including torque converter:	Imp pints	Litres	US pints
ATF fluid to M2C 33G (Duckhams Q-Matic)	14.5	8.2	17.4

TORQUE FIGURES
Model 65, 66

		lb/ft	Nm
Transmission case to torque converter housing:	Small bolts	25	34
	Large bolts	40	54
Oil pan bolts		5	7
Oil pan drain plug		10	14
Output coupling flange bolt		80	109

Oil capacities:	Imp pints	Litres	US pints
Model 8, 12, 35F including torque converter	16.5	9.4	19.68
Model 65, 66	14.5	8.2	17.4

All auto gearboxes require ATF fluid to standard M2C 33G, such as Duckhams Q-Matic.

STRIPDOWN AND REBUILD OF AUTOMATIC GEARBOX AND TORQUE CONVERTER

The stripdown and rebuild of a Type 66 Borg-Warner gearbox and its torque converter was carried out by G. Whitehouse Autos Ltd. Graham Whitehouse has over 20 years experience in dealing with Borg-Warner gearboxes as fitted by most major British manufacturers, so there's no doubt he knows his stuff. The company regularly handles Triumph, Rover and even Rolls Royce 'boxes, though the workload comprises mainly Jaguar units. Graham's input to this chapter was invaluable and the skill with which he turned our rattly, dirty collection of bits into a superb, good-as-new Borg-Warner 66 gearbox had to be seen to be believed. My thanks to him for his time and patience.

DRAINING THE OIL

Before you start work on your gearbox, make sure you drain the fluid. We drained it prior to the removal of the gearbox along with the engine (see Chapter 6) but, even so, there's bound to be some left in. Graham is obviously well-equipped with a system of large metal trays which held any oil spillage and could be drained at any time.

▲ TC1. Seen here is Graham Whitehouse and the rest of his Halesowen-based team. Whichever 'box you have, Graham will know it inside out. As well as a rebuild service, there is also a complete range of spares for all Jaguar transmissions.

TORQUE CONVERTERS

Graham advises that whenever you replace or rebuild the gearbox, you should ALWAYS replace the torque converter. If a gearbox has become worn and clogged over the years, it will have been chewing up its gears and putting hundreds of slivers of swarf into the box itself and the torque converter. So, if you replace the 'box alone, lots of swarf will find its way back from the old torque converter into the new 'box. Not good!

STRIPPING AND REBUILDING THE TORQUE CONVERTER

▲ TC2. Unlike many gearbox specialists Graham can service and uprate torque converters – most offer only service exchange. He first placed the converter into the lathe and marked both halves so that it could be put together at the same point to prevent problems with imbalance.

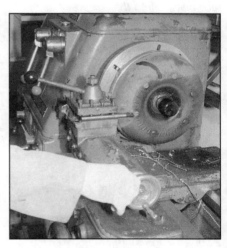

▲ TC3. He then powered up the lathe to run at a slow speed while the cutting tool evenly removed the original weld. Goggles were used to protect the eyes.

▲ TC4. He tapped it with a cold chisel and spread the component parts in a work tray.

▲ TC5. There are three typical problems; the splines tend to strip on the centre race that fits into the one-way clutch, the bearings wear and the vanes can come loose.

▲ TC6. To prevent the vanes working loose on a Whitehouse rebuilt converter, Graham hand-brazes every one to the body. As far as we're aware, this is unique and, to our knowledge, even an official Jaguar rebuilt torque converter won't have its vanes brazed in this manner.

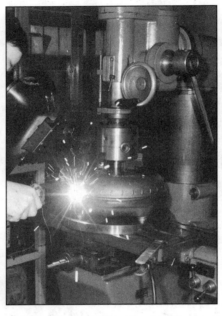

▲ TC7. When the checking, replacement and brazing procedures had been carried out, Graham took our converter to an old milling machine which had been 'doctored' for its new role in life. By using a special adaptor, the converter was held in place while he tack welded it together.

▲ TC8. When this had been carried out, he returned to the lathe where a very slow speed was selected. By fitting the welding gun to a special carrier, a perfectly even weld was created around the converter body.

▲ TC9. The next job was to check the run-out using a dial gauge. Borg-Warner originally quoted that anything less than 20 thou was acceptable, but at Whitehouse, it has to be less than 6 thou.

▲ TC10. The final test includes yet another purpose-built gadget. Graham connected an airline to the converter then immersed it in water. Any leaks show immediately as a row of bubbles. Not surprisingly, there was none here.

AUTOMATIC GEARBOX STRIPDOWN

▲ GBS1. Graham then turned his attention to the gearbox itself. The first thing he did was to check the authenticity of the box. All Series XJ6s are old enough to have had gearbox trouble at some point, and many have had gearbox swaps – often from a dismantler and often not like-for-like. It is a regular problem for Graham that a customer brings in a gearbox for rebuild only to be told that it is not the 'box it should be for the year of car! The simplest way to check this is to clean up the identification plate on the side of the gearbox, as here. The types of gearbox and the relevant reference numbers are shown below:

Engine	Date	Gearbox type	Ref. No.
2.8	10/68-9/73	35	9EG (>8924)
2.8	10/68-9/73	35	9EG (8925>)
3.4	5/75-10/80	65	033
3.4	10/80 >	66	6067
4.2	10/68-9/70	8	008
4.2	10/69-9/73	12	AS2-12J, 12A
4.2	10/80-10/83	66	6066, 6080
4.2	9/73-6/80	65	015
4.2	9/73-6/80	65	025, 056

Our Series 3, 4.2 litre car should have been fitted with a Type 66 gearbox and, as you can see from the numbering on the plate (6066), it was.

▲ GBS2. If there is any doubt, Graham examines the output shaft. The type 66 is noticeably larger in diameter and has more splines than the earlier (and often substituted) Type 65. A Type 66 shaft is seen here on the left with a Type 65 alongside. Torque converters can be identified by checking the angle of the 'fins' half way down the converter. The 4.2 litre fins are angled at 11.30am-5.30pm. The 3.4 litre fins are set at 1.30pm-7.30pm. These relate to

different stall angles of the car, the 3.4 needing more revs to pull away than the 4.2 litre model with its extra torque.

GEARBOX INTERCHANGABILITY
According to Graham, the gearboxes and corresponding torque converters for Series 2 and 3 cars are interchangeable. As mentioned, the later 'box is stronger, and so installing one of these in an earlier car is a good move, certainly from the point of view of practicality, though originality will suffer. However, though changing the other way is not advisable, some owners do it as a cheap quick fix in order to sell the car. As such, it's very important when you buy your XJ6 that you know exactly what gearbox you're getting. Series 1 cars have an obviously different box and, though it can be made to fit a later car, it requires no small amount of time, effort and money, and in truth there's little point in the exercise.

▲ GBS3. Just four bolts hold the bellhousing to the gearbox. Graham removed these using a socket and long extension, and was soon able to lift the bellhousing free. It was covered in the oil and grime of many years, and so it went straight into the steam/detergent wash whilst the rest of the dismantling process continued.

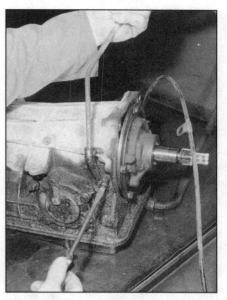

▲ GBS4. This is the gearbox breather tube – a steel tube with rubber end. This is bent in such a way to allow air out of the gearbox (because the oil expands as it gets hot) but prevent the ingress of water into the 'box. It fits into the gearbox via a plastic plug which almost always snaps as it is removed. Graham always replaces this part as a matter of course.

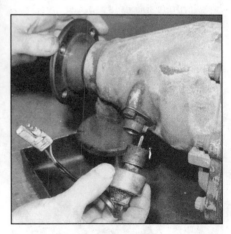

▲ GBS5. The speedometer transducer is secured by a knurled nut. If it is stiff, use large pliers or Mole grips to give more purchase. Make sure the electrical connector on the end of the two wires is clean and grease-free before replacement. Graham used a large ring spanner to remove the rear gearbox mounting pin, which is just below the prop shaft flange, and then removed the two bolts which secure the speedometer transducer housing.

▲ GBS6. The dipstick tube will certainly leak ATF fluid as it is removed.

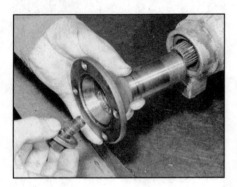

▲ GBS7. The propshaft flange is held by a single nut, and when removed it can be slid off its splines, as shown here.

▲ GBS8. There are eight fasteners on the extension case; four studs (two at the bottom, two at the top left, looking at the case head-on). They are different diameters and lengths, so note which is which. The other four bolts take sockets and ring spanners but not open-ended spanners. Actually pulling the casing off may require a few gentle taps from a rubber mallet.

▲ GBS9. The speedometer drive in the end of the casing may have to be prised gently out of its home. This is the speedometer drive complete. The rubber O-ring where it goes into the casing often fails. It's always wise to replace this, leaking or not.

▲ GBS10. Here, Graham is removing the speedometer drive gear from the output shaft. He's already removed the plug which secures the governor – note the locating pin in the plug which has to line-up with the indentation in the shaft. It's important not to confuse this with the two oil holes on the shaft.

▲ GBS11. These are the centre support bolts – two outside, one inside. At the ends of the bolts is a doweling section at the very end which locates in the centre support inside the gearbox.

▲ GBS12. Graham then removed the 12 bolts holding the sump, which gave our first glimpse of the complex innards.

▲ GBS13. At the bottom of the gearbox is the filter. Graham removed the screws, and pulled the filter free. There is also a spacer which shows that it is a model 66 gearbox which has a deeper sump than the model 65.

▲ GBS14. There are five pipes visible and they have to be removed carefully, using a screwdriver to ease them up – it's important to do this evenly to avoid bending or cracking the pipes. Make sure you know which pipes go where and in which order. Under one of the pipes you should find a round black magnet, there to pick up any pieces of swarf in the 'box and prevent them getting into the oilways and valve body. Graham often finds that it has been forgotten at a previous rebuild – a potentially expensive omission.

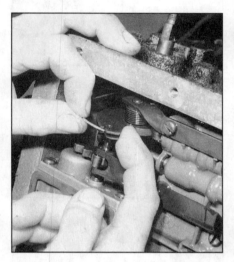

▲ GBS15. This is the kickdown mechanism with the cable being removed from the spring-loaded cam. The cable/nipple location is similar to that of a cycle brake.

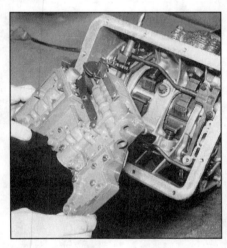

▲ GBS16. Three ⁷⁄₁₆ in bolts hold the valve body in place, which Graham removed to ease it free. This was placed carefully to one side for attention later on.

▲ GBS17. Two bolts secure the retaining plate which locates four pipes. With the plate removed the pipes followed. They simply pull out – Graham used long-nose pliers inserted gently into the bores. The longer of the two large bore aluminium tubes should have a rubber O-ring.

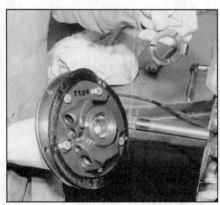

▲ GBS18. Graham removed the five bolts holding the front pump in place and eased it away along with the thrust washer (shown at top), and this was followed by …

▲ GBS19. … the front drum. Note there are two thrust washers here – one bronze and one steel.

▲ GBS20. The brake band adjusters can't be removed altogether, but they must be backed off. The adjuster for the front band is on the same side as the kickdown cable. There's a square-headed adjuster – which happens to be the same size as a Mini brake adjuster spanner – and a locking nut.

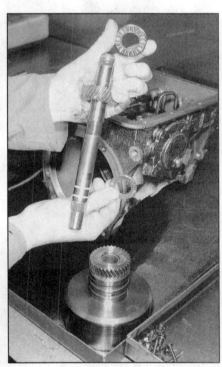

▲ GBS21. Graham pulled out the top/reverse clutch drum, the component parts of which are shown here. Note two needle roller bearings which are prone to wear.

▲ GBS22. This is a view into the gearbox looking at the front brake band and actuating strut – this is a small square-shaped piece of metal which pushes on the bottom of the brake band – other side is the adjuster. With the actuator pulled out, the brake band can be removed.

▲ GBS23. Graham removed the third centre support bolt, which allows the centre support to be pulled out, like so, followed by …

▲ GBS24. … the planetary gear set and thrust washer. According to Graham, some gearboxes have a shim for spacing, but not necessarily, so you'll need to make a note of what you've got for reassembly purposes.

▲ GBS25. The thrust washer inside the set may be round or, as here, 'triangular' – i.e. with three flats on a round washer.

▲ GBS26. Here, Graham is removing the rear band actuating pin (and strut on the opposite side). Then he was able to pull the rear band out – note that this is rigid, not flexible like the front band.

▲ GBS27. This is the output shaft coming out along with rear bronze thrust washer.

▲ GBS28. There are two servos – front and rear. The front (seen here) is secured by four bolts, the rear by six. The two assemblies are different in design though they have three main parts – cover, piston and O-ring, and a spring which slides along the shaft.

▲ GBS29. The rear piston is wider than the front, but not as deep. Tap it gently out. Graham used an S-P air blow gun, as it's quicker and less likely to damage any components.

▲ GBS30. The rear servo in its component parts.

▲ GBS31. The gear selector quadrant is held on to the gear selector shaft by spiral pin and split pin. Graham used a small punch to tap this free, and levered the shaft carefully up with a flat-bladed screwdriver. This shows the gear selector shaft and quadrant assembly. The kickdown cable is held in the casing by an expanding plastic ferule. Ideally, you should use a special tool to remove this. However, it is possible to use a 10mm socket pushed over the end and tapped lightly from the inside of the casing. This compresses the ends of the ferule and allows it to be pulled out.

▲ GBS32. The parking rod can be pulled free when the bracket, held by two screws, has been removed.

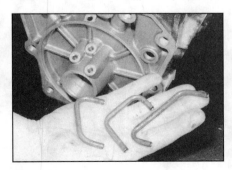

▲ GBS33. The parking pawl was then removed and Graham then pulled out the three governor pipes from the back of the 'box, followed by the remaining pipes from within the case. Ease them out very carefully, a little at a time, using a wide flat-bladed screwdriver.

▲ GBS34. This is the rear band actuating strut pin being removed. Graham checked that the pressure port plug could be turned easily – it's used for the testing procedure. He removed the brake and adjusters to check and clean the threads.

▲ GBS35. This is just part of the gearbox assembly – the torque converter has already been refurbished and the valve body has yet to be dealt with.

AUTOMATIC GEARBOX REBUILD

▲ GBR1. Cleaning the case properly is a vital part of the work. Graham works to the following regime. 'I clean the case with paraffin in a Clarke's parts washer and inspect it. It's quicker to dry it with compressed air. I check where the output shaft runs through the back of case that there are no deep groves where the sealing rings fit – if there are, the case is useless. I check where front servo moves in and out inside the casing; if there are marks, they may be able to be polished lightly with fine wet and dry paper. If not, again, the casing must be changed. The rear servo runs in its own housing rather than in the main casing. It is vital that no foreign matter gets into the 'box and so I always use cotton rags to prevent bits of fluff getting into the 'box. I use Vaseline, rather than grease, because this disperses in the fluid. Grease tends to collect in globules in the 'box and can cause problems.' He checked the case for cracks, though it is very rare to find any, and every thread was cleaned and checked for cross-threading.

◄ GBR2. From the comprehensive Whitehouse stores Graham collated a master kit of items which he includes in any gearbox rebuild. It includes: all gaskets, all rubber seals and oil rings, metal and Teflon sealing rings, friction clutch plates, front and rear metal clutch plates, front seal, rear extension seal, filter and diaphragm spring for front forward clutch. If you are working on your own gearbox, this kit, and all other parts are available on a mail order spares basis.

▲ GBR3. Graham also replaces the front and rear bands, kickdown cable and plastic breather, and fits a new filter. The bands are cheap and almost impossible to clean properly.

▲ GBR4. The clutch friction plates were soaked in ATF fluid so that the 'box doesn't start dry. The rear band handles reverse gear and it takes a lot of punishment, so Graham rebanded it with a heavy duty lining made specially for him in the USA.

▲ GBR5. Graham started the reassembly process by reinstalling the three governor pipes. They have to be tapped very gently until they are fully home.

▲ GBR6. The brake band adjuster must be fitted the right way round – one end is flat and there is a bevel on the other – because they match with the adjuster screws. The adjuster has to be screwed out to lowest tension, then the locking nuts loosely applied.

▲ GBR7. When fitting the rear band apply lever, the pin must be fitted with the machined section to the rear, followed by the parking pawl, its spring and the retaining plate which holds both of these items in place. Tighten down the retaining plate and check that the spring action of the parking pawl works correctly. If there is excess wear or chunks missing from it, the gearbox won't lock in PARK position.

▲ GBR8. The parking rod goes in next, into a hole topped off by the retaining plate. It clips into the parking selector

quadrant. Graham checked where the selector shaft runs in the seal for scores or marks which would cause oil leaks. It is sometimes possible to polish out light scoring with a little emery paper, otherwise a new shaft is required. This one proved OK and was put into position after fitting a new Vaseline-coated seal in the casing.

▲ GBR9. It is important that everything relating to this assembly is in the right order. Slide the shaft through the seal into the gearbox then add the spring steel washer, followed by the tube and gear selector quadrant. The shaft has to be turned so that the hole matches the hole in the quadrant to fit the new spiral pin and split pin. The latter has to be tapped into place, taking care not to hit the case or any other parts.

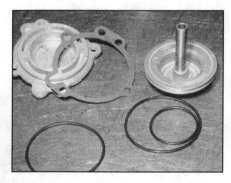

▲ GBR10. Graham checked the front servo carefully for wear and damage. Light scoring on the bore may polish out using emery paper, otherwise a new servo is required. Seen here is the casing, piston, new O-rings and gasket.

► GBR11. The complete assembly was fitted into the casing. Graham coated all moving parts and O-rings with Vaseline. He used the air gun to ensure that the piston operated correctly. A foot pump and adaptor will do the same job.

▲ GBR12. Here are the rear servo components, cleaned and checked for wear. Again, Graham used Vaseline for lubrication and to hold two small O-rings in place. Because of the spring, it is important to tighten down the bolts evenly. Once in place, it was air-pressure tested as previously.

▲ GBR13. Looking deep into the case, Graham used Vaseline to hold the rear thrust washer in place. Note that it has three lugs so can only be positioned one way.

▲ GBR14. Graham checked the surface of the output shaft for signs of wear and also that the splines were not damaged or twisted – this can happen with the prodigious torque available from the 4.2 litre engine. He then checked the internal teeth of the ring gear for chips or score marks and the bush in the centre of the ring gear for wear – normally noticeable by a lip formed at the bottom where the planetary gear that fits into it hasn't been touching. This bush was worn. Finally, he checked the machined surface inside the ring gear, where the needle roller runs, for scoring or other damage. The easiest way to remove the faulty bush was to collapse it using a suitable drift, but …

▲ GBR15. … tapping the new bush into place would damage it. Graham used the press to install it. Ensure the planetary assembly fits into the new bush housing before going any further.

▲ GBR16. The output shaft bore was coated with Vaseline to ease the passage of the shaft. Graham fitted three new sealing rings on the shaft – they're all the same size, and serve the same purpose as piston rings – and more Vaseline was applied. The shaft was 'wobbled' into the case in order to ease it and the new rings into the chamfered hole without damage to the components.

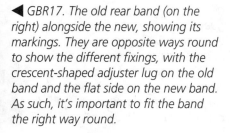

◄ GBR17. The old rear band (on the right) alongside the new, showing its markings. They are opposite ways round to show the different fixings, with the crescent-shaped adjuster lug on the old band and the flat side on the new band. As such, it's important to fit the band the right way round.

▲ GBR18. This is the planetary gear assembly, comprising the one-way clutch outer race and securing wire, and one-way clutch which goes in the centre. Graham made the usual checks for wear and damage. Blue spots on the drum surface are signs of overheating. The assembly comes as a complete unit and any problems mean a complete replacement. Graham checked the inner surface of the one-way clutch outer race for any signs of scoring, and the bush in its centre for wear. If the bush is badly worn, it can be replaced, but if it's scored, the race must be replaced. The one-way clutch has a number of sprags. Check the inner and outer surfaces of the sprags for flats worn on them. If they have flats, another one-way clutch is required. This only fits one way (naturally) and it has a lip which must face upward, away from the rear of the gearbox. The triangular thrust washer goes into the centre of the planetary assembly and Graham 'stuck' it in place using Vaseline. On the back of the assembly, the first to go on are any shims (where applicable), then the thrust washer with face upwards and finally the bearing with the lip upward.

▲ GBR19. Before fitting the centre support, Graham checked the inner surface where the three seals run on the top and reverse clutch. It can sometimes wear three grooves – if so, it must be replaced. He also checked where the one-way clutch runs on the outer part of the centre support. If it's lightly grooved or marked, it may be possible to polish it smooth. Graham fitted the centre support into the one-way clutch and checked that it was the right way round – it should turn clockwise when holding the planetary gear assembly but NOT anti-clockwise – if it does, the assembly has been fitted upside down and it's best to find out now! Before fitting the assembly, the centre support and its position in the casing was lubricated with gearbox oil. There are holes around the circumference of the centre support – three are for locating bolts (two outside, one inside) and the others are oil holes which must match exactly for obvious reasons. The locating bolts can then be fitted and tightened.

▲ GBR20. Graham then fitted the front band (this has to be fitted the correct way so that the adjusters work properly) and the driven shaft – once more using Vaseline for lubrication.

REAR CLUTCH DRUM

▲ GBR21. Remove circlip and pressure plate, turn over and check for scoring where the clutch plate has been running on it. Replace if any scoring. Take out five friction and five steel clutch plates. Graham always fits new plates, so any damage is irrelevant. Fit the Borg-Warner tool to the drum to compress the centre spring and remove the circlip. Graham has one because it's his business, but you should be able to hire one from your Jaguar club.

Turn the drum over so the gear is uppermost. Unhook three sealing rings and remove them. Apply compressed air to the hole and remove the piston from the drum. Remove the outer square section seal from the piston and the O-ring from the clutch drum.

Graham inspected the rear face of the gear where it runs on the bearing for marks, and the teeth of the gear for wear or chips on teeth. Where the band runs on the surface of the drum, he looked carefully for scoring. He checked inside the piston where it runs on a small O-ring. He advises that light scoring can be relieved with fine wet and dry or emery cloth. He checked that the ball-bearing relief valve was free and working and then put all the reusable parts into the washer.

▲ *GBR22. The three new interlocking sealing rings were snapped into place, and a new rubber O-ring was fitted. A special spring compressor was used to push the spring down far enough for the circlip to be fitted.*

▲ *GBR23. The are five steel platers and five friction plates. The steel plates are slightly dished and can go in either way round as long as they all go in the same way – the plates must be free to turn. The square section spring steel circlip went on to the clutch drum with the bronze washer, and then the whole unit was ready to be fitted into the case, wobbling slightly to ensure that sealing rings go on properly.*

FRONT CLUTCH DRUM

Remove the circlip holding the input shaft assembly in place. Pull the input shaft off and remove the fibre thrust washer. Pull out the inner clutch hub and remove five friction plates – four steel and one pressure plate. Remove the circlip above the diaphragm spring, pull out the spring and apply air pressure to

the middle of the drum at the oil drilling hole and the piston will pop up. Remove the six Belville washers and the rubber inner seal. Remove outer square section seal from the piston.

CHECKING FOR WEAR

The inner bore of the clutch drum runs on two Teflon sealing rings and needs to be checked for wear – if not perfect, it must be replaced. The inner part of the piston, which runs on a large rubber inner seal, needs to be checked for scoring, and the relief valve must be working. Graham replaces the clutch pack if it has scored the pressure plate where the friction plate runs against it. He also always changes the diaphragm spring, as they invariably crack in use, for a stronger aftermarket spring. Check that the splines are not worn or damaged on the input shaft, that the bush at the back of the shaft isn't worn and that the surface where the last clutch friction runs on it is in good order.

FRONT CLUTCH REBUILD

▲ *GBR24. The sealing ring grooves on the shaft were filled with Vaseline ready for the split Teflon sealing rings. Graham applied lots of Vaseline to the shaft and lower part of the inner drum. The piston seal goes on first, followed by six Belville washers. These are dished and have to go in alternately face-down then face-up. At the top is a steel wear ring so that the diaphragm spring presses on that rather than the soft aluminium. There is*

a square section O-ring which fits on the outside of the piston. Graham put plenty of Vaseline in the pump itself. A special tool is slotted temporarily into the housing to ensure that the piston fits squarely in the bore and that the O-ring isn't damaged in the process. This is tapped lightly with a plastic mallet until the piston is fully home.

▲ *GBR25. Then Graham fitted the diaphragm spring with the circlip – facing upwards. Before putting it back into the gearbox, Graham coated the mating surfaces with Vaseline and then installed it, tipping it from side to side and twisting to ensure that the splines fitted correctly.*

▲ *GBR26. The pressure plate is fitted with the flat surface forward and the bevelled surface to the back. The centre hub is fitted with the hollow section innermost, followed by the fibre thrust washer with yet more Vaseline. Then the nine clutch plates were installed, after which …*

▲ GBR27. ... the input shaft was fitted.

FRONT PUMP STRIPDOWN AND REBUILD

▲ GBR28. To strip the front pump you need to undo five bolts and the one flat-headed screw. Don't undo the bolts all the way, though, so you can gently tap the heads of the bolts to make the pump separate.

▲ GBR29. The pump stator is the part with the long splined shaft. Check the splines on shaft for wear, a common model 66 problem. Check the inner surface of the pump where the gears run and the bottom of the splined shaft where the inner gear runs, for wear – light scoring is acceptable, but if there's a ridge there it must be changed.

▲ GBR30. This is the pump body with gears in it. Mark the gears so they go back in the same way – Graham used a black felt tip pen. If you mismatch on rebuild, they'll be noisy and the wear patterns won't coincide. Pull the gears out and check the bush in the centre of the small gear to make sure it's not badly scored – if so, it should be replaced. Check the outer gear to make sure there is no wear and also that the pump body itself where the gears run isn't worn. There's a bush in the centre that the torque converter runs on. Any wear or

scoring here and the bush should be replaced. The front seal has to be prised out and a new one fitted when the pump is rebuilt. Remove the rubber sealing ring that runs in the groove on the outside of the pump body itself.

▲ GBR31. Graham always fits a new seal into the front of the pump body. The early type seals were slightly taller (seen on the left in this photo) and better than later ones, so he always uses early seals regardless of original fitment. Fit the two gears, making sure the marks align. The rubber O-ring is fitted to the outside of the pump body – plenty of Vaseline.

▲ GBR32. The two halves of the front are aligned, and drawn together gradually by screwing down the bolts slowly in a reversal of the procedure shown earlier. A gasket and thrust washer are fitted. The oil holes on top have to be inclined towards the plastic breather.

▲ GBR33. Check the end float on the input shaft using a dial test indicator. There should be some play to allow it to work properly, but not so much that it slops about. Officially, this should be 8-29 thou. Graham then tightened the band adjusters up. His rule of thumb is to tighten them as far as possible, then back off around ¾ of a turn.

▲ GBR34. The four pipes were fitted into the gearbox casing and secured in place by this retainer. The larger one was fitted with a new O-ring, held in place by Vaseline to prevent it dropping off during the assembly process.

COMPLETE VALVE ASSEMBLY AND COMPONENT PARTS

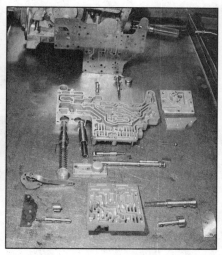

▲ GBR35. The valve body is a complex piece of equipment, and getting it wrong is very easy. Cleanliness is particularly important.

▲ GBR36. The primary pressure regulator spring usually wears and gets shorter (seen on the right alongside a new spring). By definition, if it is too short, it can't be producing the right tension and, therefore, the 'box will not work as it should.

▲ GBR37. All the valves should move freely in the bores, which should be checked for wear and scoring. Serious wear means the serious expense of a new valve body. Wear or damage to valves almost certainly means corresponding damage to bores. Another problem is that when the clutch plates have deteriorated, debris finds its way into the valve body and clogs things up. Graham checked and cleaned all parts, replacing where necessary and using the S-P air blow gun to make sure that all oilways were clear. Always protect your eyes when using compressed air like this.

▲ GBR38. Clean, fresh and as good as new, Graham replaced the valve body. Note the manual valve (seen here at top left of the photo) which must be correctly located in the indent in the selector quadrant – if it isn't, nothing at all will work!

◀ GBR39. Graham always fits a new kickdown cable assembly. He pushed it through from the outside of the casing and connected it to the spring-loaded cam.

▲ GBR40. This is the selector quadrant detent spring. Once fitted, it's advisable to try out the various selector positions to ensure that it works correctly.

▲ GBR41. It was then time for Graham to refit those five pipes so they look like this. Clearly, they must be right, otherwise you could be facing another big bill!

▲ GBR42. Then the new filter and spacer (model 66 only) were fitted. When refitting the sump, Graham recommends a gasket but no cement. It doesn't need it and if any gasket goo gets into the valve body, there'll be big trouble.

GOVERNOR, EXTENSION CASE AND SPEEDOMETER ASSEMBLY

▲ GBR43. This is the governor in its component parts. Centrifugal force caused by the speed of the shaft rotating causes the spring to compress, which in turn determines whether the gearbox selects 1, 2 or 3 (when it is in 'Drive').

▲ GBR44. Graham assembled and fitted the governor, making sure that it lined up correctly with the indent in the shaft and the two oil holes, vital for its lubrication.

▲ GBR45. Graham used an old socket and rubber mallet to tap the new seal into the extension case – it's always worth fitting a new seal. Jaguar fitted them flush to the edge of the pump body because it looked better, but Graham always drives them fully home because it is less likely to leak oil.

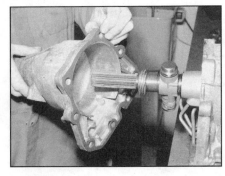

▲ GBR46. The case is put on with a new gasket – dry again, for reasons mentioned earlier. Don't forget that the fixings are studs and bolts of differing lengths and diameters. Graham put the gearbox in gear in order to tighten the propshaft flange nut.

◀ GBR47. This is the speedometer drive assembly. The rubber seal rarely gives trouble, but it's wise to replace it. The drive retaining plate (at bottom of photo) holds the cable in. Once assembled, it can be tapped gently into place whilst turning the output shaft in order to locate the gears.

TESTING THE GEARBOX

▲ *GBR48. With the gearbox fully rebuilt, it was to be painted with an incredibly tough and long-lasting German paint. At this point, the gearbox is tested on a specially imported rig from America – a procedure that sets Whitehouse gearboxes apart, for you'll have to search long and hard to find another gearbox rebuilder who has such facilities. As Graham says: 'Most of our gearboxes are exported, and we couldn't send them thousands of miles only to find that there is a slight problem that requires them to be returned!' In truth, it is Graham's total attention to detail that has gained the company so many export customers in the first place! Using a small block (5.7 litre!) Chevrolet engine, the 'box is really put through its paces, the 'load' being added at the output shaft by a connection to a special dyno.*

STALL SPEED TEST

The stall speed is the maximum speed at which the engine can drive the torque converter impeller whilst the turbine is being held stationary. To run the test, drive for around five miles, or until the engine and transmission are at normal operating temperature. Stop the car, apply the handbrake and chock the wheels. Select '1' or 'R' and fully depress the accelerator keeping an eye on the tachometer. DO NOT do this test for any more than 10 seconds or try it more than once in a half hour period, otherwise the transmission could overheat with obvious unpleasant and expensive results.

HOW TO JUDGE THE RESULTS

MODEL 8 ,12, 35F Max. rpm reading	GEARBOX MODEL 65, 66 Max. rpm reading	PROBABLE CAUSE
<1000	<1400	Stator free wheel slipping
1350-1550	circa 1600	Engine not developing full power
1600-1700	2200	Condition normal
>2100	>2400	Clutch slip or brake band fault

MANUAL TRANSMISSION AND CLUTCH

Most XJ6s were produced with automatic gearboxes, although a manual option has always been quoted. Until the late '70s, when the Rover SD1-sourced five-speed unit was used, the 'box was always a four-speed with overdrive option. Removing the gearbox is the same procedure in essence as that for removing the automatic 'box – although it is possible to remove the 'box from under the car with the engine *in situ*, it is usually recommended that they should be removed as a unit and then split outside the car.

4-SPEED ALL SYNCROMESH

Gear	Ratios
1	2.933:1 (3.238:1 on later models)
2	1.905:1
3	1.389:1
4	1.00:1
Reverse	3.378:1 (3.428:1 on later models)

Laycock de Normanville type 'A' Overdrive (where applicable)
Ratio 0.778:1 (2.753:1)

Oil capacities:		Imp pints	Litres	US pints
Early models:	Without overdrive	2.5	1.5	3
	With overdrive	4	2.25	4.75
Later models:	Without overdrive	3	1.6	3.25
	With overdrive	4.5	2.4	5

OIL TYPE Hypoid gear oil SAE 90EP

5-SPEED ALL SYNCHROMESH

Gear	Ratios
1	3.321:1
2	2.087:1
3	1.396:1
4	1.00:1
5	0.883:1
Reverse	3.428:1

Oil capacity:	Imp pints	Litres	US pints
	3.5	2.0	4.2

OIL TYPE

Drain and refill	Hypoid gear oil SAE 75
Top-up only	Hypoid gear oil SAE 80EP

However, if baulking problems are encountered, it is permissible to drain the oil and refill with Dexron II type ATF (automatic transmission fluid).

CLUTCH

A Borg and Beck 9.5 in (241mm) diaphragm spring clutch with graphite release bearing was fitted to all models. Clutch operation is hydraulic using Duckhams Universal Clutch & Brake fluid (to exceed SAE J1703D).

The diaphragm spring is riveted inside the cover-pressing with two fulcrum rings interposed between the rivets and cover-pressing. The spring pivots on the two rings. The release bearing is actuated by depressing the clutch pedal, which causes a deflection of the spring, which in turn pulls the pressure plate from the driven plate. At this point, the clutch is freed.

CLUTCH REMOVAL

Having removed and split the engine/gearbox as described previously in this chapter, unscrew the bolts securing the clutch assembly to the flywheel. Note the position of any balance weights, which must be refitted in the same positions. Withdraw the assembly and take care not to catch the driven plate as it falls from the face of the flywheel.

Examine the friction facings and expect to find a highly polished glaze through which the 'grain' of the material can be seen. If the facings have dark, highly glazed patches which hide the grain or there is a black-soaked appearance, then they have been oil-contaminated and should be replaced. Oil contaminating means oil leaks, which should be rectified before replacing the clutch – the most likely causes of leaks are from the crankshaft rear oil seal or the gearbox front oil seal. The rivets should be well below the surface of the friction material – if not, replacement is required. Make sure that the clutch springs are secure and not cracked or otherwise damaged. The splines in the centre hub should show no sign of damage – if so, the plate must be renewed.

CLUTCH RELEASE BEARING AND WITHDRAWAL MECHANISM

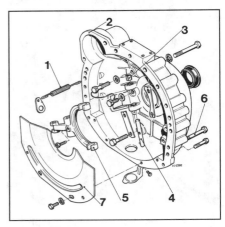

▲ SPC2. Check the withdrawal lever and release fork for signs of wear, replacing if required. Should you replace the clutch bearing? If it has done 20,000 miles, definitely so. Disconnect the small coil spring clip at each side of the release fork and lift the bearing from the fork – use new spring clips when installing the new bearing.
KEY
1. Pushrod return spring
2. Bellhousing
3. Release fork pivot bushes
4. Release fork pivot pin
5. Release fork
6. Clutch bellhousing-to-engine bolts
7. Bellhousing lower cover plate

CLUTCH ADJUSTMENT

On most XJ6s, the clutch is virtually self-adjusting and will retain the correct free-movement throughout the life of the clutch driven plate. Early models utilised a threaded pushrod for adjustment, which will probably only be required if other clutch components have been changed.

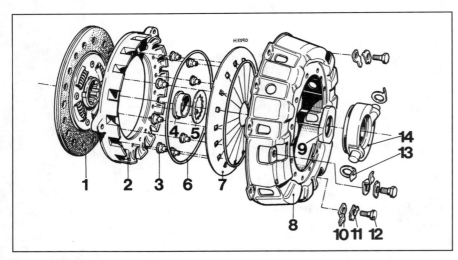

▲ SPC1. This diagram shows an exploded view of the clutch assembly. The diaphragm spring is riveted inside the pressure plate cover and has two fulcrum rings interposed between the shoulders of the rivets and the cover. The diaphragm spring pivots on these rings, and depression of the clutch pedal actuates the release bearing causing the diaphragm spring to deflect and pull the pressure plate from the driven plate (friction disc) thus freeing the clutch.
KEY

1. Driven plate	6. Fulcrum ring	11. Tab washer
2. Pressure plate	7. Diaphragm spring	12. Set screw
3. Rivet	8. Cover pressing	13. Retainer
4. Centre sleeve	9. Release plate	14. Release bearing
5. Belleville washer	10. Retainer	

CLUTCH MASTER CYLINDER AND CLUTCH PEDAL

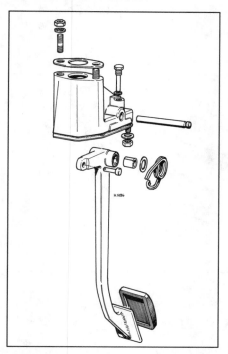

▲ SPC3. Disconnect the fluid outlet pipe from the master cylinder and remove the four setscrews (accessible from inside the car) securing the pedal box to the engine compartment rear bulkhead. Remove the pedal box and master cylinder as an assembly. Undo the setscrew and remove the pedal pivot pin, pulling the pedal back to withdraw the pin. Remove the split pin and clevis pin from the pushrod fork end, and remove the two setscrews to release the master cylinder from the pedal box.

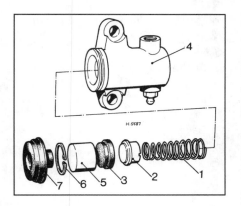

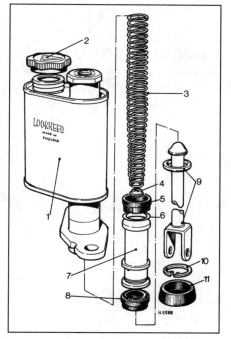

▲ SPC4. Clean the dirt from the master cylinder before dismantling it further. Pull off the rubber boot and depress the pushrod slightly to extract the circlip. The internal components will be ejected from the master cylinder body. Wash all components in clean hydraulic fluid (or methylated sprit – meths – nothing else) and examine the surfaces of the piston and cylinder for scoring or 'bright' wear areas. Any undue signs of wear means that the entire clutch cylinder assembly must be replaced. All master cylinder parts, from the complete unit to seal kits, are available from SNG Barratt.

CLUTCH SLAVE CYLINDER

◀ SPC5. Unbolt the slave cylinder cover and slacken the fluid pipe union, but leave the flexible hose in situ. Slide the rubber boot off the slave cylinder/ pushrod and disconnect the return spring (not fitted to later models). Unbolt the cylinder and withdraw it from the pushrod which will remain attached to the release lever. Unscrew the cylinder from the hose union and plug the broken connections to prevent dirt and dust getting into the works. Clean any dirt and debris from the cylinder then remove the circlip. Use air pressure from a tyre pump to 'pop' the internal components out on

to a rag laid on your bench. Once more, cleaning should be carried out using only clean hydraulic fluid or meths. As previously, 'bright' areas mean that everything should be replaced. If wear is minimal, you can use a repair kit from SNG Barratt to bring the slave cylinder up to specification. When replacing new seals, using only your fingers to put them in position – make sure you put them in the right way round. Before putting the new components into place, dip them into clean hydraulic fluid.

KEY
1. Piston return spring
2. Cup seal former
3. Cup seal
4. Body
5. Piston
6. Circlip
7. Rubber boot

INSTALLATION

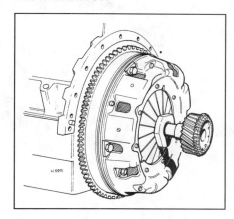

▲ SPC6. Before working with new clutch friction components, always make sure your hands are completely free from grease. Hold the driven plate against the flywheel so that the projecting side of the hub is towards the gearbox. Place the pressure plate assembly so that the 'B' stamped close to one of the dowel holes aligns with the same mark stamped on the flywheel. Insert the clutch bolts finger tight and centralise the driven plate by using a specific centralising tool or an old gearbox shaft or suitably stepped mandrel. When it has been centred, tighten the bolts evenly, a little at a time in a cross-wise pattern to the specified torque, then withdraw the centring tool.

TORQUE FIGURES

	lb/ft	Nm
Clutch bellhousing to engine bolts	35	48
Gearbox output coupling flange nut	100	136
Overdrive unit output coupling flange nut	100	136
Gearbox mainshaft front nut	120	163
Top cover bolts	14	19
Rear cover bolts	14	19
Clutch bellhousing to gearbox bolts	42	57
Oil filler plug	25	34
Oil drain plug	25	34
Propeller shaft flange nuts	34	46
Reverse lever set screw	25	34
Clutch cover bolts	20	27
Slave cylinder bolts	25	34

PROPELLER SHAFT AND UNIVERSAL JOINT

▼ UJ1. An open propeller shaft, divided in the centre, is fitted. The forward end of the rear section is supported on a rubber-mounted ball race and a universal joint (UJ) is fitted at its rear end. The front section (seen here) has a UJ at each end

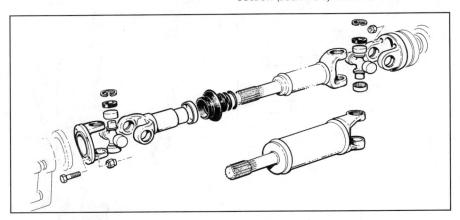

and incorporates a sliding spline within a flexible gaiter. No lubrication or maintenance is required as all joints and bearings are prepacked with grease during production. The power and, more importantly, torque of the XK engine (particularly in 4.2 litre guise) places a great strain on the propshaft UJs, and any signs of trouble (see later) should be heeded sooner rather than later. Specialists such as SNG Barratt can supply anything from a UJ rebuild kit to a complete propshaft, so spares are not a problem in this area.

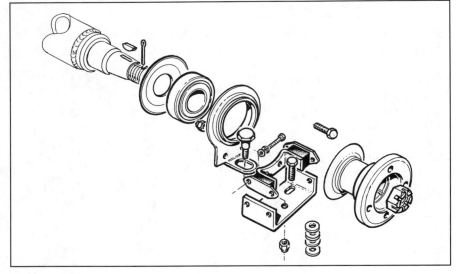

◄ UJ2. Halfway along the propshaft is a centre shaft bearing, an exploded view of which is seen here.

◄ UJ3. This diagram shows the components of the Series 3 propshaft assembly.
KEY
1. Centre yoke bolt
2. Circlips
3. Spider
4. Front section
5. Gaiter

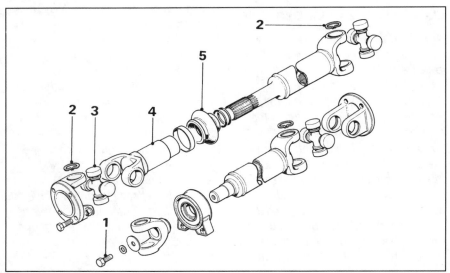

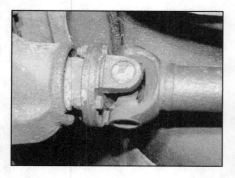

▲ UJ4. The final section of the propshaft leaves the centre bearing and goes into the differential via a conventional UJ, shown here.

▲ UJ5. Here is the propshaft to gearbox coupling on a Series 3 model (shown with the gearbox removed from the car).

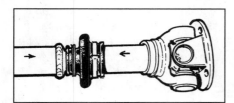

▲ UJ6. Before removing the various sections of the propshaft, it pays to mark them carefully so that they can be positioned in the same way on reassembly. This is a vital point when it comes to avoiding vibration from misalignment. Even if the parts are only slightly out, it can be enough to cause an aggravating vibration. This shows the propshaft sliding joint alignment marks.

REMOVING THE PROPSHAFT
FRONT

▲ UJ7. Before removing the propshaft, the weight at the rear of the engine should be taken by using an engine hoist to 'ease' the strain slightly. For access, the exhaust intermediate section will have to be released. The heat shield has to be removed – Phil Blundell is working here on our 'project' Series 3 car which, of course, was on its side held securely in the NBN Chassis Tilter. (Also, the engine, gearbox and entire exhaust had been removed at this stage.) If you're working with your car on the deck, you'll have to raise it and support it with axle stands. Wear gloves to protect your hands from rust, and goggles to prevent debris getting in your eyes. Disconnect the engine rear mounting plate by withdrawing the setscrews, spacers and washers. On manual cars, place a jack under the gearbox, using a strong piece of wood between the two to prevent damage, and release the self-locking nut which secures the engine rear mounting. On automatic transmission models, put the jack under the oil pan, again with a block of wood under the cast section of the transmission casing. Remove the bracket and engine mounting plate from the gear casing. Disconnect the gearbox/propshaft coupling flange and the flanges just forward of the centre bearing, and lift the front section from the car.
Early cars. Unscrew and remove the four self-locking nuts from the front and rear flanges of the propshaft and compress the shaft at the sliding splines section and withdraw it towards the rear of the car.

REAR

▲ UJ8. The front section of the propshaft is held to the centre bearing section by four bolts/self locking nuts. The centre bearing is secured by …

▲ UJ9. … two bolts to the support plate, which in turn is secured by four bolts to the underside of the car.

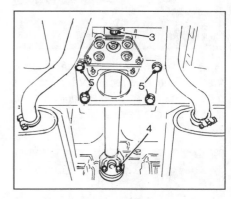

▲ UJ10. This diagram shows the location of the various fastenings.
3. Coupling flanges of front and rear sections of propshaft
4. Propshaft to final drive pinion drive flange.
5. Support plate bolts.
The flange coupling of the centre bearing is secured to the rear propshaft by two Woodruff keys and a castellated nut on early cars, or by splines on later cars. Withdraw the nut and pull off the

coupling. On early cars, take out the Woodruff keys and pull off the outer dust cover. Use a rubber mallet to drive the shaft through the bearing and its housing, then press the bearing from the housing. Remove the two self-locking nuts and bolts which secure the body mounting bracket to the centre bearing place.

▲ UJ11. This photo shows a close-up of the centre bearing with front section still in place, with the bearing cover removed.

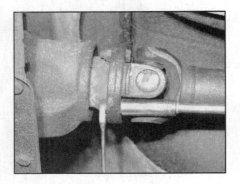

▲ UJ12. Removing the propshaft from the differential is a repeat of the previous procedures. It is secured by four nuts and bolts which can be removed as here, and …

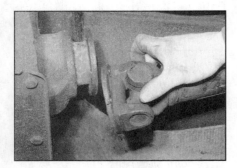

▲ UJ13. … the propshaft pulled free. Once the centre bearing has been disturbed, it is essential that the horizontal alignment is checked carefully – see Haynes Manual 242 for complete details.

UNIVERSAL JOINTS – OVERHAUL

Wear in the needle roller bearings is typified by a judder and vibration in the transmission on over-run and 'clonking' on taking up the drive. Where there has been an extreme lack of lubrication, there will be a serious metallic graunching sound, enough to set your teeth on edge.

CHECKING

With the propshaft in position, get under the car (take all the safety precautions) and try to turn the shaft with one hand and, with the other, hold the rear axle flange. Repeat this procedure for the other joints. Any movement between the shaft and the front, centre or rear couplings indicates bearing wear and/or forthcoming failure. The answer? New bearings, fitted as follows.

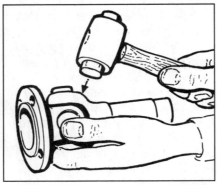

▲ UJ14. You'll have to remove the propshaft from the vehicle, as already described. Thoroughly clean the whole unit so you can see what you're doing. Remove the snap rings. The most common method is to use a small screwdriver and a pair of pliers, but always wear goggles in case the ring suddenly springs out. Where circlips are fitted, use the right size of circlip ends in circlip pliers for safe and easy removal. Hold the joint in your hand and gently tap the yoke lug as shown here – only use a rubber or copper-faced mallet. The top bearing should work outwards until you can pull it out altogether with your fingers. Repeat the procedure for the opposite bearing.

▲ UJ15. If it won't play the game, tap it gently out from inside with a small diameter punch or suitable drift, but it's easy to damage the bearing if you're not careful.

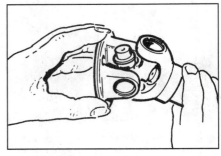

▲ UJ16. Remove the splined sleeve yoke to flange as shown here. Rest the two trunnions on wooden blocks and tap the yoke with a rubber mallet to remove the two remaining races. Check carefully the yoke cross holes for signs of ovality – this isn't common but, obviously, they need to be round, and if found to be oval they must be replaced. Early models will need new cork gaskets and gasket retainers. Smear the wall of the race with grease to keep the rollers in position in the housing during assembly. Insert the spider in the yoke holes, place the bearings in position and then lightly tap it home using a soft, flat-faced drift of slightly smaller diameter than the yoke hole. Repeat for the opposite bearings and then fit new snap rings to the bearings, making sure they are correctly fitted into the grooves. Place the mating yoke in position on the spider and fit the bearings and snap rings as described.

▲ *UJ17. When the propshaft is apart, take a good long look at the splines. Clean them up to remove all traces of dirt and grit and make sure that there is no sign of the splines being twisted – it's not unknown for the torque of the engine to have twisted them, especially where a leaden right foot has been the norm! If this is the case, it cannot be re-used or repaired – replacement is the only answer.*

TORQUE WRENCH SETTINGS

	lb/ft	Nm
Propeller shaft flange nuts	34	46
Centre bearing baseplate bolts	18	25

FINAL DRIVE
DESCRIPTION

The final drive unit is mounted independently from the hubs. Short driveshafts with a universal joint (UJ) at each end transmit the power from the final drive output shafts to the road wheels. The output shafts are carried on double row, angular contact ball bearings. The inner, splined, ends of the shafts engage with mating splines in the side gears of the differential assembly. Later cars have final drive units which may differ from earlier models as follows:

(a) Pinion shaft bearings preloaded by a collapsible spacer rather than shims.
(b) Drive shaft oil seals integral with calliper mounting bracket.
(c) Modified crownwheel and pinion design.

In addition, there was an optional limited slip differential available.

Many specific tools are needed to overhaul the final drive and, in general, it is better to renew the unit on an exchange basis with one of the many specialists. Most exchange units come less the driveshafts, hubs or brake components, so these will have to be stripped from the original and refitted or replaced as appropriate.

IMPORTANT NOTE – POWR-LOK
When working on the drive train of a vehicle equipped with the Powr-Lok limited-slip differential, it is vital to avoid jacking up one rear wheel and turning it whilst the other is still on the ground (and thus unable to turn). Doing so could cause seriously expensive damage.

The standard differential requires Hypoid SAE 90EP gear oil, such as Duckhams Hypoid 90S. Those cars with a limited-slip differential should be topped-up with the same oil, BUT when draining completely and refilling, SAE 90 oil, such as Duckhams Hypoid 90DL should be used.

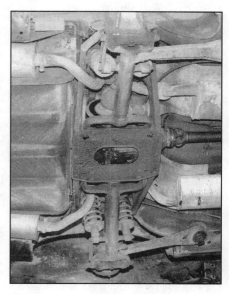

▲ *FD1. As can be seen in Chapter 8, the final drive unit is part of the IRS and this has to be removed as a piece and then the various suspension components taken off. This photo shows the whole unit (on its side with the car on the NBN Chassis Tilter), with the suspension and driveshafts still in place and propshaft connected.*

▲ *FD2. A protective plate is fitted to the underside of the IRS unit. Note the final drive drain plug in the centre. The plate is secured by no fewer than 14 nuts/bolts to the final drive unit.*

SPECIFICATIONS
AXLE RATIOS

Early models	2.8 litre		4.2 litre
4-speed manual	4.27:1		3.54:1
Overdrive	4.55:1		3.77:1
Auto transmission	4.27:1		3.54:1

Later models	2.8 litre	3.4 litre	4.2 litre
4-speed manual	4.09:1	3.54:1	3.31:1
Auto transmission	4.09:1	3.54:1	3.058:1
North America 4-speed manual			3.54:1
North America auto transmission:			
Pre 1982	N/A	N/A	3.07:1
1982 onward	N/A	N/A	2.88:1

LUBRICATION

	Imp pints	Litres	US pints
Oil capacity (all models)	2.75	1.5	3.25

DRIVESHAFTS

The overhaul of the universal joints is the same in principle as that for the UJs on the propshaft.

REMOVING THE FINAL DRIVE UNIT

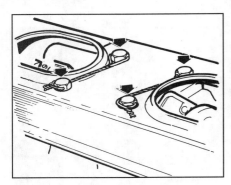

▲ FD3. The IRS should be removed from the car as detailed in Chapter 8. In essence, all appendages to the final drive must be taken off, viz. the hubs and driveshafts, damper/spring assemblies, handbrake levers, etc. Then, the final drive assembly should be inverted and the locking wire from the differential bolts cut, as shown here.

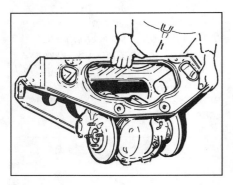

▲ FD4. Unscrew the bolts and remove the crossbeam from the carrier by tilting the crossbeam forward over the nose of the pinion. It is important that the bolts be fitted with new security wires on refitting. Note that Nylock self-locking nuts should never be substituted for the all-metal type on the output shaft flange studs.

REAR HUBS

▲ RH1. The rear hubs can be removed without the need for taking off the whole rear suspension assembly. However, it is necessary to remove the road wheel and jack up the car in order to work underneath it, so the usual safety rules must be followed. This is all the more important because some of the fasteners will require plenty of torque to remove them.

▲ RH2. Remove the suspension outer pivot grease nipple, then withdraw the split pin and unscrew the castellated nut and washer from the end of the halfshaft.

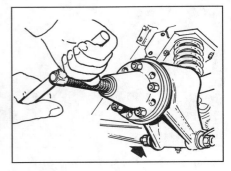

▲ RH3. You'll need a special hub extractor to push the splined end of the driveshaft out of the hub assembly. Note the location of the inner oil seal track and the endfloat spacer. Unscrew and remove the nut from the end of the lower wishbone outer pivot shaft (arrowed in this diagram), and …

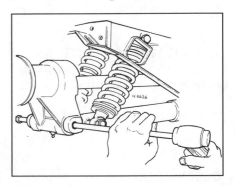

▲ RH4. … drive out the pivot shaft. This allows the hub and carrier to be lifted away.

TORQUE WRENCH SETTINGS

	lb/ft	Nm
Driveshaft castellated nut	100	136
Calliper mounting bracket bolts	70	95
Pinion nut (early cars)	120-130	163-177
Pinion nut (later cars)	100	136
Crownwheel bolts	80	109
Differential bearing cap bolts	60	82
Differential carrier bolts	75	102

Chapter 8

Brakes, Suspension and Steering

BRAKES

Hard to believe, but the braking system is often sadly neglected on older XJ6s. Bearing in mind both the weight and the performance of the car – even the relatively lowly-powered 2.8 litre cars – it should, of course, be one of your main priorities. If you've just bought your car, checking the condition and operation of the braking system is vital. If you're restoring the car, either in full or part, it will pay dividends to overhaul just about everything. All parts can be obtained from franchised dealers or specialists, such as SNG Barratt who have all braking components for all models available. Because they are as enthusiastic as you are, they can be relied on to supply parts that are not only priced right, but also totally safe – not a description that applies to everyone, unfortunately.

SAFETY: Never work on your braking system unless you are fully (and justifiably) confident of your abilities. A simple mistake on a vehicle of the Jaguar's size and capabilities could be fatal – for others, as well as yourself. If you have completed an operation but are not sure that it is totally right, ask a professional mechanic to inspect it BEFORE you use the vehicle on the road. The small cost involved will far outweigh the possible tragic consequences.

When you are working on your braking system, you should be aware of the dangers of breathing in the brake dust, especially if asbestos pads have been used; the inhalation of asbestos dust can cause cancer. Take the following precautions:
(a) Wear a particle mask.
(b) Remove brake dust from your working area by wiping and/or using a proprietary brake cleaner, never use compressed air.
(c) Don't just throw old brake pads in the bin; seal them in a plastic bag.
(d) When fitting replacement brake pads, ensure that they are asbestos-free – check before you buy.
(e) Thoroughly wash your hands when you have finished.
(f) Before using your car 'in anger', make sure you test drive the vehicle slowly and somewhere safe – just in case!

BUYING REPLACEMENT BRAKE COMPONENTS

ALWAYS buy quality brake components of known provenance – the XJ6 is a large and powerful vehicle and stopping it quickly **and** safely are vital considerations. Buy from Jaguar dealerships or specialists such as SNG Barratt, who sell brand-name (rather than cheap spurious parts) equipment. If you are uprating your brakes in any way,

again you should only use the best. There are many areas where you can save money on Jaguar restoration, but braking is definitely not one of them. NEVER buy used brake components. Your life depends on your braking system being absolutely perfect, and you simply cannot guarantee that with used parts.

RAISING YOUR CAR

In order to work on most brake components it will be necessary to raise your XJ6 which means that you should check the appropriate safety section in Chapter 2. NEVER work beneath a car supported only by a jack.

BRAKE FLUID – TYPES

'Normal' brake fluid is unpleasant stuff and will damage paintwork and skin. If you spill any, wipe it up and/or wash your hands straight away. It is hygroscopic (it absorbs water) so over a period of time, braking effectiveness is reduced, resulting in a 'longer pedal' and more effort required to stop or slow down. The water in the system will rust the steel braking components, including the brake pipes themselves, from the inside out. Completely change your brake fluid every two years, or annually if you use your Jaguar infrequently. Fluid should be top quality to SAE J1703 standard, such as Duckhams Universal Brake and Clutch fluid.

SILICONE FLUID

Silicone fluid is an alternative, as supplied by brake specialists Automec Equipment. This is harmless to skin and paintwork and doesn't absorb water at all. It will mix with standard fluid, but there's not much point. *All* the existing fluid should be drained out before filling the system with silicone fluid. The braking system should be bled in the standard manner.

Note: If the wrong type of fluid has been used, then the system should be drained and flushed out with methylated spirit – taking great care when using this volatile and toxic liquid.

SYSTEM DESCRIPTION

All XJ6 models are fitted with four-wheel disc brakes and servo assistance. The hydraulic operating system is dual circuit, in case of brake failure, with servo assistance and a tandem master cylinder. The front discs are ventilated and the rear callipers are mounted inboard on the differential housing and output flanges. The handbrake operates through a mechanical linkage to the rear callipers which incorporate an automatically adjustable handbrake mechanism.

METRICATION

On later model XJ6s, a partial metrication of the hydraulic braking components was carried out. The rear callipers, handbrake callipers, fluid supply pipes from rear three-way connection to rear callipers and the three-way connector all retained UNF threads. Assume nothing and check all threads by using a suitable nut.

TORQUE FIGURES

	lbs/ft	Nm
Disc retaining bolts	35	48
Calliper retaining bolts:		
Front	55	75
Rear	50	68
Brake pedal pivot bolt	18	25
Master cylinder banjo bolt	23	31
Master cylinder tipping valve nut	40	54

BRAKE DISCS, CALLIPERS, PADS AND PISTONS

To work on your brakes you'll need to jack up the car and remove the road wheel, as shown in Chapter 9. Always support the car on axle stands, chocking the wheels remaining on the ground. In these photos, you'll note that Phil Blundell was using the NBN Chassis Tilter to hold the whole car off the ground for most of the operations here. Brake fluid is unpleasant stuff so keep it off your hands and car paintwork. Use a brake pipe clamp to prevent fluid leaking and to remove the need for bleeding.

DISC BRAKES

All XJ6 models feature a disc brake at each corner, with the specification being as the table below.

CALLIPER REMOVAL AND REPLACEMENT

▲ CAL1. Phil sprayed Halfords Brake Cleaner to clean up the calliper and surrounding area. Remove encrusted dirt with a wire brush, but always wear a face mask to prevent inhalation of dangerous particles, especially if pads containing asbestos have been used. Before he started working on the braking system, Phil removed the top from the fluid reservoir in order to help the fluid drain more easily.

▲ CAL2. He disconnected the hydraulic hose at the junction with the rigid steel brake pipe. It's common for the union and pipe to rust together. Try soaking with WD40, but in many cases you simply have to destroy the pipe and make a new section with a new union. Phil then released the flexible pipe from its mounting. You'll need two spanners for this to prevent the whole assembly turning. Apply a brake pipe clamp to prevent most of the fluid leaking out – you'll still need a tray to collect odd drips.

DISC BRAKES

Disc data	Diameter (in/mm)	Thickness (in/mm)
Front (Series I)	11.18 (284)	0.50 (12.7)
Minimum thickness		*0.45 (11.43)*
Front (Series II & III)	11.18 (284)	0.95 (24.13)
Minimum thickness		*0.90 (22.86)*
Rear	10.375 (263.5)	0.50 (12.7)
Minimum thickness		*0.45 (11.43)*

Maximum thickness variation across the disc (any model) is 0.0005 in (0.0127mm).
Maximum disc run-out is 0.002 in (0.051mm).

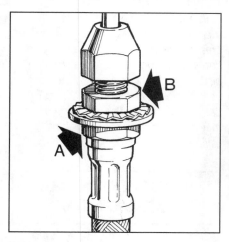

▲ *CAL3. This diagram shows clearly how the flexible hose is mounted – note the position of the washer.*
KEY
A   Flexible hose and fitting
B   Locknut

Flexible hoses eventually start to crack. Early signs of trouble are hairline cracks which can only be seen by bending the hose back hard on itself. When the system is fully connected, have a helper press hard on the brake pedal while you look at the hose. Signs of 'bulging' under pressure means a replacement hose is required.

▲ *CAL4. The calliper is secured by two bolts which are joined (for security) by a piece of twisted wire. This should always be replaced, so the simplest way to remove it is to cut it with the pliers. You'll need a ½ in drive socket and ratchet to remove the two bolts. They should be torqued up to 55 lb/ft but it's common to find that they have been tightened much more.*

▲ *CAL5. Whether you remove the pads now or later, you'll need to ease them back off the disc. Phil used a large pair of pliers to pull them back against the calliper – don't prise the pads back using a screwdriver as a lever. Phil then eased the calliper back, complete with pads.*

FRONT BRAKE CALLIPER STRIPDOWN

The procedure for stripping down a front calliper is the same in essence for the rear callipers. Use a wire brush to clean up the outside of the calliper – take care not to inhale the brake dust and wear a mask to keep any brake particles out of your lungs.

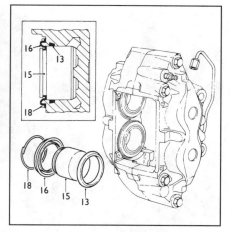

▲ *CAL7. This diagram shows the differences in the calliper design for the later four-piston callipers.*
KEY
13.   *Piston seal*
15.   *Piston*
16.   *Dust-excluding boot*
18.   *Dust-excluding boot clip*

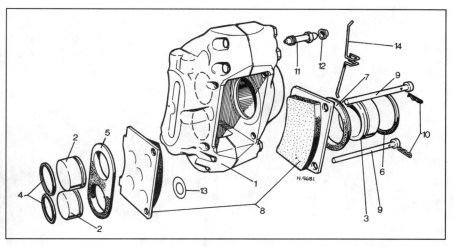

▲ *CAL6. This diagram shows an exploded view of a front disc calliper (earlier three-piston type).*
KEY

1.	Calliper body	6.	Piston seal	11.	Bleed nipple
2.	Outer pistons	7.	Dust excluder	12.	Dust cap
3.	Inner piston	8.	Friction pad	13.	Mounting shim
4.	Piston seals	9.	Pad retaining pin	14.	Anti-chatter spring
5.	Dust excluder	10.	Clip		(later models)

165

▲ CAL8. The pads are held in place by two long pins, which in turn are prevented from leaving home by R-clips. Use long-nose pliers to remove them. The pins tend to seize in place and it may be necessary to tap them out with a suitable punch and pull them right out with pliers. Before replacing the pins, clean them with sandpaper to remove the surface corrosion. Apply copper grease on replacement, but do not get any on the friction surfaces.

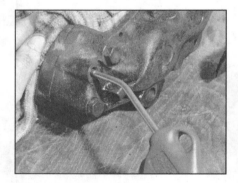

▲ CAL9. To remove the pistons, use your compressor and S-P air gun or a foot pump with suitable adaptor to apply air to the union hole. This will push the pistons out of the bores so that they can be removed easily. The rag prevents the pistons being damaged. They will come out with a loud pop, so be prepared! Keep pistons and bores together for replacement purposes. Do not unscrew the bolts which hold the two halves of the calliper together.

▲ CAL10. Detach the rubber dust excluders from their locating grooves and check their condition. Remove the inner seals from the grooves approx. 6mm inside the piston bore. Always discard these. Rust around the outside edges of the bores doesn't necessarily mean that the callipers are shot – it's the condition of the bores themselves and the pistons that counts. Carefully check the pistons for any signs of wear or scoring – as you can see here, there are rust pitting marks around the edges of both pistons. This would have led to fluid leakage and an obvious lack of braking ability. If you detect any wear or rusty areas, then the pistons and the callipers are defunct and must be discarded – they cannot be repaired. If you're going to re-use the calliper, blow through all the passageways with compressed air and ensure that there is no dirt or rust particles in the bores.

▲ CAL11. This is the SNG Barratt calliper repair kit for use when the pistons and their respective bores are OK. There's a circlip, rubber dust excluder and seal for each. Reassembly is a reversal of the procedure outlined here. Wipe the piston

seals, dust excluders and the pistons themselves with clean brake fluid before pressing them into place – use only your fingers, nothing metal. Make sure the pistons are sitting 'square' in the bore before you press them fully home. The pads can be refitted at this stage or it may be easier to fit them after the calliper has been refitted to the hub.

FRONT WHEEL BEARINGS

The front wheel bearings take a lot of stresses and strains, but are easy to access and simple to adjust. The car must be raised for dealing with the wheel bearings, so always take appropriate safety measures.

▲ FB1. The bearing is protected by a simple end cap – remove using a large pair of pliers. The hole in the cap allows excess grease to bleed out during routine greasing. Make sure that the hole is clear.

▲ FB2. Wipe off excess grease and remove and discard the split pin. The castellated cover can then be pulled off. This gives access to the securing nut …

▲ FB3. … the D-washer and the outer bearing itself. Unless you are replacing, examine the bearing carefully, cleaning off the grease and checking for signs of excessive wear or pitting on the bearing surfaces. The disc assembly can then be pulled off the stub axle and the excess grease wiped off to stop it getting everywhere as you work around it. Make sure that no dirt or grit gets on to the axle before the new grease and bearing is fitted.

CHECKING THE DISC CONDITION

With the road wheel removed, the first check is visual, looking for excess corrosion, scoring and other defects to the surface. Check the thickness of the disc, and if it's less than that stated earlier, replace it as a matter of course. If it has light damage or scoring, it may be possible to reface the discs within the prescribed limits. However, new discs are far from expensive and we would recommend a disc change wherever there's the slightest doubt as to their efficiency.

CHECKING DISC RUN-OUT

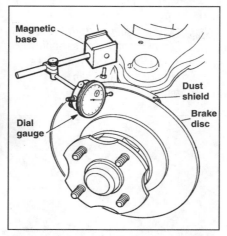

▲ FB4. Raise the car and remove the road wheels in turn. Use a dial gauge and spin the wheel to assess what, if any, the run-out is, i.e. how much the disc is 'out of true'. If it is beyond the limit stated earlier, remove the disc and position it with the holes aligned differently. Check again once the bolts have been replaced and tightened. If moving to several positions does not improve the run-out, the disc must be replaced. If you are checking for any run-out on a new disc, it should be checked after the whole assembly has been replaced. (Courtesy AP Lockheed)

▲ FB5. In this case, we were replacing the disc itself as well as the bearing – note that on early, three-piston cars, there is no need to remove the calliper to remove the disc. The disc is held by five bolts which are likely to be tight and possibly corroded in place. The disc will probably stick and need a tap from a rubber mallet.

REPLACING DISCS – IMPORTANT NOTES

With new discs (always in pairs) brake specialists AP Lockheed recommend that you avoid excessive or high-speed braking until the pads and discs are bedded-in – usually around 150-200 miles. Harsh braking during this period can cause heat spots on the disc with a subsequent reduction in braking efficiency. From 1980, Jaguar fitted discs which had a higher chrome content than previously. These have an identification code cast into the hub location face. Because of the improved friction characteristics of these discs, they must only be replaced in pairs, both discs of which must show the same identification code.

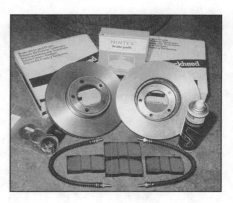

▲ FB6. SNG Barratt recommended that we used Lockheed discs together with Mintex brake pads as the best combination of price and excellent performance. Also seen here from the Barratt stores are new flexible hoses and a calliper service kit – all aspects of XJ6 brake performance are catered for.

USEFUL NOTE: In 1983, the disc brake pads (not the handbrake pads) were changed to a semi-metallic material, and these can be identified by the number FER 3401 printed on them. Though they can be fitted to any four-piston set-up it is vitally important that you do not mix them with other types of pads, either side-to-side or front-to-rear. They may only be fitted in sets of four.

▲ FB7. Phil cleaned up the hub/disc mating surfaces with a wire brush and then used a copper grease to prevent them sticking together in future, and then applied a dab to the threads of each bolt.

▲ FB8. The oil seal and inner races of the tapered roller bearings were withdrawn. Phil drifted out the outer tracks from the hub (you can't put new bearings in old tracks).

▲ FB9. SNG Barratt supplied the new wheel bearing kits (we did both wheels, of course), and seen here are the inner components (left), and the outer

components (right). Phil used plenty of clean grease before replacing the tracks and bearings – if they start dry, they could be damaged right from the start. He used an old toothbrush to apply the grease. A suitably-sized impact socket was used to gently tap them into place, not forgetting …

▲ FB10. … the oil seal on the inner bearing. This should be soaked in clean engine oil for around 12 hours prior to fitting. Replace the disc/hub assembly in a reversal of the removal procedure. Do not overtighten the hub securing nut; just finger tighten it and then check for play (this is a simpler task if the wheel is attached). Hold the wheel at top and bottom and try to rock it. If you can feel play in the bearing, tighten the nut a quarter of a turn and try it again. Take your time and progress slowly until there is no play but the wheel still turns freely with no 'tight spots'. Refit the castellated cover and a new split pin. If you have a dial gauge, you can be more accurate. The correct endfloat is between 0.002 in and 0.006 in (0.05mm and 0.15mm). Remember that, having had the hydraulic braking system 'open', it must be bled before the car is used.

REMOVING AND REPLACING FLEXIBLE HOSES

By definition, the hoses carrying the brake fluid from the rest of the system to the wheel callipers are rubber in order to be flexible. This means that over a period of time they will deteriorate.

CHECKING FLEXIBLE HOSES

The most obvious sign of dangerous wear is when cracks appear allowing fluid leakage. Sometimes these can only be seen by bending back the pipe and looking closely – even hairline cracks can be lethal, so at the first sign of this kind of wear, replace the pipe.

Sometimes the rubber becomes weak without actually cracking. What happens then is that when the brake pedal is pressed, the hose bulges and is actually absorbing some of that pressure, thus reducing the braking effect. Ultimately, this kind of hose 'ballooning' will result in a burst pipe – and some nasty consequences.

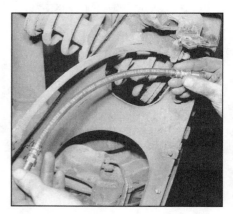

▲ H1. Seen here is a new Lucas-Girling hose alongside its predecessor. SNG Barratt can supply all the hoses required to make your XJ6 truly safe, and we would recommend that all such hoses are replaced as a matter of course unless you have documented evidence that they have been replaced recently.

RIGID BRAKE LINES

The original rigid brake lines were steel. Though it's likely that at least some of the pipework will be original, some sections will probably have been replaced – usually as a 'needs must' at MoT time. It's important, therefore, to make a thorough check over all the rigid lines to ensure that they are securely located and rust-free. It always pays to clean them up with a wire brush to reveal any rust damage that may not be immediately obvious. If the lines are solid, brush them over on a regular basis with Waxoyl to keep the rot at bay. But don't forget that because standard brake fluid is hygroscopic, the water it absorbs can rot the lines from the inside out. Unless you have evidence that the lines have been replaced very recently, it's a wise move to replace them as a matter of course.

Upgrading your rigid brake lines is always a good idea. SNG Barratt can supply stainless steel (Cunifer) pipe sets, and Automec can supply copper sets or individual lengths.

STEEL BRAKE PIPES

▲ H2. As the brake pipes pass under and around your Jaguar, you'll see that they are held in place by various clips. The pipes should always be in place in these, not just for safety reasons but also because it is an MoT test requirement. Remember that water can accumulate around these clips, so check carefully for signs of corrosion, and brush plenty of Waxoyl into the area. Even if you're not removing the pipes, it pays to wire brush

dirt and surface rust from them and coat them with Waxoyl to prevent damage between times and to make it easier for when you do need to get the connections undone.

▲ H3. Always use two spanners when undoing brake unions, like this, otherwise you run the risk or damaging the brake pipe, the union, or both. Apply lots of releasing agent and ease the connections apart slowly, so as not to cause distortion of the pipe (which would lead to a loss of braking performance).

BENDING AND CUTTING BRAKE PIPES

▲ H4. Cutting any brake pipe is best achieved with a purpose-made tool, like this one from Sykes-Pickavant. If you use a saw, there's the possibility you won't get a right-angled cut and, of course, if you get any bits of swarf in the tube, it will eventually find its way into your braking system – not good! As you can see here, the tool is simply applied to the tube where the cut is required and the handle turned clockwise. Turn the tool around the pipe, applying extra turns as required and …

▲ H5. … it takes just seconds to make the perfect cut.

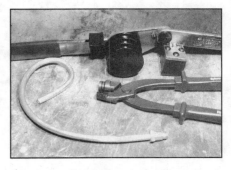

▲ H6. Bending brake pipes without a special tool is extremely difficult and not recommended – it is very easy to distort the tube so that its internal diameter is too small. Moreover, it could also 'crease' and create a weak point. Two S-P variants are shown here, at the front is the simpler version and at the rear is the more complex model designed to cope with various tube sizes. Both allow perfect bends to be made very easily indeed.

▲ H7. You can buy sections of brake pipe specifically made for certain applications. If you're buying pipe 'on the roll' you can make your own union joins, but you'll need the right equipment. The S-P brake flaring kit allows you to make any connection you like.

MASTER CYLINDER

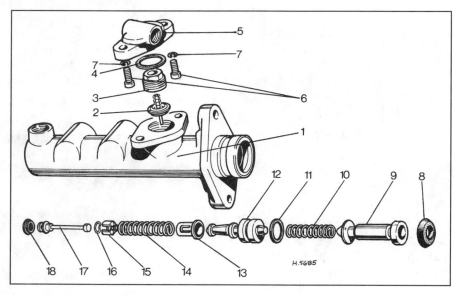

REMOVING THE MASTER CYLINDER

Take a piece of plastic pipe (as you would use to bleed the brakes) and fit one end to the front bleed screw and the other to a suitable container. Undo the screw a little and depress the brake pedal several times to expel the fluid from the front part of the master cylinder. Repeat the operation with the rear bleed screw (dual circuit brakes, don't forget) and then disconnect the pipes from the master cylinder, which is secured to the servo by two nuts. Remove these and lift the whole unit clear, taking care not to drip any brake fluid on to the bodywork.

Before dismantling, thoroughly wash the outside of the unit in Girling cleaning fluid or methylated spirits – not paraffin or petrol, etc. When taking it apart, be aware that there are two springs in each set-up and when released, these can pop out and jump across your garage floor! Take careful note of the order the components come out. SNG Barratt can supply overhaul kits for both types, but it's no use fitting one if the cylinder bores are rusted or scored. Check the bores and the pistons for signs of wear. If any is found, the master cylinder and all components must be replaced.

If you are fitting an overhaul kit, use only your fingers to assemble the parts – resist the temptation to use small screwdrivers, etc. to fit the fiddly bits! Immerse the parts in clean brake fluid and assemble only when wet.Clearly, once the master cylinder has been replaced, the braking system must be bled in the conventional manner.

▲ SER1. This is an exploded view of early type master cylinder.
KEY
1. Body
2. Tipping valve
3. Tipping valve securing nut
4. Tipping valve cover seal
5. Cover
6. Screw
7. Spring washer
8. Gland nut
9. Primary plunger
10. Intermediate spring
11. Ring seal
12. Secondary plunger
13. Thimble
14. Spring
15. Valve spacer
16. Spring washer
17. Valve stem
18. Valve seal
Compare this with …

▶ SER2. … the later type master cylinder, as shown here.
KEY
2. Fluid pipe adaptor
3. Grommets
4. Lock pin
40. Secondary piston
21. Primary piston

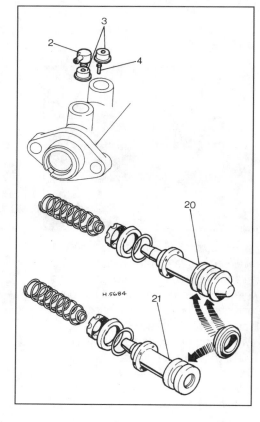

▲ SER3. This is the master cylinder on a Series 3 car. Note the wiring to the cap which must be removed before the cap is unscrewed. *The filter should be cleaned on a regular basis, for obvious reasons. When it's necessary for the cap to be off, whether it's for bleeding the entire system or just topping up, always take great care to keep all foreign bodies out of the fluid.*

BRAKE SERVO UNIT

All models are fitted with a servo which boosts brake pedal pressure. The unit operates by vacuum obtained from the induction manifold and comprises basically a booster diaphragm and a non-return valve. The servo and master cylinder are connected so that the servo unit piston rod acts also as the master cylinder pushrod.

The servo unit piston does not fit tightly into the cylinder but it has a strong diaphragm to keep its edges in constant contact with the cylinder wall, giving an air-tight seal between the two parts. The forward chamber is held under vacuum conditions created in the inlet manifold, and during periods when the brake pedal is not in use, the controls open a passage to the rear chamber, placing it under vacuum conditions as well.

From the facelift models (1979/1980 model year), there was a dash-mounted warning light to warn of brake vacuum loss.

SERVO TESTING

To test, turn the ignition off and press down hard on the brake pedal several times to expel all the air from the servo. Hold the pedal whilst turning on the ignition and starting the car. As the vacuum pressure starts to assist the braking effect, the pedal should go down further. If it doesn't, then there is a problem. This could be a blocked or leaking pipe to the servo, a blocked non-return valve or, most expensive of all, the servo is faulty. Whatever it is, the fault should be identified and solved before

driving the vehicle further. It pays to make regular checks on the condition of the servo hoses and their securing bolts.

NOTE: The servo cannot be repaired – if it is found to be faulty, it MUST be replaced.

REAR DISCS, PADS AND CALLIPERS, AND HANDBRAKE

Most of the photos here are with the rear suspension unit removed from the car. Although some operations are possible with this *in situ*, for most it is essential to remove it – see later in this chapter. In the photos, we have removed the suspension unit from our project Series 3 car, which was on its side in the NBN Chassis Tilter. As such, it was actually being held on the engine hoist which made life easier for Phil Blundell to work on it.

REMOVING THE REAR PADS

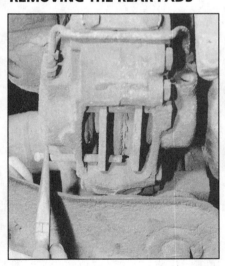

▲ *BRK1. The basic operating principles of the rear callipers and pads are the same as those for the front, albeit the rears are only single piston units. After removing the split pins, the pad retaining pins can be removed. They often seize and will almost certainly need to be wiggled enthusiastically with a pair of pliers. A squirt of WD40 helps, too.*

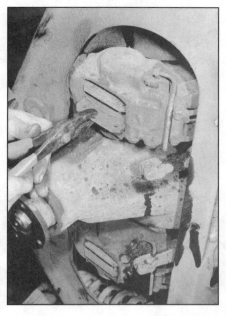

▲ *BRK2. The pliers can be used again to pull the old pads out.*

HANDBRAKE

The handbrake is cable-operated and acts on the rear brake discs. It's unlikely that anyone will ever wear their handbrake pads out, but they should still be checked at service intervals. The simplest way to check them is to use a torch or inspection light. There is no official minimum thickness specified, but look for them to have at least ⅛ in (3mm). It should be noted that the handbrake pads, discs and operation of the cable mechanism are totally independent of the four hydraulically operated discs. When the pads are replaced, it is important that the retraction fingers must also be renewed. To remove the handbrake assembly, the rear complete suspension must be taken from the car.

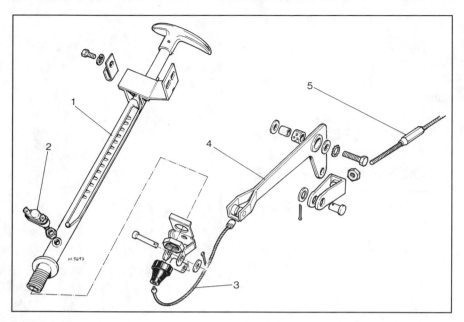

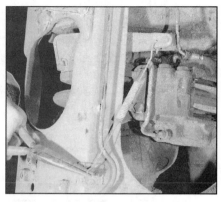

▲ *BRK4. Extract the split pin and clevis pin and disconnect the handbrake cable from the compensator linkage. On later cars, it is necessary to remove the suspension tie plate. Disconnect the pull-off springs, and …*

▲ *BRK3. There is a handbrake 'on' warning light on the dashboard. In order that it comes on and goes off as it should, it will be necessary to make periodic adjustments. This diagram shows the general layout of the handbrake assembly, but it should be noted that this light is also connected to two level switches in the master cylinder reservoirs and lights when either one has a low fluid level – this should be checked BEFORE carrying out the following sequence.*

KEY

1. *Handbrake control*
2. *Warning switch*
3. *Primary cable*
4. *Intermediate lever*
5. *Secondary cable*

Earlier models used a pulley, into which the primary cable was engaged. The light operation is by a simple plunger switch – when the handbrake is fully down, it presses on the switch and the light goes out. If the light stays on with the handbrake released, check first that it is going to the end of its travel and pressing on the switch. If so, remove the control and cable, disconnect the wires from the switch and then unscrew the switch itself. You can check the operation of the switch by connecting your multimeter to the two terminals of the switch.

Select resistance (Ohms) and note the readings. With the plunger 'down', there should be a circuit, but when it is released, the reading should be nothing or 'open circuit'. If it doesn't react like this, there is the possibility that the switch itself is faulty internally, and should be replaced.

If it is OK, it will almost certainly just require adjustment. If the light stays on too long, the switch is too far down, meaning that the handbrake is not touching it and so breaking the light circuit. Replace the switch but unscrew it approximately half a turn further than its original position. Temporarily replace the wiring connections and check its operation. Repeat this until the correct position has been reached, and tighten the locknut carefully to prevent it moving again.

▲ *BRK5. … lift the locking tabs for access to the pivot bolts.*

▲ *BRK6. Remove these, and then …*

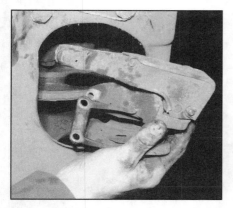

▲ BRK7. … the assembly can be withdrawn, as shown here.

CABLE ADJUSTMENT

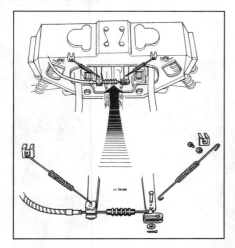

▲ BRK8. The handbrake on the XJ6 is self-adjusting, but cable stretch means that some adjustment may be necessary from time to time, as follows: Under the car, slacken the locknut at the forked end of the cable adjuster and remove the split pin, clevis pin and washer. This will enable you to disconnect the fork from the handbrake lever. Make sure the actuating arms are fully released by pressing inwards toward the callipers. Then unscrew the clevis fork on the end of the cable until it can be reconnected to the handbrake lever and the clevis pin can be inserted without the cable pulling on the calliper actuating levers.

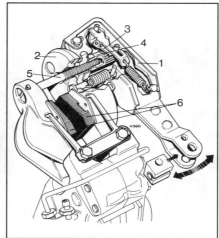

▲ BRK9. The handbrake mechanism/pads is attached to the rear caliper, as shown here.
KEY
1. Operating lever
2. Pad carrier assembly
3. Pawl assembly
5. Adjuster bolt
4. Adjuster nut
6. Friction pad

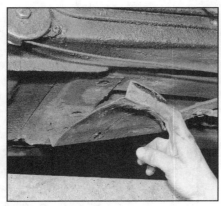

▲ BRK10. Under the centre of the car is a plate which protects the vulnerable mechanism from damage. However, over the years it can often be found adrift, as here. If this looks like yours, it should be re-fastened as soon as possible – it was put there for a reason, and that reason is safety.

REMOVING REAR CALLIPERS

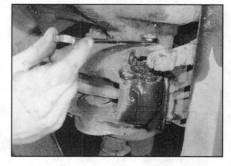

▲ BRK11. Disconnect the hydraulic pipe union from the calliper and cut the wire that secures the two calliper mounting bolts. There's very little room to work, as can be seen here, and you'll need a thin pair of snips to cut the wire, and a quality ring spanner (no space for a socket/ratchet) to get at the bolts.

▲ BRK12. Once they have been removed, the calliper can be eased out of place. Procedure relating to the checking of the pistons and bores and fitting of a calliper repair kit (where possible) are the same as those for front callipers – but with fewer pistons, of course.

▲ BRK13. This photo shows the relationship of the calliper and handbrake mechanism – out of the vehicle for obvious reasons.

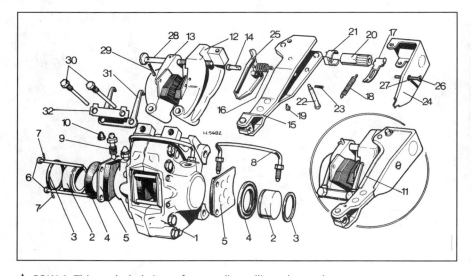

▲ BRK14. This exploded view of a rear disc calliper shows the component parts.

1. Calliper body
2. Piston
3. Piston seal
4. Dust excluder
5. Friction pad
6. Pad retaining pin
7. Clip
8 Bridge pipe
9. Bleed nipple
10. Dust cap
11. Handbrake mechanism
12. Pad carrier assembly
13. Pad carrier assembly
14. Anchor pin
15. Operating lever
16. Return spring
17. Pawl assembly
18. Tension spring
19. Anchor pin
20. Adjuster
21. Friction spring
22. Hinge pin
23. Split pin
24. Protection cover
25. Protection cover
26. Bolt
27. Washer
28. Bolt
29. Split pin
30. Bolt
31. Retraction plate
32. Tab washer

▲ BRK16. He tapped the bolts gently backwards towards the final drive unit …

REMOVING AND REPLACING THE REAR DISCS

Basic inspection of the discs can be made *in situ*, but to remove and replace the discs, the entire rear suspension assembly has to be removed beforehand.

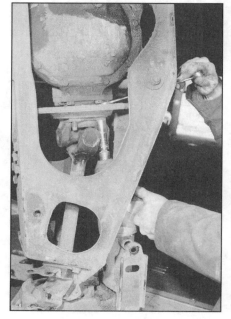

▶ BRK15. With the brake calliper removed (as described earlier), the object is to clear enough room for access to the disc securing bolts. In this photo, the halfshaft inner universal joint cover, the suspension units and radius arm have been removed (see elsewhere in this chapter). As you can see, the XJ6 set-up is different from most vehicles, in that the disc is 'sandwiched' between the final drive unit and UJ. Phil is removing the nuts here using a pneumatic hammer socket (they're tight!) and preventing them from turning all round by using a ring spanner on the bolt heads.

▲ BRK17. … releasing the disc and the camber shims. Do take great care not to shear these bolts as they are demons to get out if they do. Take your time and use plenty of releasing agent. Out of interest, we discovered that if you require bolts for a Series XJ6, they can only be purchased from a Jaguar dealer as part of the complete brake assembly – with a commensurate price tag. However, if you want studs for a later model XJ6 (née XJ40) they can be purchased individually. As the studs are the same for both vehicles, you now know what to ask for!

▲ BRK18. SNG Barratt recommended that we used Lockheed replacement brake products. Here is the new disc (at top!) and, of course …

▲ BRK19. … we fitted new brake pads (at top) at the same time.

▲ BRK20. Don't forget that new discs are covered in a fine layer of grease to prevent them rusting. Phil used a spray-on degreasing compound to get the grease off.

▲ BRK21. Fitting the new disc is a reversal of taking the old one off, and just as fiddly! Note here the shims included between the UJ and the disc. It is vital that the disc runs centrally in the calliper aperture. If this is not the case, add or remove shims to suit, but always balance up the shims at either side of the disc. For example, if a shim of 0.04 in (1mm) was added between the disc and the output flange, one of the same thickness must be removed from between the disc and the driveshaft.

BLEEDING THE BRAKES

Brake fluid type: Hydraulic fluid to SAE J1703D such as Duckhams Universal Brake and Clutch fluid.

How you bleed the system will depend on the general situation. If you cannot be sure when they were last bled, it is wise to totally flush out the existing fluid and replace it with new fluid, as specified earlier. If you are bleeding the system because you have opened it at some point in order to replace components or make adjustments, then you need only bleed the circuit that has been open. Of course, if you have removed/replaced the master cylinder, the whole system will need to be bled. Note that there is a slightly different procedure relating to those cars with a pressure differential warning actuator – see below.

Clean up the area around the bleed nipples with a wire brush, to ensure that no dirt gets in there. Apply a little

releasing agent (the nipples often seize) and use a ring spanner to undo it slightly. Be patient, as it's very easy to damage the flats or, worse still, strip off the head of the nipple because it's seized. Start with the rear calliper diagonally opposite the master cylinder, placing a piece of tube over the bleed nipple, and place the other end of the tube into a see-through container (an ideal use for all those old coffee jars!) in which there is some fresh brake fluid. Do **not** use a milk bottle! Have an assistant press down the brake pedal quickly and release it slowly. Check the fluid coming out of the nipple – it should be clean and there should be no sign of air bubbles. Repeat the operation until only clear fluid emerges, when the nipple can be tightened again when the pedal is fully depressed. Don't forget to keep the fluid reservoir topped up.

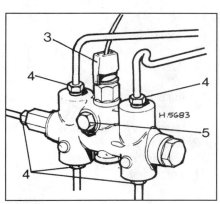

▲ BLD1. This is the brake pressure differential warning actuator.
KEY
3. Electrical connector
4. Fluid pipe unions
5. Actuator mounting bolt
   The aim of this device is to give a visual warning (a light on the dashboard) of a difference in pressure between the two hydraulic circuits. Essentially, it is a piston, kept in balance by equal pressures within the circuits. If the pressure in one circuit falls, the piston moves and triggers the electrical circuit which powers the warning lamp. There are two types, the later of which automatically resets after there has been a pressure difference, either through a problem or, say, because the master cylinder has been drained and overhauled.

The earlier type must be reset as follows; place your plastic pipe on the front right calliper bleed nipple and run it to a clear jar with clean brake fluid in it. Run the engine at idling speed and put your foot on the brake pedal while your assistant opens the nipple slowly. Gradually, the piston in the warning actuator will shift to the centre and the warning light will go off. It's important to tighten the nipple quickly, otherwise it will go over centre and the warning light will come back on. If this happens, repeat this operation, but with the left-hand front calliper.

FSU1. *Jaguar front suspension.*

1. Crossmember assembly
2. Mounting rubber
3. Mounting rubber
4. Set screw
5. Suspension assembly
6. Front upper wishbone lever
7. Bush
8. Distance washer
9. Self-locking nut
10. Adjusting camber angle washer
11. Upper fulcrum shaft
12. Washer
13. Bolt
14. Upper wishbone lever – rear
15. Washer
16. Self-locking nut
17. Adjusting castor angle shim
18. Upper ball joint assembly
19. Distance piece
20. Rebound rubber
21. Slotted nut
22. Split pin
23. Washer
24. Lower fulcrum shaft
25. Keeper plate
26. Rubber bush
27. Bracket
28. Anti-roll bar
29. Rubber bush
30. Link
31. Retaining washer
32. Rubber pad
33. Distance piece
34. Rubber pad
35. Retaining washer
36. Tie rod lever
37. Gaiter assembly
38. Ring
39. Insert
40. Spigot
41. Ball pin
42. Railko socket
43. Shim
44. Cap
45. Nylon washer
46. Grease nipple
47. Tab washer
48. Bolt
49. Stub axle carrier
50. Water deflector
51. Stub axle shaft
52. Oil seal
53. Water deflector
54. Inner bearing
55. Front hub
56. Outer bearing
57. 'D' washer
58. Split pin
59. Slotted nut
60. End cap
61. Locknut
62. Nut
63. Outer washer
64. Rubber buffer
65. Inner washer
66. Spacing collar
67. Hydraulic damper
68. Bracket
69. Bolt
70. Bracket
71. Rubber bump stop
72. Lower wishbone lever
73. Coil spring seal
74. Coil spring

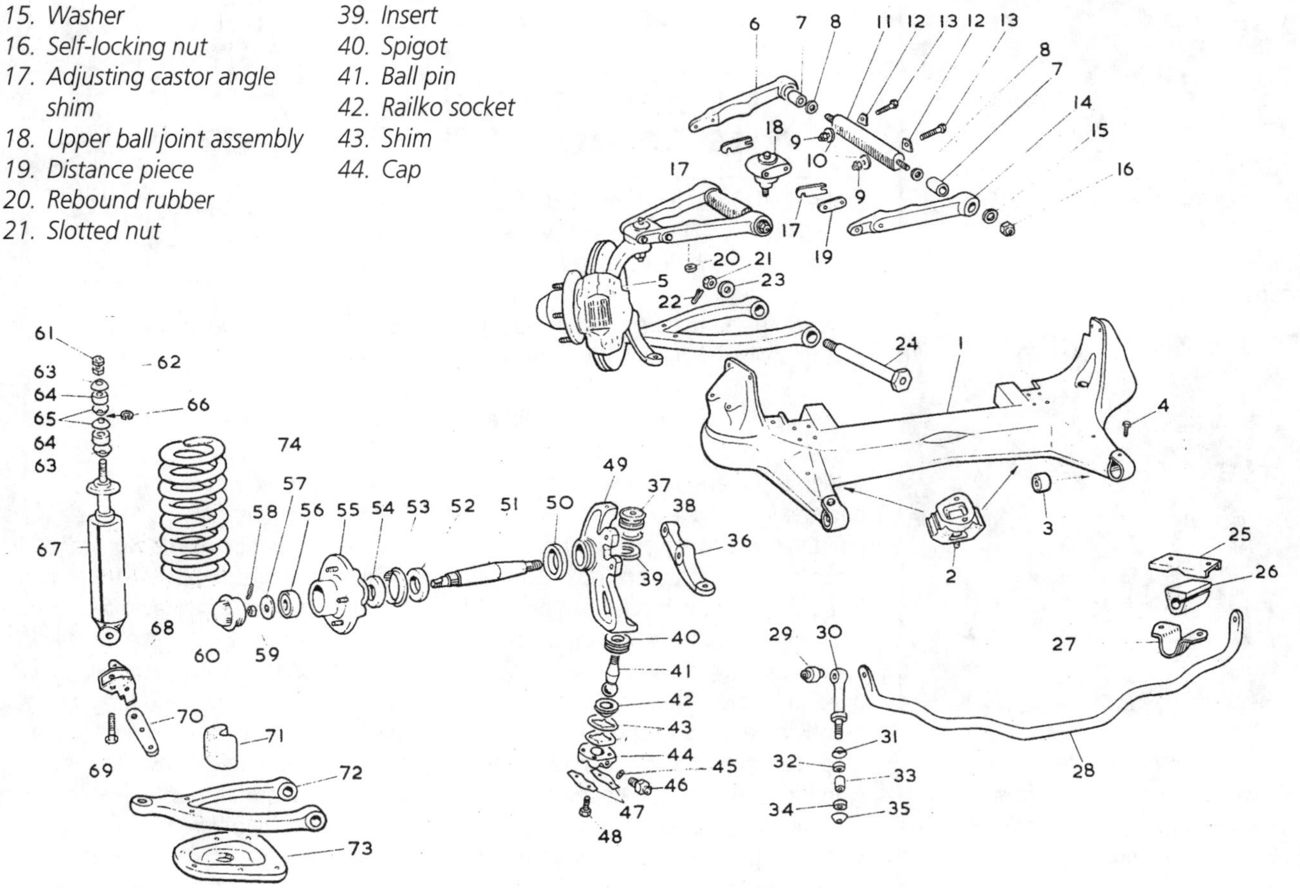

FRONT SUSPENSION

BUYING

All suspension and steering parts have a difficult job controlling the XJ6. Again, buy from Jaguar dealerships or specialists such as SNG Barratt to ensure that you are fitting only quality parts to your big cat. We do not advise buying second-hand suspension components, however cheap they may seem.

DESCRIPTION

The front suspension assembly comprises a pressed steel crossmember to which is attached the steering mechanism and the upper and lower wishbones. The unit also incorporates coil springs, hydraulic telescopic dampers and an anti-roll bar (fitted between the two lower wishbones). Series 2 cars have gas-pressurised hydraulic dampers.

◀ FSU1. As this diagram shows, there are a lot of components comprising a Jaguar front suspension.

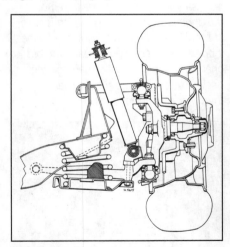

▲ FSU2. The operation of the front suspension can be better understood by studying this sectional view through one side.

TRACK ROD ENDS

▲ FSU3. The track rod end assemblies are sealed units and need no greasing at routine service intervals. Phil unscrewed and removed the taper pin nut, and separated the balljoint from the steering arm, using an extractor. He held the track rod end with an open-ended spanner and unscrewed the locknut a quarter of a turn. He then held the track rod whilst the end was unscrewed from it. Check the condition of the rubber bellows – if they are split or cut, they must be removed, as dust and dirt could get in and cause dangerous wear. The bellows are secured by Jubilee clips.

STUB AXLE CARRIER

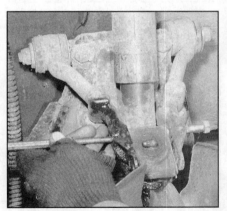

▲ FSU4. To remove the stub axle carrier, you first have to remove the brake calliper, disc and hub assembly. If the condition of the top ball joint is OK, simply undo the self-locking nut securing the ball joint to the carrier. We were replacing both the ball joints and the upper wishbone bushes, so Phil removed the nuts from the bolts securing the top ball joint to the wishbone. It will

probably be necessary to drift out the bolts – they tend to seize. There will be a number of shims situated as shown ...

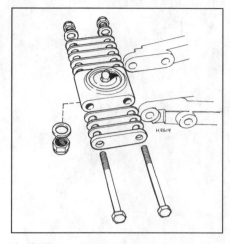

▲ FSU5. ... in this diagram.

▲ FSU6. The carrier is secured by the lower ball joint. There's a small protective cover there and, if removed, offers better access to the self-locking ball joint nut.

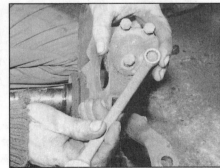

▲ FSU7. Phil removed the four bolts securing the bottom ball joint.

▲ FSU8. This is what it looks like in 'exploded' form. The originals have grease nipples, but the more modern versions supplied by SNG Barratt are sealed for life, thus reducing the maintenance.

▲ FSU9. Phil removed three steel shims – and that's how many he put back! Always keep track of such items if you're storing for any length of time.

▲ FSU10. Phil removed the single Nylock nut holding the upper ball joint. If the whole lot swivels, use a ball joint splitter to hold it steady. Note that there is a washer under the nut – it must be replaced with the new ball joint …

▲ FSU11. … seen here replacing its worn-out compatriot.

▲ FSU12. The finished stub axle carrier, a relatively simple job but one which is highly beneficial in terms of driveability and safety.

▲ FSU13. Back at the top wishbone, this is in two halves, both secured by a single nut and two washers.

▲ FSU14. It will almost certainly be necessary to use some force to remove the original bushes, one of which is seen at top. When you're replacing the bushes, it doesn't matter if you damage the old ones, but take care not to damage the sleeve itself. Compare the original with the shiny new part alongside.

▲ FSU15. Before fitting the new bush, Phil rubbed down the sleeve with a very fine Scotchbrite pad. It is only necessary to remove any fine surface rust – you don't want score marks from the abrasive material. He sprayed WD40 into the sleeve, and then, having placed one half of the bush into the sleeve, he eased the second half into place by using the vice. It's important to get everything absolutely square at this stage, to prevent damage to bush and/or sleeve.

▲ FSU16. To prevent future seizures, Phil 'painted' some copper grease on to the pivot shaft, before …

▲ FSU17. … tightening up the securing nut. Don't forget to try out the newly installed wishbones for the correct movement.

▲ FSU18. The lower wishbone bushes may also need replacing. The lower wishbone is held by a shaft with a castellated nut at one end, secured by a

split pin which Phil removed and discarded. He removed the nut and wishbone, replacing the bushes in a repeat of the earlier operation.

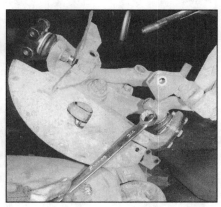

▲ FSU19. With the wishbones in place and re-bushed, Phil fitted the carrier back on to the lower wishbone by the lower balljoint. Again, if the ball pin turns, use a ball joint splitter (more carefully this time) to hold it steady while the nut is tightened.

▲ FSU20. At the top, the ball joint was fitted back in between the upper wishbone arms, making sure to replace the right number of castor-adjusting shims.

SPRINGS AND DAMPERS

Check your springs (cracks and security) and dampers (oil leakage) regularly. Jaguar recommends that dampers are changed at 30,000 mile intervals. Remember that springs and dampers are safety items – a well-worn damper can affect not only handling, but also braking performance, by two metres or more.

MONROE SENSA-TRAC SHOCK ABSORBERS

We used Monroe Sensa-Trac dampers. We were keen to retain the smooth, unruffled ride, but we also wanted to improve the cornering ability when 'pressing on'. Using a unique system of seals, valves and grooves called Position Sensitive Damping (PSD) the Sensa-Trac shock absorbers automatically change to suit the road and driving conditions. When you're wafting along, they're luxury soft, soaking up small deflections, but when cornering hard, the dampers stiffen up to prevent excessive roll.

Technically, when you're driving in the 'comfort zone', the damping fluid flows freely around the piston via a fine groove in the damper wall, hence a smooth and comfortable ride. But when greater deflections push the piston past the PSD groove, the normal firm damping comes into play and the suspension stiffens up, giving better control.

SNG Barratt supplied the original specification springs. It's usually the case that in the search for improved road-holding, it is better to uprate the dampers more than the springs. Greatly uprated springs and dampers can often lead to a harsh, choppy ride, especially over bumpy surfaces. The combination we fitted here offers an excellent compromise between better handling on the one hand and a luxury smooth ride on the other.

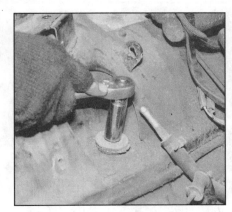

▲ FSU21. Before removing the damper, Phil placed a trolley jack under the front wishbone because the first job is to remove the upper mounting nut, accessed from within the engine bay.

SPRINGS

▲ FSU22. With this released, the damper is free to drop down – which is the reason for the trolley jack. Note the rubber cushion and washer at the top of the damper. It's important to get the cushions and washers back in the right order.

▲ FSU23. A single bolt holds the damper at its lower mounting point.

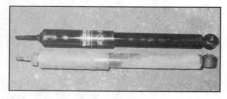

▲ FSU24. Compare the old and the new. The wet patch at the bottom of the damper is the WD40 Phil used to ease the bolt/nut. However, the rust shows the general age of the damper and, although it wasn't actually leaking, its efficiency wouldn't be anywhere near as good as it should be, and failure wouldn't be long coming.

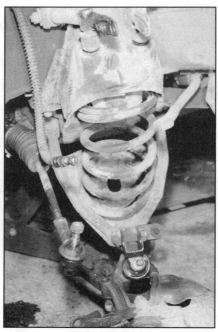

▲ FSU25. This is the view with the damper removed and the stub axle carrier unbolted from the top wishbone.

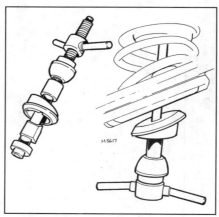

▲ FSU26. You'll need a coil spring compressor to remove the front springs. Either use a proprietary model or make one up from a length of suitably threaded rod using nuts and large washers or cross-pieces. The compressor has to be inserted from underneath through the hole in the spring pan, and the spring tightened. It can then be manoeuvred out of position and ...

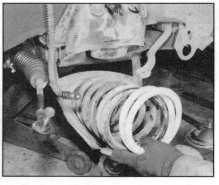

▲ FSU27. ... the compression released – slowly; do not underestimate the effect of a spring flying off unchecked. Note that there are packing rings here. These may or may not be present, but if they are, take note of how many are present. They are used to adjust the side-to-side ride height which should be 611mm (24 ⅝ in). This is measured from ground level to the headlamp centres. Each packing piece is 7.93mm (⁵⁄₁₆ in) thick.

▲ FSU28. Though not visible from the outside, this spring had broken off, the lower coil being rusted solid in the spring pan!

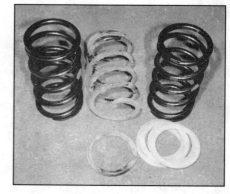

▲ FSU29. Once more, the old and the new. The springs from SNG Barratt are marked as per Jaguar specification and *come with enough packing rings to fit any model. The springs are colour-coded with blobs of paint to ensure that you get the right springs for your car.*

REAR SUSPENSION

The rear suspension assembly comprises a pressed steel crossmember. It is located by radius arms and rubber mounted to the body. The driveshafts are open and

located transversely by two links. The suspension is conventional dampers and springs, although it is unusual in that two assemblies per side are used. Series 2 cars utilised gas-filled dampers as standard fitment.

▼ *RUS1. Exploded view of the rear suspension.*

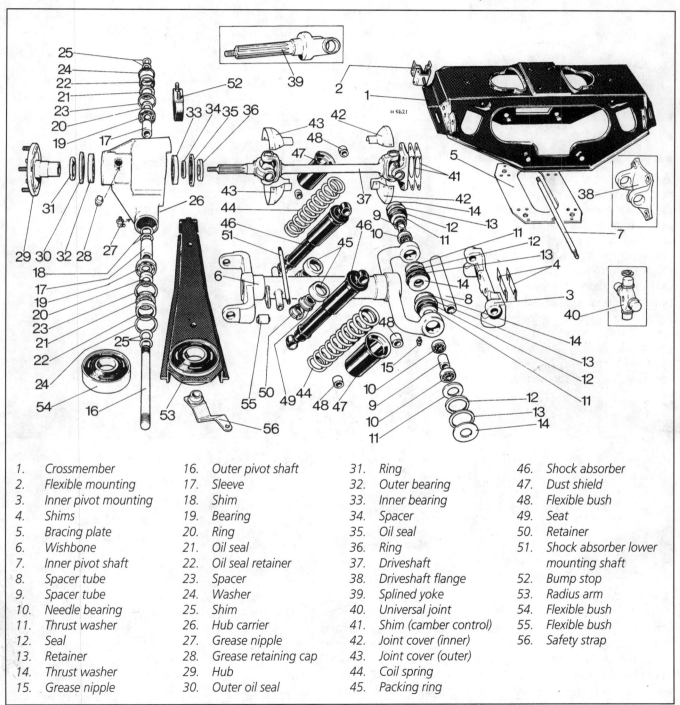

1.	Crossmember	16.	Outer pivot shaft	31.	Ring	46.	Shock absorber
2.	Flexible mounting	17.	Sleeve	32.	Outer bearing	47.	Dust shield
3.	Inner pivot mounting	18.	Shim	33.	Inner bearing	48.	Flexible bush
4.	Shims	19.	Bearing	34.	Spacer	49.	Seat
5.	Bracing plate	20.	Ring	35.	Oil seal	50.	Retainer
6.	Wishbone	21.	Oil seal	36.	Ring	51.	Shock absorber lower mounting shaft
7.	Inner pivot shaft	22.	Oil seal retainer	37.	Driveshaft	52.	Bump stop
8.	Spacer tube	23.	Spacer	38.	Driveshaft flange	53.	Radius arm
9.	Spacer tube	24.	Washer	39.	Splined yoke	54.	Flexible bush
10.	Needle bearing	25.	Shim	40.	Universal joint	55.	Flexible bush
11.	Thrust washer	26.	Hub carrier	41.	Shim (camber control)	56.	Safety strap
12.	Seal	27.	Grease nipple	42.	Joint cover (inner)		
13.	Retainer	28.	Grease retaining cap	43.	Joint cover (outer)		
14.	Thrust washer	29.	Hub	44.	Coil spring		
15.	Grease nipple	30.	Outer oil seal	45.	Packing ring		

▲ RUS2. What would seem like a fairly drastic step on most cars, is necessary on the XJ6 for many brake/suspension procedures. We had the luxury of working with the NBN Chassis Tilter and having our car on its side made life very much easier. However, working with the car in a typical garage demands some care. It is necessary to raise the car far higher than would normally be the case for routine maintenance. You must work with at least one assistant, and safety must be your main concern. The complete assembly is shown here.

▲ RUS3. The propshaft has to be uncoupled from the final drive and the handbrake cables disconnected – both shown elsewhere in this chapter. The radius arm has to be disconnected at its front mounting point. The security wire passing through the centre bolt has to be snipped before the bolt can be removed.

▲ RUS4. The bolt securing the safety plate to the underside of the car has to be removed, and then the plate can be removed.

▲ RUS5. Use a pry bar if necessary to ease the radius arm away. The arm can be left in place on the suspension unit if required, for later removal at its opposite end.

▲ RUS6. There are four mountings, two at either side, each with two bolts/nuts per mounting. They are rubber bonded to metal and vital to the car. Phil used his pneumatic hammer and a ring spanner to remove the mountings – don't forget the car in these photos is on its side in the chassis tilter. He had taken the precaution of chaining the unit to the engine hoist to take the load.

▲ RUS7. Always inspect the mountings carefully. If they have been in place for years, replace as a matter of course. Here are the four new SNG Barratt mountings we used, surrounding one of the old ones. Ours, incredibly, weren't in bad condition – it's usual to find them literally hanging by a thread on cars of any age.

▲ RUS8. Another common item notable by its absence is the bump stop – an MoT failure point, too. Again, it's a rubber bush bonded to a metal plate with two studs in it. Eventually, metal and rubber part company, leaving the plate in situ and the rubber bush in a hedge bottom. They cannot be repaired and if yours look even the slightest bit dodgy, replace them. Getting the nuts off the original mounting plate is almost certain to be tricky and usually calls for patience and lots of WD40.

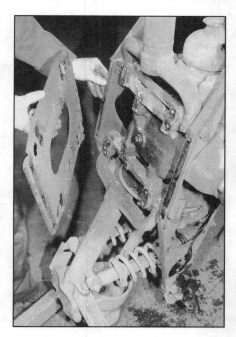

▲ RUS9. We needed access to the discs and callipers which meant that the protective tie plate had to be removed. There are six self-locking nuts/bolts at either end of the plate securing it to the cross beam, and eight self-locking nuts/bolts holding it to the inner pivot mounting brackets. Remove the lot and pull off the plate. The plate itself needed a thorough degreasing. Though most such items will usually need wire-brushing and repainting, the tie plate is often covered in a layer of oil (from a leaking differential) which provides a protective coating against rust, and cleaning may be all that is required.

▲ RUS10. The inner and outer universal joints on each half shaft are protected by two-part metal shrouds. These are secured by Jubilee clips on to the drive shaft.

▲ RUS11. If you need to remove the shroud altogether, drill out the rivets holding the two halves together.

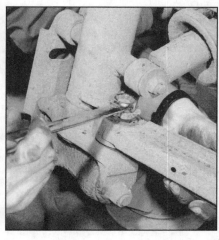

▲ RUS12. To remove the radius arm, the tab washer has to be bent back first, but, as is shown in this photo, the nut cannot be removed with the lower suspension mountings in place.

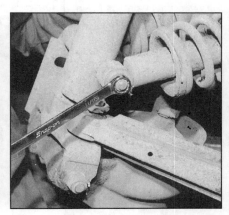

▲ RUS13. Phil removed the nut from here, whilst using a ring spanner to prevent the head of the bolt from turning.

▲ RUS14. He was then able to tap the bolt through using a suitable drift.

▲ RUS15. This is the complete assembly – note that there's a spacer at one end (nearest to camera), necessary so that the nut will clear the head of the radius arm mounting bolt.

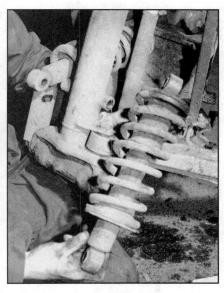

▲ RUS16. A single nut/bolt secures the suspension unit at the top mounting.

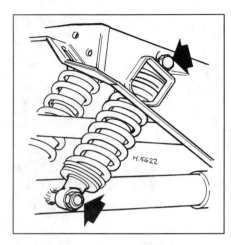

▲ RUS17. This diagram shows the rear shock absorber mountings.

▲ RUS18. With them removed, attention could then be paid to the radius arm. Note that the bolt head is shaped on one side to clear the front suspension mounting, which itself is shorter at this point than its rearmost opposite number, compensated for by a spacer.

▲ RUS19. SNG Barratt have a complete range of rubber bushes for the various suspension components.

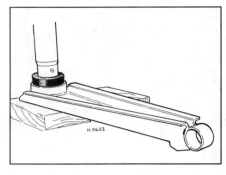

▲ RUS20. Getting the old bushes out of the radius arm is no easy task and the best way is to use a press. Their cost puts them beyond most of us, but your friendly local garage should be able to do them for you for only a small charge. Balance the cash cost against hours of hard work – and even then, you may not be able to remove some of the more stubborn bushes.

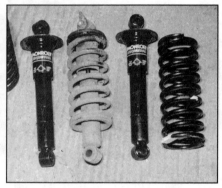

▲ RUS21. We fitted Monroe Sensa-trac shock absorbers and springs at the rear to match those already fitted at the front. They are seen here, with the old unit in the centre.

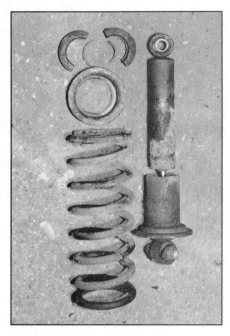

▲ RUS22. Always use a spring compressor (with appropriate safety precautions) to remove the springs from the rear dampers. This simple circlip is all that holds the spring in place, although it's likely to be rusted in place and will probably need tapping free. This is the original, well-rusted damper with its spring and associated components. The retainer, and seat are required for the fitting of the new dampers.

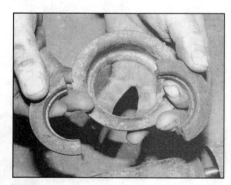

▲ RUS23. This is the seat and two-part retainer – all three parts were cleaned-up for re-use.

◀ RUS24. Phil used the S-P compressors again to get the spring down to a manageable length before inserting the new damper, the seat, and the two halves of the retainer.

▲ RUS25. Here, the seat and retainer are in place, and the circlip has been fitted. The spring compressor was then released slowly and evenly.

▲ RUS26. Before and after – no prizes for guessing which is which!

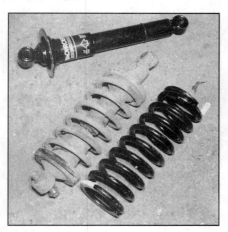

▲ RUS27. For reference, this shot shows just how much the spring has to be compressed. It's a lot, so please take great care – the effect of such a spring uncompressing at speed does not bear thinking about.

STEERING

REAR SUSPENSION TORQUE FIGURES

	lbs/ft	kg/m
Bottom plate to crossbeam/inner fulcrum mtg	14/18	1.94/2.48
Inner fulcrum mounting to drive unit	60/65	8.30/8.98
Drive unit to crossbeam	70/77	9.68/10.64
Calliper to drive unit flanges	49/55	6.78/7.60
Fulcrum pin (inner)	45/50	6.23/6.91
Outer pivot pin	97/107	13.41/14.80
Drive unit to drive shaft	49/55	6.78/7.60
Half shaft to hub carrier (bearing)	100/120	13.83/16.60
Radius rods to wishbones	60/70	8.30/9.68
Safety strap and radius rods to body	40/45	5.54/6.62
Safety strap to floor panel	27/32	3.74/4.42
Rear shock absorbers	32/36	4.43/4.97

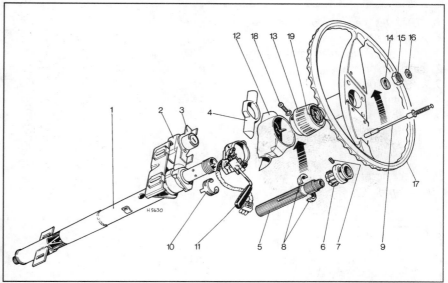

▲ STR1. All models have a rack and pinion steering system, power assisted on all but a few 2.8 litre Series 1 cars. The steering column is collapsible, incorporating shear plugs and universal joints. The power steering was of Adwest manufacture on all XJ6 variants until 1974, when Alford and Adler power steering was fitted as an alternative. This diagram shows an exploded view of a Series 1 upper steering column assembly.
KEY
1. Column
2. Steering column
3. Cowl support bracket
4. Cowl
5. Upper shaft
6. Cone
7. Grub screw
8. Split collets*
9. Horn contact
10. Striker Plate
11. Direction indicator switch
12. Switch cover
13. Lock nut
14. Washer
15. Nut
16. Lock washer
17. Steering wheel
18. Screw
19. Circlip
*Collets are reversed for Series 2 cars.

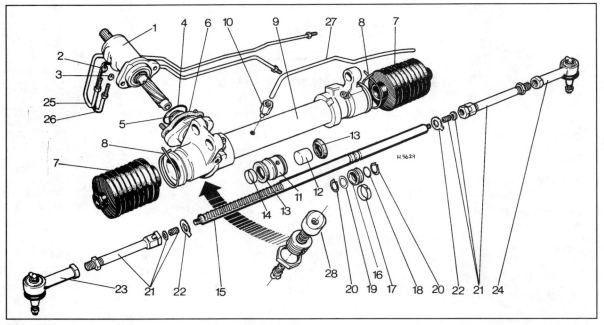

▲ STR2. This is an exploded view of Adwest power steering gear.

Key

1. Valve and pinion assembly
2. Pipe union seat
3. Pipe union seat
4. O-ring
5. Seal
6. Gasket
7. Bellows
8. Clip
9. Rack housing
10. Adaptor

11. Seal housing
12. Special 'Chevite' bearing
13. Seal
14. Seal retainer
15. Rack
16. Piston
17. Piston ring
18. O-ring
19. Shim
20. Circlip

21. Inner balljoint assembly
22. Tab washer
23. Track rod end
24. Rack rod end
25. Outlet pipe
26. Inlet pipe
27. Air transfer tube
28. Rack damper assembly

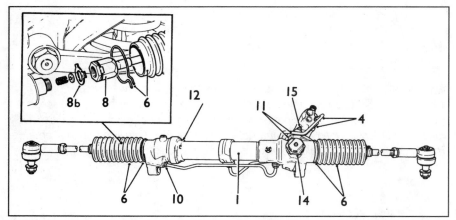

▲ STR3. This is an exploded view of Alford and Adler power steering gear.

KEY

1. Rack housing
4. Valve housing
6. Bellows and clip
8. Inner balljoint assemblies
8b. Lock plates

10. Air transfer pipe
11. Valve-to-cylinder connecting pipes
12. Rack housing ring nut
14. Rack damper assembly
15. Valve assembly lock nuts

REPLACING THE STEERING RACK

As the engine was out being rebuilt at VSE at the time, fitting the rack was very simple – and much clearer from a photographic point of view. However, it isn't that difficult anyway, the main problem areas being simply those of lack of space and the awkwardness of working from beneath the car. Don't forget the safety precautions.

▲ STR4. Phil uncoupled the hydraulic pipes (clearly not a requirement on a non-power steering system) and then removed the pinch bolt from the lower steering column universal joint. We had already removed the tie rods from the wheels.

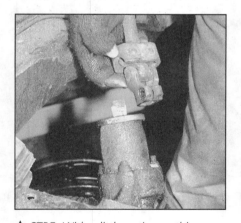

▲ STR5. With a little patience, this was waggled off the splines.

▲ STR6. The rack itself can be removed as a complete unit. It is held by two nuts/bolts on the left, just here, and …

▲ STR7. … by one nut/bolt on the right. It's a tight fit so, even with the fasteners removed, it should still stay in place. It's worth having an assistant on hand just in case, though.

▼ STR8. The old unit at top, with the SNG Barratt-supplied replacement. Steering racks are supplied on an exchange basis, which would normally mean a delay whilst the old one was removed and returned and the new one was supplied. However, in order to help enthusiasts keep their cars on the road, the company operates a system whereby the new rack can be supplied with a surcharge, refundable on the return of the old rack.

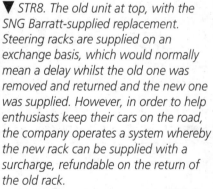

▲ STR9. Barratts supplied new bearings and seals for the mountings – it's pointless fitting a new rack with old bearings.

▲ STR10. Fitting was simply a reversal of the removal procedure, with the bolts being tightened to the correct torque.

▲ STR11. Naturally, we fitted new track rod ends – not to do so would be to spoil the ship for a ha'p'orth of tar.

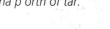

POWER STEERING PUMP

▶ *STR12. Overhauling a power steering pump is tricky and involved, as you can imagine from this exploded view. Moreover, the cost of exchange units makes it more logical to do a straight swap and use your time more constructively. Remove the pump by disconnecting the hose from the outlet at the rear of the pump reservoir and allowing the fluid to drain into a container. Disconnect the high pressure hose from the reservoir and the pump adjusting link from the water pump. Press the pump inwards, lift the jockey pulley against the spring pressure and ease the drivebelt off the pump pulley. Lift the pump outwards and disconnect the bottom pivot mounting bolt which will enable the pump to be lifted up and away.*
KEY

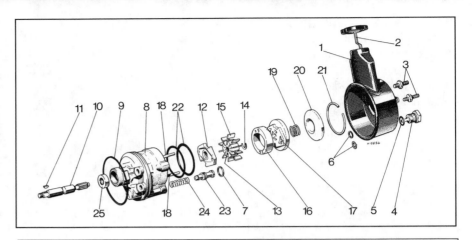

1. Reservoir	15. Pump rotor
2. Dipstick	vanes
3. Stud	16. Pump ring
4. Union	17. Pressure plate
5. O-ring	18. Pin
6. Seal	19. Spring
7. Seal	20. End plate
8. Pump body	21. Clip
9. O-ring	22. O-ring
10. Shaft	23. Flow control
11. Key	valve
12. Thrust plate	24. Spring
13. Rotor	25. Oil seal
14. Clip	

BLEEDING THE POWER STEERING

Using a block of wood to protect the subframe, jack up the front of the car so that both wheels are off the ground. Top up the power steering fluid reservoir and start the engine. At idle, turn the wheels from lock to lock and have an assistant watch the fluid level. Top up where required and continue the procedure until the fluid level does not drop further.

STEERING ANGLES AND FRONT WHEEL ALIGNMENT

Contributing factors are correct tyre pressures, serviceable bearings (correctly adjusted) and other steering linkage components in good order. The four

SPECIFICATIONS

Castor angle	2.25 degrees +/– 0.25 degree positive
Camber angle	0.5 degrees +/ 0.25 degree positive
Front wheel toe-in	1/16 in.-1/8 in. (1.6mm-3.2mm)
Steering axis inclination	1.5 degrees

TORQUE FIGURES

	lb/ft	kg/m
Pinion housing cover plate	14/18	1.94/2.48
Track rod end ball joint	45/50	6.22/6.91
Bolt in tie-rod end assembly	6/7	0.83/0.96
Mounting bolts	14/18	1.94/2.48
Universal joints	14/18	1.94/2.48
Column transverse strut to body	8/10	1.10/1.38
Steering wheel to shaft	25/32	3.46/4.42
Steering column to lower bracket	14/18	1.94/2.48
Steering column to upper bracket	14/18	1.94/2.48
Steering wheel clamp bolt	10/12	1.40/1.65
Locknut – collet adaptor retaining screw	6/7	0.83/0.96
Longitudinal strut to body	11/13	1.53/1.79
Vertical strut to body	14/18	1.92/2.48
Vertical strut to longitudinal strut	8/10	1.10/1.38
PAS feed hose	14/16	1.94/2.21
PAS return hose	18/20	2.48/2.76
PAS hose assembly valve to pump	18/20	2.48/2.76
Rack locking bolt	27/32	3.74/4.42
Rack adaptor	49/55	6.78/7.60
Horizontal strut to vertical bracket	8/10	1.10/1.38

major aspects to wheel alignment are as follows:

CAMBER is the angle at which the front wheels are set from the vertical when viewed from the front of the car. Positive camber is the amount in degrees that the wheels are tilted outwards at the top from the vertical.

CASTOR is the angle between the steering axis and a vertical line when viewed from each side of the car. Positive castor is when the steering axis

is inclined rearwards.

STEERING AXIS INCLINATION is the angle when viewed from the front of the car, between the vertical and an imaginary line drawn between the upper and lower suspension swivels.

TOE-IN is the amount by which the distance between the front inside edges of the road wheels (measured at hub height) is less than the diametrically opposite distance measured between the rear inside edges of the front road wheels.

Chapter 9

Wheels and Tyres

Much of the technical information and specifications given in this chapter were kindly provided by Goodyear Great Britain Limited.

GENERAL WHEEL SPECIFICATIONS

Road wheels, all 5 studs/nuts.
Pressed steel disc   6J x 15
Alloy wheels   6J x 15

BUYING WHEELS

Buying new steel or alloy wheels is easy – if you've got the cash! Franchised Jaguar dealers have access to the range of O/E wheels and there are a number of wheel companies who can supply them. It is obviously important that you buy wheels which are suited to the weight and capabilities of your Jaguar – not all are. Make sure that the rim profile and offset are correct, and pay great attention to the wheel nuts, especially where alloy wheels are concerned, as it is vital that they seat properly.

There are always plenty of second-hand wheels for sale in the specialist magazines. When buying wheels in this way, make sure that they are not seriously damaged – very likely, particularly if they are any age. Alloy wheels can be damaged very easily and this can lead to gradual tyre deflation, uneven tracking, inaccurate steering or uneven tyre wear – or the whole lot! If you're not sure what to look for, take along someone who is.

WIDE BOYS?

Fitting larger wheels and huge, low profile 'rubber band' tyres to the XJ6 is a popular option. The most obvious reason for doing so is the 'mean' look it gives the car, especially if the suspension is lowered. However, there are drawbacks, the most obvious being that this kind of treatment will almost always destroy the XJ6's legendary ride comfort, especially as big tyres tend to create lots more bump-thump. And whilst good low-profile tyres will add to the grip in the dry, they are naturally more prone to aquaplaning in the wet. A larger wheel/tyre combination will place more strain on the associated components, i.e. steering, suspension, transmission and brakes, so making any great changes should be considered very carefully, preferably with some unbiased professional advice.

▲ W1. The design of the steel wheels changed somewhat over the years, but they are interchangeable, model to model. This is the chrome centre trim as fitted to Series 1 and 2 cars.

▲ W2. The famous 'pepperpot' alloy wheel was available on Series 3 models from 1982 but can be retro-fitted as required.

▲ W3. If you have an air-powered wrench, now is the time to make it work for a living. After 'cracking' the five nuts with the wheel wrench, it makes short work of removing them. It's OK to use your air ratchet to replace them again because it won't be able to overtighten them. However, don't use a pneumatic impact driver for this job and always check the final tightness with a torque wrench. This is a Series 3 wheel with stainless steel wheel trim.

▲ W4. Teng's magnetic tool tray is one of the most useful tools you can have and it's ideal for keeping your wheel nuts together and out of the dirt and grime on the garage floor. This type of chrome wheel nut suffers badly at the hands of rust because few owners are fussy enough to remove and clean them on a regular basis. Polishing with a quality cleaner such as Solvol's Autosol will bring off most surface rust, but if there is pitting it's a case for re-chroming or, more realistically, a new set of nuts from your dealer or a specialist such as SNG Barratt.

▲ W5. This horrible sight is typical of older XJ6s – that attractive trim covers up a multitude of sins. It's not a difficult job to respray steel wheels, as shown next. It's important to at least remove the trim for periodic checks to ensure that there are no cracks in the wheel and no signs of wheel bearing leakage which may not be apparent with the trim in place.

▲ W6. When putting the wheel cover back, you'll need to hold it in place against its natural spring to get the nuts to locate centrally in their holes. Don't forget to line up the valve hole!

▲ W7. All wheel nuts should be torqued up to the right figure. Never rely on guesswork, and if you have new tyres fitted at a tyre centre, always check the torque figures when you get home – they can often be enthusiastic with those pneumatic impact guns and the nuts can often be incredibly tight as a result. It's better to find out in your garage where you've got plenty of tools than on a dark, rainy country road with just the wheel-changing brace and jack! If they're not tight enough there's the possibility of wheel wobble and stress on the various suspension and steering components, not to mention the obvious danger to life and limb. Alloy wheel nuts should be torqued to a higher figure than steel wheels, which have more 'spring' in them. Tighten the nuts in a cross-wise sequence to avoid the risk of distortion.

Apply a little copper grease to the threads each time you replace a wheel. Make sure you don't get grease of any description on the brake discs or pads. If you have alloy wheels, it pays to dab a little on the hub in-between the studs in order to prevent the wheel sticking to it.

WHEEL NUT TORQUE FIGURES

Alloy wheels	75 lb/ft (101 Nm)
Steel wheels	45 lb/ft (61 Nm)

SPRAYING STEEL WHEELS

SAFETY NOTE: There will be plenty of flaking paint, rust and dirt in the air, so it pays to wear goggles. When using thinners and/or spray paints, ALWAYS wear a mask, goggles and gloves and make sure that there is some ventilation.

It is possible to spray the wheel whilst on the car, but it means there are several areas that can't be properly de-rusted and much more attention must be paid to masking off to prevent overspray getting on to the bodywork.

▲ W8. Bead blasting is the best way to clean up scruffy steel wheels. Companies such as Pristine (see later in this chapter), who specialise in alloy wheel refurbishment, can often offer this facility. However, it is possible to make a reasonable job of such a wheel at home, though you'll need plenty of patience and energy.

Start by using a degreasant to clean them and remove as much brake dust as possible. Wash off, ideally using a high pressure washer, such as the SIP Lunarstorm. Use a wire brush (a cordless drill makes life easier) to get the loose stuff off, and then use emery paper around the rim to provide a key for the paint and to get into any areas of rust.

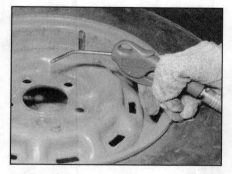

▲ W9. We used the S-P air gun to blast all the debris from those awkward nooks and crannies – there's no point in painting over rust! Rusted areas, of which there will probably be plenty, should be treated with a proprietary anti-rust agent, such as Jenolite. Always follow the instructions carefully and, as most such preparations are designed to eat into the rust, you should keep them off your hands in case they do the same thing to your skin!

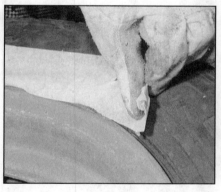

▲ W10. We masked off the tyre from the wheel by using lots of short strips of 2 in masking tape, pressed well down behind the rim. If you're an accurate sprayer, this is all that will be required – if not, tag large sections of newspaper along the outer edges of the original masking tape.

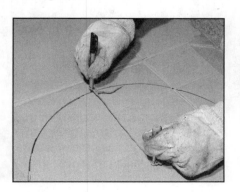

▲ W11. Using standard spraying techniques with a proprietary 'steel wheel' aerosol can produce a gleaming finish like this. Don't try to cover everything in one go – apply several light coats. Let the wheel dry fully, preferably overnight, before fitting it to the car.

▲ W12. An alternative method of masking is to take a large sheet of cardboard (a folded out cardboard box is ideal), cut a wheel-size hole in it and then tape it to the wheel. If you're doing all five wheels, this will make life much easier. Measure the rim exactly (don't forget, this measurement is more than the nominal 15 in), and then transfer it to …

◄ W13. … a piece of string. Fix the string at the centre point by using a screwdriver or punch and then put a pen in a loop at the opposite end. Hold the 'driver and draw the circle – simple, isn't it? Cut out the circle and you have an instant single-piece wheel mask.

KEEPING YOUR WHEELS UP TO SCRATCH

When fitting steel (and some alloy) wheels, it's easy to damage the paint surface with the edge of the socket as it turns. Get around this by simply inserting a large rubber washer into the end of the socket, so that it still fits on to the nut but now can't go down far enough to touch the wheel.

REFURBISHING ALLOY WHEELS

Jaguar alloy wheels are as prone as most others to corrosion, and the UK climate, in particular, doesn't help at all. If the vehicle has been used for even a small mileage during the winter, the effects of cold, damp and, worst of all, the rock salt used for de-icing the roads, will soon cause damage.

▲ ALL1. Whilst the wheel doesn't rust in the same way as steel, it will still suffer corrosion in the form of a white 'fur' which forms on the surface, as the protective coat of lacquer starts to break-up. This can be treated to some extent by using a metal polish, but it will soon start to 'pit'. The DIY enthusiast can do nothing about serious pitting. This wheel shows the effects of many winters and little cleaning with 'scuffing' around the edges where successive drivers have employed the Braille-driving technique when parking close up to kerbs. A set of new wheels is far from cheap, and buying used wheels is difficult; they'll probably also be pitted and, more seriously, could well be damaged and/or bent and therefore dangerous. Unless you really know your stuff, leave second-hand wheel purchase alone.

▲ ALL2. A third option is usually more viable – have your original alloys professionally cleaned. Under the leadership of David James, Pristine in Woburn Sands, Beds, can handle absolutely any type of alloy for any type of car, whether original or aftermarket. This is just a few of the wheels being processed at the time of writing. For most popular wheels, Pristine offer an exchange service, and this includes the 6 in. alloy as fitted to Series 3 XJ6s. With its bespoke service, it is possible for an owner to make advance arrangements and make the old to new wheel transformation in an hour. And all for much less cost than buying new wheels – even aftermarket copies.

Pristine have such a high turnover of wheels that they keep a huge selection of the most popular alloys in stock. Naturally, this includes the Jaguar 'pepperpots' and means that, as a rule, you can drive in with your old alloys and drive away with refurbished wheels.

▲ ALL3. This shot shows the four stages of preparation and finishing which, from lower centre clockwise are: (a) straight

off the car and looking the worse for wear; (b) newly beadblasted; (c) machined; (d) sprayed and lacquered. The sequence here follows a wheel around the Pristine factory, where it was transformed from ugly duckling to swan.

▲ ALL4. The first job is to put the damaged and corroded wheel into the beadblasting machine.

▲ ALL5. The turntable makes sure that all of the top surface rim gets the full treatment.

▲ ALL6. It only takes about two minutes at full power to produce what is already a much better-looking wheel.

▲ ALL7. The difference is even more pronounced when we look at the original pitted and dirty surface of the inner rim before …

▲ ALL8. … and after. This process removes almost all the loose lacquer, dirt and brake dust, but not quite all, which is why it needs to be given …

▲ ALL9. … a quick dip in the acid bath which removes any vestiges of the original paint finish. Note the serious protective gear, necessary when dealing with unpleasant acids, etc. Then it was pressure-sprayed to blast away all traces of acid so that it can be handled safely for the next operation, which is …

▲ ALL10. … a trip to the comprehensive machine room. Here, it is expertly set-up so that around one thou is removed from the top surface of the wheel. The lathes are all computer controlled. Special programmes are available to enable the device to work to the exact contours of the individual wheel. All clever stuff!

▲ ALL11. After this it goes into the pre-treatment bay. In here, there are four operations, starting with a spell in the hot degreasing jet-blast cabinet,

followed by …
▲ ALL12. … a dunking in the cold bath. Note the bubbles, caused by compressed air being forced into the bath in order to give a 'swirl' effect and get the water

into all the nooks and crannies.
▲ ALL13. The wheel then goes for a swim in the etch primer, necessary for the powder coating finish to get a grip, and after another dunking in cold clear

water …
▲ ALL14. … it goes into the huge oven to be baked at a sweltering 225°C (437°F) in order to remove all traces of inherent gasses contained in the metal. If this were not carried out, the final

coating would soon lift off the wheel.
▲ ALL15. The wheel then comes straight out of the oven and is powder coated while it is still hot, which means that the

coating cures as it is applied. The powder coating is an electro-magnetic process with a 12v positive charge coming through the gun, and the wheel being earthed via the rail in the spray booth. When the spraying process is complete, the wheel goes into a separate oven where it is baked at 180°C (356°F) for 10 minutes. After being hung to dry it is lacquered cold and then heated to 200°C (392°F) to cure it. The results are staggering; wheels that look as good as new for a fraction of the new cost.

TYRES

It is extremely important that you fit high quality tyres to your XJ6. It is a powerful, heavy car, designed to be driven at high speeds – where limits allow – and this means that the most stressed items on the car are those black circles at each corner. All the acceleration, braking and cornering forces are turned into positive action via four hand-size patches of rubber, so that rubber had better be up to the job in hand!

ORIGINAL TYRE SPECIFICATIONS

UK models	Dunlop E70. VR15 SP Sport or Pirelli P5 205/70 VR15
US models	Pirelli P5 205/70 VR15 or P5 215/70 VR15

It has to be remembered that though these were ahead of their time, they were designed in the early 1960s and that tyre design and composition has changed radically since. Most notable is the introduction of sticky, low profile tyres. According to Paul Bould at Goodyear, the original sizes are getting tricky to find, but it is possible to substitute a lower-profile tyre as long as the rolling circumference remains the same. If the overall height of the wheel/tyre combination is much different (higher or lower) this will affect the gearing of the car and the accuracy of the speedometer reading – no policeman will accept your choice of tyres as a reason for exceeding a speed limit!

▲ TY1. Paul suggested that we treat our newly refurbished alloy wheels to a set of Goodyear Eagle NCT 2 tyres, 225/60 15, which would be only slightly different from the original overall sizes and would not be enough to make any discernible difference.

▲ TY2. These are superbly 'grippy' and

as you might guess from the tyre tread pattern, are excellent for dispersing water on the road. It's important to consider the general climate the car will be driven in – very wide, ultra low profile tyres will give better grip in the dry but in some instances this can lead to aquaplaning in extreme circumstances.

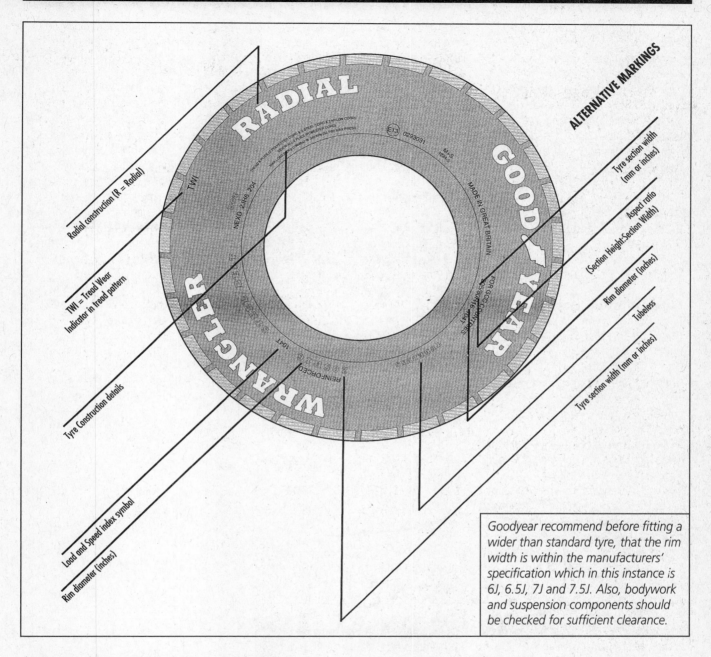

ALTERNATIVE MARKINGS

RADIAL

GOOD YEAR

WRANGLER

Radial construction (R = Radial)

TWI = Tread Wear Indicator in tread pattern

Tyre Construction details

Load and Speed index symbol

Rim diameter (inches)

Tyre section width (mm or inches)

Aspect ratio (Section Height:Section Width)

Rim diameter (inches)

Tubeless

Tyre section width (mm or inches)

Goodyear recommend before fitting a wider than standard tyre, that the rim width is within the manufacturers' specification which in this instance is 6J, 6.5J, 7J and 7.5J. Also, bodywork and suspension components should be checked for sufficient clearance.

▲ *TY3. We had the new tyres fitted at the local Hi-Q branch of tyre fitters. They took great care not to damage the newly refurbished alloy wheels and checked both the inside of the tyre and rim for anything untoward; even though both were new, you cannot take safety checks too far with wheels and tyres.*

▲ *TY4. Sophisticated electronic machinery means that it is impossible to have an out of balance wheel and tyre. The correct number and weight required to balance the wheel are put into exactly the right position.*

▲ *TY5. We made sure that the balancing weights were put on to the inside of the rim. Although some tyre-fitting establishments fit them on the outside, there is no need for this – just ask, and they'll put them out of the way. If you need or choose to fit even more capable Goodyears on your XJ6, you may find that they are directional. This will be denoted around the outside of the casing as an arrow, pointing forward. It is vital that directional tyres are never fitted the wrong way round!*

▶ TY6. All tyres come with all sorts of writing and symbols on the sidewalls. What do they mean? You can decipher the code easily with the aid of this diagram. Note that all new tyres now come with an 'E' or 'e' in a circle or square respectively, denoting that they meet European standards for speed and durability. (Courtesy Goodyear Great Britain Limited)

LEGALITIES
- Don't fit crossply and radial ply tyres on the same axle.
- If you have radial ply tyres fitted on the front axle, don't fit crossply tyres on the rear.
- Make sure you are aware of local tyre laws and regulations; in some parts of the world, it is illegal to mix radial and crossply tyres in any combination.

In the UK and throughout the EC,

Level 4, which means there is a compulsory three-points on the driving licence and the option to impose a ban. Moreover, each offence carries a maximum fine of £2,500 – and each faulty tyre is counted as a single offence!

So, apart from the obvious safety reasons, it's more essential than ever to check your tyres on a regular basis, looking for:
- Tread depth above the legal requirement.
- Correct inflation.
- Exposed ply or cord.
- Cuts and bulges.
All the above can render the driver liable to prosecution.

SECOND-HAND TYRES
Buying used tyres is a tricky business; unless you're experienced in looking for cuts, uneven wear and other damage (especially inside the tyre) it's best to

always be spot-on and changed to suit the type of driving you're doing and the number of passengers/amount of luggage you're carrying. In general, gauges on garage forecourts should be treated with some suspicion as they have a hard life, and buying a gauge of your own is recommended – a pocket gauge, perhaps, or if you have a compressor, it's worth buying a pressure gauge attachment which enables you to top-up your tyres at home as part of your normal service schedule.

SPEED SYMBOL TABLE

Speed symbol	Max speed (km/h)	Max speed (mph)
L	120	75
M	130	81
N	140	86
P	150	93
Q	160	100
R	170	105
S	180	113
T	190	118
H	210	130

Model	Front	Rear
2.8 litre model	psi/ksm*	psi/ksm*
Driver, 2 passengers, speeds >100 mph**	24/1.68	26/1.8
Full loads + luggage, speeds >100 mph**	24/1.68	30/2.1
3.4 and 4.2 litre models		
Driver, 2 passengers, speeds >100 mph**	27/1.9	26/1.8
Full loads + luggage, speeds >100 mph**	27/1.9	30/2.1

*pse – pounds per square inch
*ksm – kilograms per square metre
**Where speeds of more than 100 mph are sustained for any distance, increase the pressures by 4 psi (0.28 ksm) for the 2.8 litre and 6 psi (0.42 ksm) for the 3.4 and 4.2 litre models.

there must be AT LEAST 1.6mm of tread throughout a continuous band comprising the centre three-quarters of the tread and around the entire circumference of the tyre. However, 1.6mm is hardly any tread at all, and the difference in roadholding and braking on an XJ6 would be extremely marked. As such, you are well-advised to change your tyres long before they get down to that level.

PENALTIES
The penalties which can be imposed for tyre offences are much more severe than is generally recognised. They are rated at

steer clear of second-hand tyres. Regulations from 1 June 1995 require part-worn tyres to be examined internally and externally to check for cuts, bulges, etc. The tread depth must be at least 2mm across the whole breadth of the tread and they must be marked 'PART-WORN' alongside the 'E' or 'e' marking. In general, it cannot be advised that you run such a powerful, heavy car as an XJ6 on second-hand tyres unless you have sought professional advice.

PRESSURES
With a heavy performance car like the XJ6, it is vital that tyre pressures should

Chapter 10

The Interior

DOOR TRIM PANELS

Most interior trim and fittings are all still readily available from Jaguar dealers and specialists such as SNG Barratt. However, many enthusiasts scour auto-jumbles and Jaguar meetings for odds and sods that aren't required *now*, but come under the heading of 'you never know'. Control knobs, instrument clusters, switches, door mechanisms and locks; even reasonable condition leather trim items. Buying items cheaply now could save you lots of expense in the future.

▲ *IN2. A typical 19-year-old XJ6 door trim panel; dirty, scruffy, and hacked about, as you can see from this rough aluminium cover plate.*

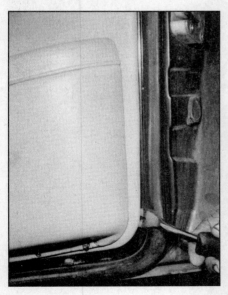

▲ *IN1. Almost all the trim and interior can be removed by using a selection of screwdrivers and combination spanners. For releasing the 'poppers' on trim panels, the Sykes-Pickavant trim tool is a must to prevent trim damage.*

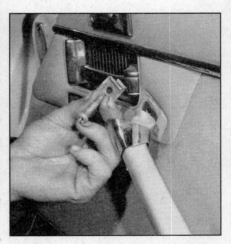

▲ *IN3. There's a chrome trim piece at the top of the armrest which has to be eased back to allow access to the crosshead securing bolt.*

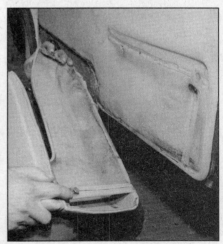

▲ *IN4. In the centre of the armrest, there is a large screw to remove, and then the armrest can be unhooked from the door trim.*

▲ IN5. The door trim is secured by pop studs. Ease the door carefully back a little

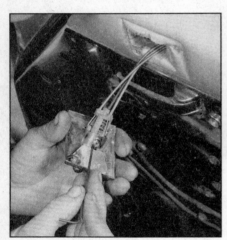

at a time to free them.
▲ IN6. Remove the two screws from the cable-operated remote mirror control surround. You'll need a small Allen key to remove the control unit from the

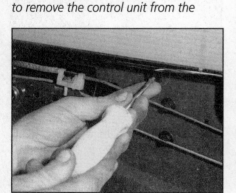

mechanism.
▲ IN7. Three self-tapping screws hold

the top trim piece in place.
▲ IN8. A typical front door trim set. Note the differences in colour of the main door trim, especially where the dirt is ditched in around the armrest area. Proprietary cleaners such as Gliptone will

do wonders for most leather.
▲ IN9. The rear door trims are usually in much better condition because the back is used less. Two self-tapping screws secure the armrest/speaker console to

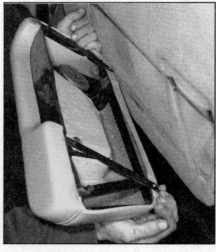
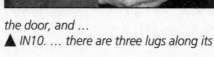

the door, and …
▲ IN10. … there are three lugs along its

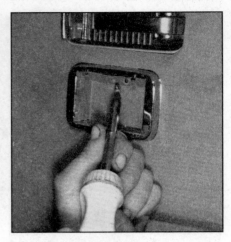

top edge which 'hang' it in place.
▲ IN11. Remove the ashtray to access

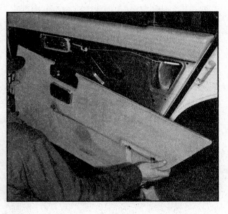

the self-tapping screw in the housing.
▲ IN12. The main trim panel can then

be un-popped like the front panel.
▲ IN13. Three self-tapping screws hold the top trim section in place, which leaves us with the three main rear door trim sections.

CARPETS

▲ CA1. If your project XJ6 has its original carpets, the odds are that they will either be very worn or damaged by damp, or both. This is a front and rear carpet section – hardly complex shapes. These are available from a number of sources, and whilst it may be tempting to buy carpet off the roll and cut out your own, the effort involved, particularly when it comes to leather-trimming the edges, would probably not be cost-effective.

▲ CA2. Better spend your time on sorting out the problems revealed by removing the carpets! This is a typical sight. XJ6s were always prone to leaks from various sources and, when left unchecked, the damp held on to the floor by the carpets leaving a horrible rusty mess like this. The first requirement here would be to use a wire brush in a drill to get somewhere near to good metal. If there were no perforations (which would have to be patch-welded), an application of anti-rust treatment should be followed by an anti-rust primer and a hard paint, such as Hammerite.

▲ CA3. At the rear, the first signs were favourable, with the original carpet, sound-deadening mat and rubber strips being in place.

▲ CA4. However, at the rear, the sound-deadening had deteriorated quite badly, as had …

▲ CA5. … the rubber strips laid into the flutes in the floor, again to reduce resonance and vibration noise. The

attention to quietness was admirable, but it all tended to hold the moisture to the floor and cause masses of rust, as you can see. Don't worry too much about the damaged sound-deadening, as companies such as BJ Acoustics have a huge selection of different materials available cut to size or off the roll.

SEATS

▲ SE1. This is a typical leather driver's seat. It looks fairly ropy but, in fact, this is mostly superficial and it would clean up well. There were no areas of split

stitching or, more important, damaged leather. Where a seat needs a really good clean, it's best to take it out

altogether.

▲ SE2. The front seats are secured to the floor by four bolts, one either side at the front, and …

▲ SE3. … one either side at the rear.

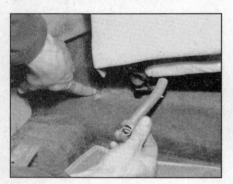

Note how the seat has to be moved fore and aft to allow access. A combination spanner was used because of the lack of space.

▲ SE4. Phil is pointing here to the bolt

mounting hole on the floor crossmember and holding one of the two springs. Both must be unhooked before the seat is

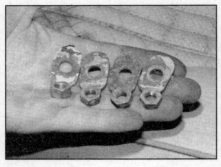

removed. At the right, you can see how the spring fixes to the crossmember.

▲ SE5. Ease the seat carefully out, making sure you don't damage other

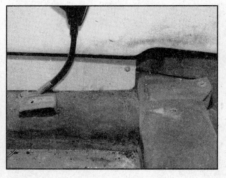

trim or paintwork in the process.

▲ SE6. These are the nuts and spacers from the four securing bolts, duly removed – make sure they all go back after being cleaned up.

▲ SE7. This photo clearly shows the two LH mounting points. Note how the rear mounting is actually on a bracket – this is

covered by a flap of carpet when the seat is in place.

▲ SE9. The rear seat squab is secured by

▲ SE8. The rear seats, too, were in need of nothing much more than some cleaning and general sprucing up. Again, it's best to remove them altogether – it doesn't take long and it will allow you to examine several parts of the car not normally seen for corrosion damage.

a crosshead screw in a bracket at each side. With them removed …

▲ *SE10. … the seat can be lifted out. It's remarkably light, but watch you don't damage any paintwork with the springs.*

▲ *SE11. The rear seat backrest should be fastened to the rear bulkhead by a bracket at each side at the lower edge of the backrest. However, it is common to find that the brackets have rusted off or that a previous owner has had the backrest out and not bothered to replace the screws. The top of the backrest is held to the rear bulkhead by slotting this metal rod over the bracket in the bulkhead.*

CLEANING AND TREATING LEATHER TRIM

Most Jaguars were produced with leather trim which, in general, is extremely hard-wearing and, if treated well (i.e. if the leather is cleaned and 'fed' on a regular basis), it should last for well over 20 years without needing more than the odd stitch or two.

The patina of age and a few wrinkles add to its charm, and the rich leather aroma has no equal. However, if it has been ignored, the lovely smell will be long gone and the seats, in particular, will be looking very dog-eared. Apart from the wear and possible damage, another area of failure is the stitching. Split seams are usually caused by ill-treatment and the use of lots of water to clean the seats – it gets into the stitching and rots the thread. Buy suitable thread (and a suitably large needle) from a specialist leather restorer, and with a little care you should be able to overcome such problems. Badly damaged leather means that the specialist must be called in on a more serious basis – and that's far from cheap.

MENDING RIPS AND TEARS

Small rips and tears can often be solved by using a proprietary adhesive, such as Loctite's Vinyl Bond. Squeeze a small amount of the glue on to the rip which will then 'melt' the two parts together.

Where the rip is larger, place a piece of masking tape beneath it to hold the two halves together before applying the Vinyl Bond. As ever, it's as well to try the technique in an area that can't be seen.

▲ *CL1. Some of the best leather treatment products we've come across are those from Gliptone. The company*

emphasises that all its cleaners and conditioners are PH neutral, which means there are no chemicals in the liquids to attack either the leather or the

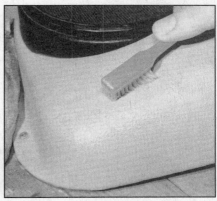

stitching. It's so user-friendly, that you can use it without skin protection.

▲ *CL2. Use a damp cloth to wipe any*

surface dust and dirt from the leather and, when dry, apply the Gliptone cleaner, rubbing it well into the surface.

▲ *CL3. An old toothbrush is ideal for*

getting the cleaner right into the 'grain' of the leather.

▲ CL4. Finally, an application of Gliptone's Liquid Leather conditioner was given. Incredibly, the magic aroma of leather comes straight out of the bottle!

PAINTING INTERIOR TRIM AND LEATHER

▲ PA1. There comes a time when no amount of cleaning can bring your leather trim back to life. In particular, it tends to fade, something which becomes apparent if you remove, say, the seat squab and compare the rear 'hidden' section that slides under the backrest with the rest of the squab. If the leatherwork is damaged or seriously worn, then replacement is probably the best answer, albeit not a cheap answer. However, if it is just looking scruffy, there's an alternative – paint it! Odd though it sounds, using a special paint

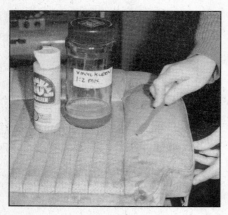

such as Vinylkote actually works. It is available in aerosol spray or in larger cans for use with your own spraying equipment. As ever, when spraying, obey the safety rules with regard to skin

protection and ventilation, etc.
▲ PA2. It's that toothbrush again! With a very dirty seat, you'll definitely need one to get all the dirt out of the grain. Here, we're using Vinylkleen in a 1:2 mixture with water. Use such things as

old coffee jars for storage, but label it clearly and keep it out of the reach of small children. This is very effective but very harsh and therefore specifically not recommended for regular cleaning purposes.

▲ PA3. This is a black aerosol finish, largely so that it shows in the photos. The aerosol can should be held about 8 in away from the workpiece. Apply a number of light coats rather than trying to cover in one pass.
▲ PA4. Whilst most owners would want to keep the original biscuit colour, it has to be said that black leather does look good. The paint won't flake off because it actually penetrates the material it's sprayed on to, thus becoming part of the seat.

Vinylkote not only works on all leather items but also on 'plastic' trim. It's always sensible to spray a test piece to ensure (a) it's the colour you want and (b) that there is no adverse reaction, as

not all 'plastics' are the same chemical composition.

SEAT DIAPHRAGM

▲ DI1. Whilst the cushion in the front squabs give the comfort, the springiness and support comes from a rubber

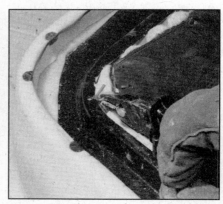

diaphragm. Over the years, this can deteriorate to the extent that it provides little or no support. Changing it is quite simple, with replacements being available at a reasonable price from specialists such as SNG Barratt.
▲ DI2. Removal and replacement is quite simple. Upend the squab and you'll see that there are seven hog rings securing it to the metal frame. Note that the rings at the front of the squab are inverted compared to those at the rear and around the edges – they should be replaced in the same way. Use a strong pair of pliers to ease these off the frame (not off the diaphragm at this point),

wear gloves to protect your hands, and goggles for your eyes.

▲ DI3. The diaphragm is likely to 'stick' to the foam seat filling as it is pulled away. Use a sharp craft knife and some care to prevent it wrecking the foam altogether. The new diaphragm is fitted in a reverse of the above procedure.

WOODEN TRIM

▼ WD1. Damaged or just old and shabby wooden trim is extremely difficult to repair on a DIY basis. Without doubt, the best policy with regard to wooden trim is to keep it clean and in good condition in the first place! Where the veneer is splitting and crazing, as on this Series 2 glovebox lid, there is little the owner can do except to approach a specialist trimmer. A used glovebox lid from another vehicle would normally be an option, but seldom in the case of an XJ6 because matching the grain of the wood is important – note how the grain 'flows' from the central section on to the lid.

Although serious work of this nature requires professional help, here are a few tips for dealing with some of the more simple to deal with ailments:
– Where you have a stubborn mark or stain on wooden trim, rub the area with equal parts of linseed oil and cleaning fluid, then wipe off.
– If you have a problem with blistered wood veneer, carefully cut along the blister with a sharp knife and squeeze PVA adhesive carefully into the cut. It's a very fiddly job, and great care is required. Cover the blister with aluminium foil and blotting paper and secure it in place using masking tape. Apply a heat source – a hot air gun or hair dryer and at the same time press on the area with something flat – your sanding block, for example. It's a good idea to wear a thick glove to protect the hand that's doing the pressing from the heat. You'll only need to heat for around a minute, but keep the pressure on until the area has cooled and the glue set.
– Dents in wood can usually be removed by placing a wet cloth over the affected area and then applying a hot iron. The steam produced causes the wood to swell. It's best to run this procedure several times, bringing the depression out slowly, rather than trying to do the job all at once.
– You can sometimes fill a depression or damaged area by using 'plastic wood', of the type available from domestic DIY stores. Make sure you get the type that will absorb varnish and stain so that you can blend it in to its surroundings.
– An alternative method is to melt a stick of coloured Shellac into the depression. This can be obtained from most artists/craft shops.
– If your wooden trim has been scarred by a cigarette burn, very carefully scrape the blackened area away and use a small brush to apply bleach to it. This will gradually bring back the colour of the wood. Use a wood dye to get exactly the right shade.

STAIN REMOVAL GUIDE

Removing stains from cloth seats, trim and the carpets of your XJ6 can prove problematical, as there are different ways to deal with different stains. However, it is most important to try out any 'remedy' on a small piece of out-of-the-way material/carpet first, in case it causes the colour to run or has a

bleaching effect. This applies particularly when using proprietary cleaners with a solvent base. Always take great care when using cleaning chemicals of any description – many of them are highly dangerous when used incorrectly and/or inhaled. Make sure that they are clearly labelled and stored safely.

BLOOD

Soak the stained area for as long as possible, using cold water (never hot or even warm). An alternative is to use a dilution of cold water and ammonia. Whichever you choose, 'blot' rather than rub the stain out.

CHEWING GUM

Children, cars and chewing gum make poor partners! The best way to solve the chewing gum problem is to ban it, totally, from the car. If it's too late, then pull as much of it off the fabric as possible – don't rub it, you'll just make it worse. The gum is easier to manage when it's solid, so place a bag of ice cubes over it for a while. When solid, you can pick it off more easily. You may need several applications and considerable patience to get the area gum-free.

MILK

The smell of spilt milk in a car can be absolutely overpowering, so clearing it up is a matter of some urgency. Soak up the milk as much as possible, with a sponge or a cloth and then use a proprietary carpet/upholstery cleaner on the affected areas. If the smell remains, wipe over with a water/ammonia mixture.

TAR

Many companies market a tar remover, though you must be careful that you don't just dilute the tar and make things worse by spreading it around. Use an absorbent cloth or piece of blotting paper to 'dab' the stain out. Eucalyptus oil, available from most chemists, also

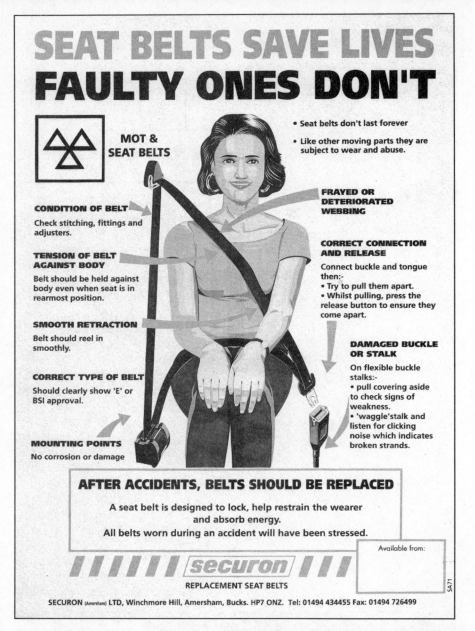

▲ SB1. This diagram shows everything that should be checked on a regular basis. Where you have any doubts at all about your seat belts, the mechanisms or their mountings, replacement is the safest answer. (Courtesy Securon (Amersham) Ltd)

works well. Finish by wiping the area with a mixture of hot water and washing powder/liquid.

TEA/COFFEE

If the stain is still wet, mop up the excess and treat the area with a borax/warm water solution. Where the stain has been allowed to dry for some while, use a 50/50 solution of water and glycerine and leave for an hour. Sponge off and then treat the area with a proprietary cleaner.

VOMIT

Unpleasant, but a fact of life, particularly if children are regular travellers. Sponge the area with water/carpet cleaner/disinfectant solution. For stubborn marks, clean with a solution of washing powder in water and then sponge off using clean water.

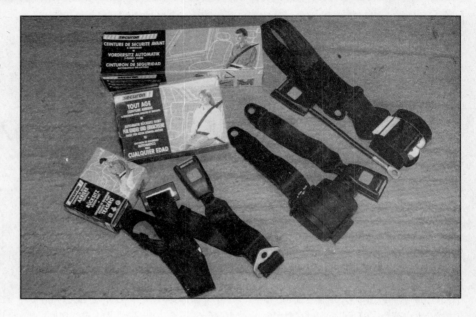

▲ SB2. Securon has seat belts available for all XJ6 requirements. Seen here are front

▲ SB3. Fitting is simply a matter of unbolting the old and replacing with the new. It is vital, however, to use the new bolts, washers, etc., supplied and to ensure that the fastener sequence is maintained. Torque up as specified in your Haynes workshop manual.

SEAT BELTS

Unless you know for certain (a) that the seat belts in your XJ6 have been replaced recently *and* (b) that the car has not been in an accident where one or more of the belts has been used*, you should look at seat belt replacement as a matter of course. The MoT test now includes specific requirements for seat belts, and

205

Chapter 11

Security

Vehicle security is, sadly, an area in which Britain leads Europe – and most of the world. According to figures from Norwich Union at the time of writing, we had almost 10 times as many car thefts as Germany. All luxury vehicles are prime targets as there is a healthy market for 'used' spares and for complete vehicles.

Though the latest model Jaguars are admirably well-equipped security wise, unfortunately XJ6 models fare nowhere near as well. That means that extra security should be viewed as a priority, especially if you've spent some time and money on your pride and joy.

THATCHAM

This is the insurance industry's testing body (based at Thatcham in Berks). Security devices are submitted by the manufacturers and undergo many harsh tests to ensure that they are of the highest quality. This includes moisture and vibration tests and resistance to physical attack. Thatcham has three categories defined as follows:

CATEGORY 1
Combined alarm/immobiliser
   Alarm with full perimetric and volumetric detection, and stand-by power supply. Immobiliser isolating a minimum of two circuits, passively armed. Anti-scan, anti-grab resistance of codes.

CATEGORY 2
Electronic/Electromechanical immobiliser
   Immobiliser isolating a minimum of two circuits, passively armed. Anti-scan, anti-grab resistance of codes.

CATEGORY 2>1
Electronic/Electromechanical immobiliser
   Immobiliser as Category 2 but which can easily be upgraded to Category 1 specification.

CATEGORY 3
Mechanical immobiliser
   Immobiliser isolating a minimum of one operating system. Easy to arm and disarm. Attack resistance to five minutes minimum using comprehensive range of hand tools. Can be permanently fitted, or temporary DIY (temporary DIY mechanical immobilisers are listed as devices intended as supplementary security or security appropriate to lower risk vehicles).

INSURANCE DISCOUNTS
The fitting of a Thatcham Category 1 or 2 device will, in many cases, bring with it an insurance discount (and/or a lowering of theft excess, etc.). However, it is important that you check with your insurers BEFORE fitting the product; discounting remains somewhat muddled, and not all companies offer the same discounts and terms. Moreover, any discount has to be related to the gross figure, and shopping around remains as important as ever. One important aspect for Category 1 and 2 products (i.e., electronic alarms/immobilisers) is that they MUST be installed professionally. A full list of the latest approved Thatcham products can be obtained by sending a large SAE to: Department VS, Association of British Insurers, 51 Gresham Street, London EC2V 7HQ.

SOLID SECURE

This is a non-profit making organisation backed by various concerns, including the Police, the Master Locksmith's Association and the Home Office. Again, products are tested, and if they stand up to a sustained five-minute attack, they achieve Sold Secure 'recognition'. This can (but not necessarily) lead to insurance discounts being available – check beforehand what is on offer for any particular product. Ring the freephone telephone line (0800 192192) for advice about what is available, nearest dealers and insurance companies linked into Sold Secure.

THE TRUE COSTS
The true cost of having your XJ6 stolen is far more than you would at first imagine. First, there's the inconvenience of having no vehicle – taking public transport is expensive and awkward, hiring a car is incredibly expensive. And as a car is only 'stolen not recovered' after 30 days, that's a whole month's inconvenience to start with. Then there's the haggling with your insurers over the value of the vehicle. This can be protracted, and almost always leaves a deficit to be made up by the owner in order to replace the vehicle with one of equal standing. It's at this point you should be considering getting an 'agreed value' policy on your car. This will, of course, require proof of its worth (receipts, photographs, etc.) but if it comes to the crunch, you'll be glad you did it.

The excess – the first amount of any claim paid by the insured – can be as low as £50, but is usually much more than that, in some cases as much as £500.

Then there's the matter of no-claims discount (NCD). Most companies set the insured back two years NCD for a claim, usually 20 per cent. Add one fifth to your last year's gross premium to see how much difference that would make. And don't forget that whilst you go *back* 20 per cent, you only go *forward* 10 per cent per year, so you're penalised for TWO years. In addition, the insurers could impose special terms if they feel the circumstances of the claim demanded it.

For drivers with a suitable driving history, it is often possible to 'protect' the NCD. However, insurers are always at liberty to refuse to offer a renewal to anyone they feel is an unacceptable risk, and any other insurer will penalise you for your claims history.

All this is expensive and inconvenient and is the reason why you should secure your XJ6 – now!

BASIC RULES

– Park sensibly – down a dark alley is asking for trouble.
– Don't leave valuables in the car, especially credit cards, cheque books, etc.
– If you've installed an alarm, use it! It's surprising how many don't.
– If you must leave anything in the car, put it out of sight.
– Always lock/secure your car even when at home or in the garage.
– Don't leave documents such as the V5 or MoT certificate in the car.
– Don't leave anything with your name and address, or worse still your signature, in the car.

GETTING PHYSICAL

Despite being in a modern age, many drivers are still mistrustful of electronic security products. There is also the problem of false-alarms, though this is almost always down to poor quality equipment and/or poor DIY installation. Owners concerned with originality and/or concours competitions will not want to drill holes in their cars, regardless of the security risks. The option is some form of physical security product – some are portable and can be swapped between cars, some, like alarms, are there to stay.

In general, steering wheel bars and handbrake gearlever locks are not particularly effective in stopping the thief from taking your XJ6. Attack tests in major magazines show that many can be bypassed by a determined thief in less than a minute – some less than 10 seconds! Ideally, you should look for a product that has passed either the Thatcham or Sold Secure (some have both) testing procedure. To pass this, a device must stand up to prolonged and violent attack for at least five minutes. Though this may not seem like much, a car thief measures his available time in seconds. Remember that, however effective any immobiliser is, it will not stop a thief stealing *from* your vehicle. Here are some of the better ones.

▲ SC1. The Autolok 2000 has passed the tests set by both Thatcham and Sold Secure and that of the Dutch TNO organisation. It's very effective, covering most of the steering wheel and with a projecting 'tongue' at the lower edge to prevent the car being driven with the device fitted, even if the steering lock is broken. One of its best features is that it is very light and thus easier to use and store than some products. As is typical, the bright yellow colouring is intended as a deterrent to the would-be thief.

▼ SC2. The Low Loc is a strong steel case (bright yellow, the standard deterrent colour) which fits over the pedals. The lock is positioned so it can't be drilled from above and has 16 million combinations. Interchangeable fitting plates make it suitable for either manual or automatic cars and the bulkhead staybar prevents vertical movement under force, so the accelerator can't be depressed. The hinge is retained by hardened steel bolts that can't be chiselled.

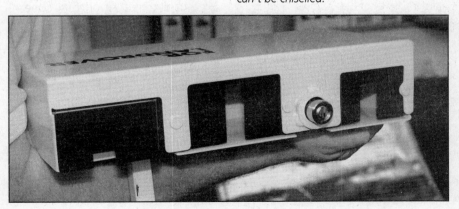

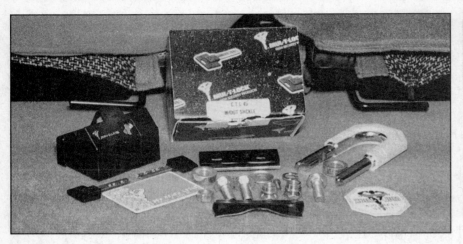

▲ SC3. One of the most effective permanent physical products on the market is the Mul-T-Lok GearLock 45. A bracket is fitted to the centre console with shear bolts, which means the bolts cannot be removed from underneath the car (or inside, of course). The gear lever is locked into neutral (or Park) by a chromed 'U' section secured by a high security Mul-T-Lok, lock.

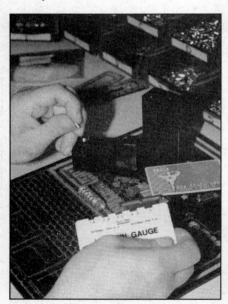

▲ SC4. A great benefit of using the company's products is that any number of items can be 'keyed alike'; i.e., the same key could operate a padlock for the workshop, a GearLock 45 on a second car, a motorcycle lock and even your front door lock. For ultimate peace of mind, a security card comes with each lock, and without it no-one can obtain an extra key.

▲ SC5. In the same league, and one of the first devices of its type on the market in the early '90s, the Barrier Deadlock is a simple, but very secure, lock fitted into the centre console in the passenger footwell. Underneath the car, the device is welded to a special bracket and on to the gearchange mechanism. Simply by pressing in the lock, the car is immobilised, and …

▲ SC6. … this high security key is required to open it. Drilling or attacking the lock is generally useless because of the hardening techniques used on the components.

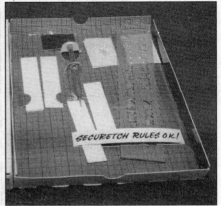

▲ SC7. Etching all the side and rear window glass is an excellent idea. It won't stop the thief, but it will give him some hassle should he want to resell your car or break the vehicle to sell its component parts. A proprietary kit like this from Automaxi costs very little and is easy to use.

▲ SC8. Use the small cutter and the stencil to etch your registration number on to the glass. Do all the separate sections of glass including the quarterlights. Red stickers are supplied and placed above the etching as a warning to thieves. Clearly, it won't help if the thief is looking to 'joy ride' or wants the car to perform a robbery, but many thieves steal to profit from the car (by ringing, etc.) and they'll probably find a car with all the glass etched more trouble than it's worth.

ELECTRONICS

▲ SC9. The Dis-car-nect is a simple immobiliser which certainly won't gain you any insurance discounts but it may fool a thief in a hurry. Moreover, it can also be used as it was originally intended, as a battery-saver for vehicles which are laid up for long periods. The device fits on to one battery terminal and features an in-line fuse. When the knurled knob is removed, all power to the car goes with it, except for a trickle sufficient to power an electric clock and keep a radio memory going. Obviously, this will reduce the current drain on the battery considerably. However, should a thief attempt to start the engine, the huge current demanded will cause the in-line fuse to blow and act as an immobiliser.

IMMOBILISERS AND THE NEED FOR NOISE

As all insurers would agree, the first priority is to immobilise the vehicle. Whilst repairing attack damage (broken side windows, ravaged trim) can be costly and inconvenient, it's unlikely in most cases to be anywhere near the cost of replacing the vehicle itself.

Engine immobilisers should be regarded as professionally fitted items unless you are extremely well-qualified in vehicle electrics. Whilst physical and electronic immobilisers are good for keeping your car, they won't help if a thief is stealing *from* your car. Professional thieves often work in teams

of up to six members and can strip out your Jaguar in an incredibly short time. Because they are relatively numerous, XJ6s are also a favourite for 'ringing' – giving a stolen car a false identity in order to sell it on to an unsuspecting buyer.

THE FULL WORKS

▲ SC10. The very latest Jaguars have extremely complex anti-theft measures, including ECUs (electronic control units) that 'talk' to each other. This is to prevent thieves simply removing the immobiliser ECU and substituting it with 'one they bought earlier'. The engine management system is coded to work only with the original immobiliser, so substitution will not work.

▼ SC11. Ideally, you should fit a full alarm system. Despite general thinking

that no-one takes any notice of sirens, research by the police with convicted car thieves reveals that they definitely don't want a siren sounding while they are 'working', potentially attracting attention. If you fit an extra internal siren, he'll still have to work in the car with a deafening racket going on. False alarms can usually be avoided by (a) choosing a quality product and (b) having it professionally installed. There is a body which sets standards for installers called the VSIB (vehicle security installation board) and they can advise as to the nearest dealers to you.

Of course, if you fit a good-name alarm, it means you'll also be able to link in electric windows, central locking and even an electric sunroof which means (a) you can always be sure of total security at the press of a button and (b) you'll look really good as you get out and walk away from your car as it quietly locks itself and sets the alarm! This is the Conlog 300, a three-circuit combined alarm/immobiliser with built-in wiring for central locking, electric windows and the increasingly important anti hi-jack. The latter is an unpleasant form of car theft where the thief steals the car whilst you're in it, thus avoiding the need to bypass any security – unless it has anti hi-jack. As he usually has some form of weapon, often a knife, it's a situation to avoid if possible – locking all the doors when town-driving is recommended – and these 'heroes' favour lone female drivers for obvious reasons, and so they

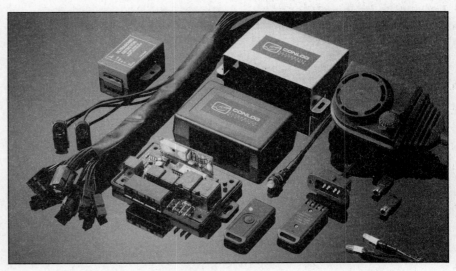

should take particular care.

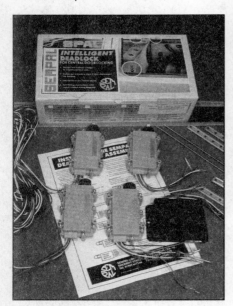

TRACKING

DEADLOCKING

▲ *SC12. Deadlocking is one of the single most effective methods of securing your doors. In essence, deadlocks are similar to the mortise locks fitted to a domestic front door. With 'normal' car locks, all a thief has to do is break a side window, reach inside and unlock the door from the inside. And, of course, if standard central locking is fitted, this simple act also unlocks all other doors on the system and (on later models) the boot lid, too.*

When deadlocking is fitted, the thief can still break the glass, but pulling on that locking knob will be to no avail. He could crawl through the window, but working in all that broken glass won't appeal and it wouldn't be a furtive manoeuvre. Deadlocking on new cars is now commonplace, but that doesn't help those of us with older models. The answer, however, is to fit the only (currently) aftermarket electronic deadlocking system.

It has been designed by Sempal and can be used with any remote control device – this could be an immobiliser, alarm system or even just remote control central locking. It is available for purchase on a DIY basis and could be fitted quite easily by anyone proficient in DIY motoring electronics. Quite appropriately for the XJ6, it is British-designed and the

electronic software is made in Britain.

▲ *SC13. This photo shows how the Sempal assembly differs from conventional locks, as it includes two motors. One pulls down the locking rod as usual and then a second pushes a locking pin across into the bottom of the locking rod. As such, the rod just cannot be pulled up to open the door. If it's a really cold night and your battery goes flat overnight, the central control box measures the battery voltage and if it gets too low, it withdraws the locking pin from one front door solenoid, but does not actually unlock the door. As such, if the battery hasn't enough power to operate the central locking, you will be able to open one door manually with the key.*

Crafty thieves who remove the battery power cable hoping to fool the system will be disappointed – it can recognise the difference between a gradual power loss and a sudden power loss. Also, when reconnected, the system will 'remember' what state it was in beforehand.

The deadlocking kits come in two-door and four-door formats, with extra locks available to add the boot into the system.

▲ *SC14. There are several electronic vehicle tracking systems available, though the main players are TrakBak from Securicor and Tracker. Being able to locate your car utilising this kind of clever electronic technology is impressive and effective but not cheap, so it pays to investigate fully all systems to decide which is more appropriate to your needs. Certainly, one of them should be on your list if your car is particularly valuable.*

WHEELS AND TYRES

Alloy wheels are a favourite target of the thief. Unprotected, they are relatively simple to remove and extremely easy to resell on the illegal aftermarket. Even steel wheels can be valuable, and all large tyres of the kind used on any XJ6 model are expensive items, especially top-brand names. Physically, a set of locking wheel nuts is the first defence. Whilst not infallible, they do add some extra hardship to the thief's life. It is VITAL that the unlocking 'key' be kept in the car, otherwise a puncture will render you stranded.

Electronically, it's a good idea to fit an alarm tilt sensor; this recognises the angle at which the vehicle was parked and triggers the siren if it varies by more than a few degrees. Clearly, this will be the case if the vehicle is being jacked up to remove the wheels.

SAFE AT HOME?

Not at all – an enormous number of car thefts take place at or near the owner's home. Even the most security-minded XJ6 owner has a tendency to 'switch off' once the car is on the driveway, and often leaves it unlocked/unalarmed and/or with expensive goodies inside. Thieves know this and target accordingly. ALWAYS lock and secure your car and remove valuables.

GARAGE

▶ SC15. How safe is your garage? Most standard-fit garage door locks would only deter a good thief for a few seconds. Consider fitting some kind of specific garage door security system – several have sections which bolt into the concrete. Shown here is one of many aftermarket devices, the Autolok Stoppa. It's suitable for metal or roller shutter doors and is a rigid security arm that rotates at the turn of a key to secure firmly into its own baseplate. This effectively braces the garage door against external attack and from the outside, the lock is drill resistant.

Think also about what's in your garage apart from your car; tools, washing machine, welder, compressor, freezer, etc. Remember to lock/secure your car even in the garage, and if you have a personal door into the house, always keep it locked. There are many cases where a thief has gained access to the house via the poor garage door lock and then used the family car to carry away the video and TV!

SECURITY HINTS AND TIPS

- Most insurance discounts come from Thatcham or Sold Secure products which must be professionally installed. Balance the saving you make by DIY fitting against discounts.
- **Never** use self-stripping connectors when wiring any immobiliser or alarm components.
- Regard ECU wiring as strictly for the professionals.
- Simple alarms/immobilisers with 'hidden' override switches are simple for a thief, too.
- Check before you buy whether you'll get an insurance discount – there's no clear-cut policy.
- Forget voltage-drop systems which commonly false alarm on cold nights.
- Always lock your doors/boot when driving in heavy traffic.
- Always lock/secure your car at home, even in the garage.
- Check out specialist magazines, such as CS&S and Car Hi-fi, for details of the latest in security products.

Appendix

SPECIALIST SUPPLIERS, CLUBS AND MAGAZINES

As well as the conventional address and telephone number for each company, the website address and e-mail address have also been included where available. If you are buying 'online', it is important to ensure that the site is 'secure' and that your credit card details cannot be stolen by a third party. In addition, we would not recommend any Internet connection or e-mail communication without some form of anti-virus protection to inhibit potentially dangerous computer 'bugs' getting onto your machine and wreaking havoc. A personal 'firewall' should prevent computer hackers breaking and entering your machine and stealing card and PIN numbers etc. All addresses and sites were correct at the time of writing but are subject to change.

SPECIALIST SUPPLIERS

Aldridge Trimming
Specialists in interior trimming.
Castle House, Drayton Street,
Wolverhampton, West Midlands, WV2 4EF
Phone: 01902 710805/710408
www.aldridge.co.uk
mail@aldridge.co.uk

Association of British Insurers (ABI)
Eponymous organisation which can supply details of car insurance companies and Thatcham-approved security products.
51 Gresham Street, London, EC2V 7HS
Phone: 0207 600 3333
www.abi.org.uk
info@abi.org.uk

Automec Equipment and Parts Limited
Copper brake pipe sets made for all models; silicone brake fluid. Also copper replacement petrol and clutch pipes.
36 Ballmoor, Buckingham, MK18 1RT
Phone: 01280 822818
www.automec.co.uk
sales@automec.co.uk

Barratt, SNG
Suppliers of all XJ6 repair and maintenance parts, from nuts and bolts to a complete body shell. A vital contributor to this book.
The Heritage Building, Stourbridge Road,
Bridgnorth, Shropshire WV15 6AP
Phone: 01746 765432
www.sngbarratt.org.uk
sales.uk@sngbarratt.com

Bedford Auto Panels
A family-owned business producing some great paint finishes and body repairs/refurbishment, using Standox paints.
Unit 7, Alexa Court, Aston, Off
Cambridge Road, Bedford, MK42 0LW
Phone: 01234 217338

Burlen Fuel Systems Limited
SU/Stromberg, Weber and Zenith carburettors sales and spares.
Spitfire House, Castle Road, Salisbury,
Wilts SP1 3SA
Phone: 01722 412500
www.burlen.co.uk
info@burlen.co.uk

Carburettor Exchange
Carburettor specialist, offering rebuilds and reconditioned units.
28F High Street, Leighton Buzzard, Beds
LU7 7EA
Phone: 01525 371369
www.carbex.demon.co.uk
sales@carbex.demon.co.uk

Cibié
See UK distributors, Valeo Distribution (UK) Ltd.

CJ Autos (Heywood) Ltd
(Previously known as NBN Designs Limited) Manufacturers of the NBN Chassis Tilter, used for much of this book.
Mission Street, Heywood, Lancs,
OL10 1HY
Phone: 01706 367649
www.cjautos.org.uk
c.j.autos@easynet.co.uk

Clarke International
A wide range of restoration equipment including MIG/ARC welders, compressors and pneumatic tools, hoists, grinders, drills, etc.
Hemnal Street, Epping, Essex CM16 4LG
Phone: 01992 565300
www.clarkeinternational.com
sales@clarkeinternational.com

W David & Sons Limited
Manufacturers of David's Isopon, plastic/metal filler and glassfibre repair kits etc.
1 Totteridge Lane, Whetstone, London,
N20 0AY
Phone: 0208 445 0372

Dis-car-nect (Richbrook International)
See Richbrook International Ltd.

Disklok UK
Disklok is a highly effective physical security device which covers the whole steering wheel.
Preston Road, Charnock Richard,
Chorley, Lancs, PR7 8HH
Phone: 01257 795100
www.disklokuk.co.uk
sales@disklokuk.co.uk

Falcon stainless steel exhausts
See SC Parts Group

Gliptone Leathercare UK
Leather care products to clean and restore leather without the use of harsh chemicals.
250 Halifax Road, Todmorden, West Yorks OL14 5SQ
Phone: 01706 819365
www.liquidleather.com
pparkinson@ndirect.co.uk

Goodyear GB Ltd
A complete range of quality tyres in various sizes and specifications.
TyreFort, 88-89 Wingfoot Way, Erdington, Birmingham, B24 9HY
Phone: 08453 453 453
www.goodyear.co.uk

Halfords Limited
High street motor accessory stores with a large number of XJ6 parts available, including batteries, cooling parts, wiper blades and Metex dust covers.
Phone: 08457 626625 for nearest store
www.Halfords.com

K&N Filters (Europe) Ltd
Range of long-life air filters for better breathing and improved torque and power.
John Street, Warrington, Cheshire, WA2 7UB
Phone: 01925 636950
www.knfilters.co.uk
uk.sales@knfilters.com

Kenlowe Limited
Electric fan replacement kits and Hot Start warm up device, both designed to aid efficiency and improve mpg.
Burchetts Green, Maidenhead, Berks SL6 6QU
Phone: 01628 823303
www.kenlowe.com
sales@kenlowe.com

Mountney Ltd
A wide range of Automaxi roof racks and roof boxes, Mountney steering wheels, locking wheel nuts and SecureEtch window security etching kits.
Unit 10, Chartmoor Road, Leighton Buzzard, Bedfordshire LU7 4WG
Phone: 01525 383055
www.mountneyltd.com
info@mountneyltd.com

Mul-T-Lok
The Gearlever car security lock and all kinds of of high security locks and keys including heavy-duty garage locks.
Welland House, North Folds Road, Corby, Northants NN18 9QB
Phone: 01536 461111
www.mul-t-lock.com

Tenneco Automotive UK Ltd
Monroe replacement shock absorbers for all XJ6 models, and indeed, the complete Jaguar range, all products having full availability.
Units 6 Tafarnaubach Industrial estate, Tredegar, NP22 3CA
Phone: 01495 723400
www.tenneco.com

Mr Fast'ner
A vast range of fasteners and 'Recoil' thread repair system.
M&P Direct, Pheonix Way, Garngoch Ind Estate, Gorseinon, Swansea, SA4 9HN
Phone: 0871 222 1122

Northampton Autorads
Established in 1968, specialists in repair, rebuilding and manufacture of all types of radiator, air-conditioning condensers and water pipes. Supply of all Jaguar radiators worldwide and O/E radiators to Aston Martin Lagonda.
51-53 Robert Street, Northampton, NN1 2NQ
Phone: 01604 630191
www.jagweb.com/autorads
autorads@jagweb.com

PB Restorations
Instrumental in producing most of the practical sections of this book.
The Workshop, Broadways Farm, Newton Road, Drayton Parslow, Bucks MK17 0JZ
Phone: 01908 365560

Pristine Alloy Wheel Refurbishers Ltd
Refurbishers of all types of alloy wheel to as-good-as-new standards, including colour-coding or machined-only finish.
Newport Road, Woburn Sands, Beds MK17 8UD
Phone: 01908 282628
www.pristinealloywheels.co.uk

Richbrook International Ltd
Dis-car-nect security device and a rabge of quality accessories for your XJ6.
3 Millers Close, Fakenham, Norfolk NR21 8NW
Phone: 01328 862387
www.richbrook.co.uk
sales@richbrook.co.uk

Ross Autotronics Ltd
Distributors of Datatag security marking and transponder tagging system for cars, tools and equipment.
Wainwright Road, Shire Business Park, Worcester, WR4 9FA
01905 756900

SC Parts Group
A whole range of parts for the Jaguar owner including, Falcon stainless steel exhaust systems as featured in this book.
14 Cobham Way, Gatwick Road, Crawley, West Sussex RH10 9RX
Phone: 01293 847200
www.scparts.co.uk
enquiries@scparts.co.uk

Securon Ltd
Replacement standard front and rear seat belts and sporting harnesses.
Winchmore Hill, Amersham, Bucks HP7 0NZ
Phone: 01494 434455
www.securon.co.uk
enquiries@securon.co.uk

Sempal
Unique aftermarket remote central deadlocking systems and Spal electric windows.
Unit 3 Great Western Business Park, McKenzie Way, Tolladine Road, Worcester WR4 9PT
Phone: 01905 613714
www.spalautomotive.co.uk
sales@spalautomotive.co.uk

SIP (Industrial Products Ltd)
Range of power and hand tools, pressure washers and Omega trolley jacks.
Gelders Hall Road, Shepshed, Loughborough, Leics LE12 9NH
Phone: 01509 500300
www.sip-group.com
info@sip-group.com

Standox
Europe's leading brand of car refinishing paints, with 40,000 colours and ancillaries listed, including solid colours, metallic, pearl and special-effect basecoats. Conventional solvent and low-emission high solids and water-based systems are available.
Freshwater Road, Dagenham, Essex RM8 1RU
Phone: 0208 590 6030
www.standox.co.uk
info@standox.co.uk

SU Carburettors
See Burlen Fuel Systems Limited.

Techno-Weld
Low heat aluminium welding system.
Aston Works, Back lane, Aston, Oxon OX18 2BX
Phone: 01993 851028
www.techno-weld.co.uk
enquiries@techno-weld.co.uk

Teng Tools
Suppliers of high-quality hand tools for all aspects of Jaguar restoration.
Unit 5, Flitwick Industrial Estate, Maulden Road, Flitwick, Beds, MK45 1UF
Phone: 01525 711500
www.tengtools.co.uk
sales@tengtools.co.uk

Thatcham (Motor Insurance Repair Research Centre)
The insurance industry's testing and approval centre for vehicle alarms/immobilisers and other security products.
Colthrop Lane, Thatcham, Newbury, Berks RG19 4NP
Phone: 01635 868855
www.thatcham.org
security@thatcham.org

Vinylkote
Interior trim paint for leather, PVC and vinyl.
Bradleys, Eastlands Industrial Estate, Leiston, Suffolk IP16 4LL
Phone: 01449 6161223

VSE Engineering
Jaguar XK engine specialist. Rebuilds, tuning, engine component sales, unleaded conversions, etc. Instrumental in the production of the engine chapter of this book.
Llanbister, Llandindrod Wells, Powys LD1 6TL
Phone: 01597 840308
www.vse-engines.com
vsekemp@btconnect.com

G Whitehouse Autos Ltd.
Automatic and gearbox specialists, with many years of Borg-Warner experience and top-class testing facilities.
Brooklands House, Nimmings Road, Halesowen, West Midlands B62 9JE
Phone: 0121 559 9800
www.gwautos.com
info@gwautos.com

PRE-BUYING CHECKS

Checking the provenance is an essential pre-purchase procedure for XJ6s; you will get information about the vehicle including whether or not it's been written-off or stolen, whether it has finance owing and the full details of the car for you to match up. Some operators offer large cash warranties.

HPI Equifax
Phone: 01722 422 422
www.hpicheck.com

AA Used Car Data Check
Phone: 0870 600 0838
www.theaa.com

RAC
Phone: 0870 533 3660
www.rac.co.uk

CLUBS AND ORGANISATIONS & MAGAZINES

Jaguar Car Club
Graham Bradshaw,
Highways, Hanley William, Tenbury Wells, Worcs WR15 8QT
Phone: 01584 781713
www.j-c-c.org.uk

Jaguar Drivers Club
Jaguar House, 18 Stuart Street, Luton, Beds LU1 2SL
Phone: 01582 419332
www.jaguardriver.co.uk
jaguar_drivers_club@lineone.net

Jaguar Enthusiasts' Club Ltd
Abbeywood Office Park, Emma Chris Way, Filton, Bristol, BS34 7JU
Phone 01179 698186
www.jec.org.uk
jechq@btopenworld.com

Jaguar World
Kelsey Publishing Ltd., PO Box 13, Westerham, Kent, TN16 3WT
Magazine dealing solely with Jaguar matters.
Phone: 01959 541444
www.jaguar-world.com
jwm.ed@kelsey.co.uk

Haynes
Restoration
Manuals

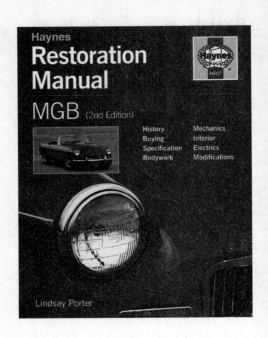

For more information on books please contact: Customer Services,
Haynes Publishing, Sparkford, Yeovil, Somerset BA22 7JJ, UK
Tel. **01963 442030** Fax: **01963 440001**
Int. tel: **+44 1963 442030** Fax: **+44 1963 440001**
E-mail: **sales@haynes.co.uk** Website: **www.haynes.co.uk**

CONTACT BREAKER   PLUGS
PAGE. 135

COMPRESSION TESTING PAGE. 46.

CONTACT BREAKER   PLUGS